STAYIN' SAFE

The Art and Science
of Riding Really Well

Lawrence Grodsky

Edited by Pete Tamblyn

Whitehorse Press
Center Conway, New Hampshire

Illustrations by Hector Cademartori

We recognize that some words, model names, and designations mentioned herein are the property of the trademark holder. We use them for identification purposes only.

Whitehorse Press books are also available at discounts in bulk quantity for sales and promotional use. For details about special sales or for a catalog of motorcycling books and videos, write to the publisher:

Whitehorse Press
107 East Conway Road
Center Conway, New Hampshire 03813-4012
Phone: 603-356-6556 or 800-531-1133
E-mail: CustomerService@WhitehorsePress.com
Internet: www.WhitehorsePress.com

ISBN: 978-1-884313-72-1

5 4 3 2 1

Printed in U.S.A.

The articles making up this book first appeared in *Rider* magazine.

All contact information (telephone numbers, web addresses, etc.) found in the columns has been checked for accuracy and updated where necessary.

Contents

Introduction

When Pete asked me to introduce this compilation of Larry Grodsky's Stayin' Safe columns from *Rider* magazine, I was truly flattered. I was Larry's editor for most of his work in *Rider*, but really in name only—Larry's writing rarely needed more than small changes to suit *Rider's* style, and I looked forward to leaning back and reading it every month (rather than leaning forward and editing it). I also didn't know Larry personally as well as some of his friends nearby in the northeast, yet as they can attest, meeting and knowing Larry even a little was a life-changing experience, similar I imagine to sharing a meal with someone like Einstein or van Gogh—afterward you never looked at most things the same way again.

Larry's genius, his art, and his passion were, of course, motorcycle skills and safety, and his Stayin' Safe column brought life to the subject in a way we aren't likely to experience in the pages of *Rider* or any other magazine again. Larry used his deep expertise and took this potentially dull but oh-so-important subject and made it entertaining, personal, and meaningful as well as informative, imparting vital tips and tricks for safer riding with wit and craftsmanship in every column.

Ironically, in person Larry was easy-going and charmingly disorganized, not much like his precise and tightly focused writing at all. Upon meeting him for the first time people were both captivated and confused by his often quiet, then suddenly effusive manner, the dry wit and those searching eyes that seemed to be looking for the answers to a thousand questions all at once. A visit from Larry was like an intelligent whirlwind dropping by, shedding a few personal belongings he would reclaim some other time . . . 'cause he's gotta go, gotta present a white paper to the board, and oh-by-the-way can he have a ride to the airport? My wife and I once watched in amusement as Larry used nearly our entire driveway to repack the contents of two saddlebags, and then couldn't find the bike keys or his glasses. "He was the kind of person, he had friends on every continent," Larry's sister told the *Associated Press*. "He could walk into a cafe in Pittsburgh or Kosovo, and within 10 minutes he had made a friend for life."

Among the *Rider* staff we loved Larry like a brother, and were devastated when he died. We still are in many ways. Through his column and Stayin' Safe Motorcycle Training program, Larry inspired and trained thousands to be better motorcycle riders, many of whom wrote *Rider* magazine when he died to express condolences and share stories about him. Some wished to thank him for literally saving their lives with his advice and guidance. In April 2006 Larry was on his way home to Pittsburgh from California after attending the International Motorcycle Safety Conference there when, at night on an arrow-straight rural highway in Texas, a deer collided with his motorcycle and he was thrown from the bike. He died at the scene. There was no evidence of any wrongdoing or neglect on Larry's part. Deer are one of those things over which we as motorcyclists have little or no control. "This is the one thing he knew he couldn't do anything about," his girlfriend told the *Pittsburgh Post-Gazette.* "Just a few weeks ago he said to me, 'That's how I'm going to go, it's going to be a deer.' He could deal with all the idiot drivers, but at night when a deer jumps in your path, that's it and he knew that." Riders from as far away as Georgia joined more than 100 of Larry's family and friends for his funeral in Pittsburgh, the processional to which was led by nearly 30 motorcycles.

The man packed a lot into 55 years. Growing up in Monroeville, Pennsylvania, Larry graduated from high school with a scholarship from Future Teachers of America. A champion wrestler, his passion for motorcycles began at Ohio University, where he earned a teaching degree. He taught high school and was a wrestling coach in Cambridge, Ohio, for several years, then worked at the Job Corps after returning to Pittsburgh. Larry's love of motorcycles eventually inspired him to become an instructor with the upstart Pennsylvania Motorcycle Safety Foundation, for which he ran a Monroeville training site. Sometime after he started writing for *Rider,* Larry launched his Stayin' Safe Motorcycle Training Program. Between it and his early work, it's estimated that he trained some 5,000 riders. Some were celebrities, but all were equally important fellow motorcycle enthusiasts to Larry.

The heart and soul of Larry's lifetime of work, what he learned from all of those students and his own piercing and astute research and observations, are in this book.

The *Rider* staff and I are extremely grateful to Whitehorse Press, Pete Tamblyn and the others who made this anthology possible. I only wish Larry were around to see it, maybe get a head-start on Volume II. If he were here, he'd probably want to update some of what he wrote with the very latest motorcycle safety information, or perfect and nitpick this and that . . . then would probably forget to tell us the page numbers.

This book is an invaluable treasure of motorcycle skills and safety information. Learn from it, but most of all enjoy it. I know I did.

Mark Tuttle Jr, Editor, Rider *magazine*

Preface

There's something irresistible about a guy who can't wait to leap from his saddle, jumbo chalk in hand, and turn the next rest stop into a roadside classroom. Teacher to the core, Larry Grodsky was fond of visual enhancements to the spoken word. Striking dramatic arcs across the pavement to represent the Roadway and You, he would diagram alternative lane positions for optimizing the view or avoiding potential hazards. Shunning the shut-up-and-listen approach, he encouraged students to raise questions from their own experiences. Larry also had a keen sense for the saturation point. Detecting when ears might soon glaze over he would promise to continue, pronouncing, Hey; that's enough chit-chat; let's ride!

Beyond the many students Larry touched, there was a much larger number of fans who knew him only through his monthly safety column.

Upon accepting the Safety Editor position at *Rider* magazine, his broad directive from then-editor Tash Matsuoka was to make them think; make them laugh. The selected columns which comprise this anthology illustrate how well he did just that. Tash might have simply said, Be yourself. Larry was an obsessive researcher, formulating theories backed with his own observations, often taken on the street with clipboard and stopwatch. He presented his ideas in a manner that invited deliberation. You could count on a grin whether he was poking fun at fellow staffers (I would rather listen to Salvadori talk about opera than. . .) or other sources (. . .contained about as much information as a 3-year-old *National Enquirer*.). Pounding the keys of the word processor, or pouring guests a second glass of vino after dinner, Larry was an entertaining story-teller.

From late in the 1980s until mid-2006, Larry's monthly safety columns generated more than 220 pieces of work. That's a lot of safety advice. You would think that after a bit his columns would have become mostly boring and repetitive, but you would be wrong. They mostly got better. In a style that avoids both repetition and wordiness, he used his broad vocabulary to great advantage. He loved to insert obscure adjectives like ineffable; that one applies well to him. Part of the fun of Larry was that his writing is packed with delightful surprises. Few columns have a single focus from which they never stray, posing an editorial challenge the equivalent of herding waterbugs.

These selected columns first introduce the environment in which we all ride: the bikes, the roads and regulations, the risks. The main body then discusses how we can manage that environment: braking and cornering, tips and drills, gear, street strategies, and training. Finally comes a potpourri which illuminates various aspects of a guy with a zest for living, who marched to his own drummer. Larry was a person who lived to ask why? and then relentlessly investigated more sides of the issue than you realized existed. He projected an inseparable combination of perennial student and dedicated teacher.

This book is not intended to be a cookbook how-to guide to motorcycling proficiency, nor does it address just the beginner or only the more expert among us. Most who read it will come away with a much deeper appreciation for managing the myriad issues facing today's motorcycle enthusiasts. Where it seemed especially appropriate, guest contributors familiar with the column's subject—and most often good friends—have been asked to enrich this volume with comments of their own. The editor owes his deep gratitude to those writers, with an apology for the occasional brutal edits.

But hey; thats enough chit-chat—let's read.

I wish to thank my friend, supporter, and my own brutal editor Donnie Brous for her encouragement throughout this project. Also, Fred Applegate and Tom Bellhouse for similar, but gentler, assistance.

Pete Tamblyn

The Bikes

Use(d)ful

May 1996

Perhaps due to the suffix "sky" on his name, Larry Grodsky was like a bird that was always flying about. He would often roost at Battley Cycles, where we were familiar with his penchant for inexpensive, reliable, and simple motorcycles. Larry was a walking, talking encyclopedia of motorcycle knowledge.

Even though he always maintained at least one premium motorcycle, he frequently had a simple motorcycle or two in the back of his compact pickup truck. He once needed a major part for a precious Yamaha Exciter 185. I just happened to have a crusty version of that entire bike I rescued from the junk pile. The part that he needed and many other parts were good on this bike. I told him that he could buy my Exciter 185 for half the price of the new part. He agreed, asking if we could deliver this bike to the garage where he needed it since his schedule did not afford the time to pick it up. When he took delivery he objected to the price since the bike was so ugly. When I explained to him that I was giving him the bike for free and that all he was paying me for was delivery, he said fair enough and paid me.

He was always a pleasure to deal with.

Devin Battley, owner, Battley Cycles

I'm tellin' ya—this little unit was *clean*. Not a scratch, and the owner still had shelves full of accessory boxes he hadn't even opened! Why was he selling it? The usual: wanted something bigger and faster, with more features. Guy told me right up front it would need a battery soon, but the price was right, so how could I go wrong?

Well, would you believe *a hundred and seven bucks* for a battery?! And that was nothing. I'd have never dreamed something that clean on the outside could be so screwed-up on the inside. And there I was—2,000 miles from home and I'd *given* away my old machine, which had never caused me a whit of trouble.

I've always fancied myself a pretty savvy used bike shopper . . . but don't ask me for advice on secondhand computers. Though they're essential tools in this age, computers are the recipe books of vampires who can never sate their bloody appetites for speed and power. The coldest place on the planet is the computer store where you dare bring a question about a three-year-old machine.

I went through a period, back when motorcycles were a lot cheaper, when I *had* to have a new one yearly, but I've mellowed. Visit the markets and fields of almost any Third World country and you'll see how much intrinsic value older motorcycles have.

Today's bikes are cleaner, quieter, and more reliable than ever, but take a look at the advancements of the past decade: ABS, traction control, linked braking systems, fuel injection, catalytic converters, forkless front ends. Not one of these features is found on more than a handful of models, and among all of the manufacturers only BMW has committed its full marketing efforts to the new technologies.

If you left motorcycling's orbit 20 years ago, your old skills are still applicable on re-entry. I wouldn't recommend buying a 20-year old bike as a primary ride, but between the showroom and the crusher, a motorcycle has a lot it can teach a man . . . or a woman . . . or a number of men and women.

I've never bought a used BMW or Harley or Honda Gold Wing—the bikes which maintain high resale value regardless of mileage—so I wouldn't know what to advise potential buyers in terms of possible mechanical gremlins. My success "secret" for purchasing secondhand is really no secret at all. I like bikes that are relatively recent and have very low mileage—3,000 has been my average, and I've bought some with mileage down in the hundreds.

It's tougher than it used to be, because used motorcycles are selling well. I've bought a lot of secondhand bikes, and whenever I browse the classifieds, I find the same models still fetching what I paid 10 years ago. Sure, new bikes have gone up—significantly—but if you buy a used bike in today's market, keep it clean and ride it 3,000 to 4,000 miles annually (the national average), you can reasonably expect to lose little more than the interest your money would have accrued in the bank.

What's the number one thing to look out for when buying secondhand?

Your friends! There are tons of bad bikes out there and the only proven method of getting rid of one is to sell it to an unsuspecting friend. Get yourself a NADA guide and/or a *Kelley Blue Book*—and maybe a list of new tire prices. Then ask if that Yamaha XS750 (worst Yamaha ever made!) in your friend's garage is such a steal at $500.

Find a mentor. Someone with no basement to clear out. Someone who is mechanically inclined but who would rather ride than fix motorcycles. He should be someone who has enjoyed a broad spectrum of riding activities, i.e. not someone who only lives for Wing Ding or the next BMW rally. You want someone who handles a bike skillfully but beware of "natural" riders; they often don't understand the stumbling of ordinary mortals. And lastly, he should be someone who respects your tastes, even if they sometimes confound him.

Prioritize. Make three lists: 1) how you plan to use the bike; 2) the features and characteristics you desire; and 3) specific models (you can obtain magazine road test reprints from Ian Smith Information, PO. Box 9440, Denver, Colorado 80209-0440; (303) 777-2385), or on the web at www.mcreports.com.

Don't search by price. "Valuable," said Cook Nielson, the former editor of *Cycle,* " . . . is when two rich guys want the same thing." If it's way too much money, politely leave your name and number. You may be pleasantly surprised.

Stock is best. Bolt-on accessories usually add nothing to a bike's value, and major modifications are bad news. Original owner's manual, tools, and service records are good signs.

The machine is just the starting point. You need to be warm, dry, and well protected to enjoy riding. And I'd rather ride almost any $1,000 bike with premium tires and shocks than I would a $10,000 machine with marginal rubber.

Any good models to watch for? Sure. This is by no means a definitive list:

Suzuki VX800. Friendly V-twin engine, shaft drive, stable handling. Good choice for large riders who want to live simply. Nice examples run $2,500 to $3,000.

Kawasaki EX500. sport-bike which doubles as commuter. Nimble, comfortable, plenty of pep. "Prelude to a Superbike." Depending upon year and condition, $1,600 to $3,500.

Suzuki GS500E. Although I own one of these, I recommend it with reservation, since it has a carburetion glitch and slightly nervous handling. Nimble, easy to maintain, great brakes. Tons of them out there, but young riders often savage them quickly. $1,500 to $3,000.

Honda Hawk GT (647cc). If you can find a nice one, skip the GS500E for this bike. Better engine, more stable, and overall higher quality. Seller's market, but some go for $2,000.

Yamaha XT600. Been around since dirt; newer ones have lower seat height and electric start. Fabulous pothole dodger and curb leaper. Great for a tall "short hop" rider. If you're smaller or curious about off-roading, consider the XT350. Depending upon year and condition, $900 to $2,800.

Honda 250 (and 450) Rebel. A bit chopperized, but low seat, disc brake, and electric start have introduced thousands to motorcycling. $1,000 and rising.

H-D 883 Sportster (*post* AMF era!). Vibration and Spartan accommodations lead many 883 owners to upgrade after a year, thus ensuring a continued supply of used ones. Because of high resale, consider buying from a respected Harley dealer. $3,000 to $4,500.

Older motorcycles require a sharper eye, since they'll have more miles or may have atrophied from sitting. Honda's CX series (500 and 650 Moto Guzzi-style twins, with liquid cooling and shaft drive) are tanks— for nearly two decades the workhorse of London's barbarous dispatch riders. The parallel-twin 400cc standard, of which boatloads were sold in the early '80s, is a much-missed genre. Each Japanese manufacturer made one, but stay away from Kawasaki's KZ400 (later 440s and 454s were fine). There were so many Yamaha Exciters (185s and 250s) built in the early '80s that it's still possible to find good runners. One with the integral top box is the ultimate pizza delivery bike!

You may have noticed that there are no multicylinder bikes on my short list; all are simple designs, with ergonomics close to the middle. It's just my personal belief that a year with a slower revving engine and a neutral control layout will prepare most riders for whatever else they pursue—including a quick switch if it turns out they've made a wrong choice.

A lot of people—God bless 'em—want their purchases to be brand new, untouched and fully warranted. Plenty of them bought motorcycles in the early '80s, when new bikes were cheap and plentiful, but never rolled them over into newer models . . . perhaps because their trade-in values were so low.

Used bikes are an integral part of the total motorcycle market, enabling newer, less sophisticated buyers to cultivate tastes of their own. Savvy dealers realize this and actively work to put people on the road on safe, reliable machines. They're called *dealers* because it's their job to recognize value and cultivate a market for it. What would you call someone who would discard the *Mona Lisa* because it's 500 years old and a little faded?

A computer salesman.

What is Handling?

October 1995

As Larry says in his column, motorcycle handling is one of those elusive concepts that's hard to define, but to paraphrase Judge Potter Stewart I know it when I feel it. In my 45 years of riding and 30-year career as a motorcycle journalist I've tested hundreds of bikes, then had to put the complex combinations of their actions into words. In that time, I have discovered a basic truism about handling.

The main positive component in handling is predictability. You enter a certain type of turn at a certain range of speed and know from experience that this bike will take this line through and exit . . . there. It's not acceptable for a bike to give the impression that it does not seem to know where it's going—or if it does, it won't tell you. I've experienced certain machines that would enter a turn, require a certain amount of effort to initiate the turn, then suddenly everything changes. The bike either wants to fall into the turn and exchange its expected line for a tighter one, or it leans over but requires a firm hand to lean it farther yet, as it is reluctant to turn. These types of predicaments are often a function of tire choice, which is fairly easy to correct—with a new tire.

Worn front suspension components (fork springs or fork oil) can result in a bobbing motion over bumps, or excess dive under braking. Both can be easily addressed with a change of fork oil and fork springs.

Bill Stermer, contributor, Rider *magazine*

During my formative years, when my favorite motorcycle magazine (RIP) regularly ranked the top five handlers, I held their findings to be immutable as the freezing point of water. It didn't matter that these were the same machines which sprayed one's pant legs with oil or produced spark only intermittently. It *did* matter that one of the machines came from the wrong country, made that ring-a-ding sound, and left behind an acrid cloud of blue smoke . . . but I bought that one, too. It handled.

Two highly respected Brits, designer/builder Tony Foale and technical journalist Vic Willoughby, have authored a 160-page treatise entitled *Motorcycle Chassis Design: The Theory and Practice.* How do these experts define handling?

" . . . the ease, style, and feel with which the motorcycle does our bidding."

Ease . . . style . . . feel? Rather vague, and yet the phrase "does our bidding" sheds light (albeit flickering) on a crucial element overlooked in so many road tests. If you insist on seeing six seconds through a bend (half the distance recommended by MSF), will a Bimota Tesi "do your bidding" any better than a Harley Fat Boy? The authors go on to list steering geometry, chassis stiffness, weight distribution, and tires as some of the mechanical elements.

Anybody with a six-foot tape measure can make some reasonable predictions about a bike's handling. Motorcycles with long wheelbases tend to be more stable, i.e. require less attention to maintain a straight (or curved) line. Conversely, their steering is slower, more deliberate.

But even bikes with identical wheelbases sometimes have vastly different steering properties. Take rake and trail, for example. The rake is the angle between a vertical line and the motorcycle's steering stem. A Kawasaki Vulcan VN800 has a rake angle of 34 degrees; the current repli-racers are 24.5 to 26, almost by decree.

Trail is the measured distance between the contact patch (a point directly under the axle) of the front tire and the point where the extended plane of the steering axis intersects the road. That same Vulcan has 5.9 inches of trail; a Kawasaki ZX-6R only 3.4. Bikes with less rake and less trail are thought to steer more quickly at a cost of reduced stability. However, when Foale built an experimental bike with a rake angle adjustable to 15 and even *zero* degrees, he found it retained excellent stability at all speeds and markedly improved stability over rutted roads.

The penalty for the steep rake angle was severe shuddering under braking, a situation he attributed to the poor structural rigidity of conventional forks.

Ah, the telescopic fork: despite piles of damning evidence and "superior" designs dating back to the hub-centered 1920 Ner-a-Car, it remains a seminal force in motorcycle design. The biker wants a longer one; the racer wants his more rigid. The Type 259 Boxer owner's isn't fully functional, but he still insists on the appearance of one.

Possessed of no such hang-ups, Foale built a double wishbone suspension which allowed for variable trail values of between 2 and 4 inches. His conclusion: "Results were satisfactory throughout the full test range, so making personal preference the decisive factor."

Tires and wheels can be equally perplexing. Large diameter for gyroscopic stability and cooler running. Small ones for quick steering. Narrower tires steer more easily and are less easily deflected by surface irregularities such as stones. Wider tires grip more (good), have more unsprung weight (bad), are more supple (good), and have more "rolling cone effect"—the self-steering characteristic that occurs when a tire is leaned onto its smaller inner circumference. Stickier rubber is good if you don't mind the wear. Of course, higher performance tires may stick *less* if they're not warmed-up sufficiently.

Before modern suspensions, we thought that heavy vehicles "held the road" better, but additional weight means additional steering effort and puts greater demands on suspension. Of course, weight management is at least as important as total avoirdupois. Placing it low makes the bike feel "planted" when cornering . . . but carrying it higher enables you to lean further.

Regardless of whether you prefer to flick 'em or lean 'em, you probably want your wheels to track together. So, an area of handling which is free of such equivocations is chassis rigidity. Flexing along the frame may cause the bike to "weave," a condition that requires compensations in steering. Even when everything is built stoutly, hard usage eventually loosens bearings and bushings. Trouble spots are steering head, fork legs, wheel bearings, and swingarm pivots.

Because a motorcycle rides on two gyroscopes, it is self-stabilizing . . . generally. Tire condition greatly affects this ability; poor rubber or excessive looseness in the chassis can cause the wheels to move rapidly to and fro. This can cause what is called a "wobble." Even when everything works, bumps in the road can cause a "head shake." This is good in the sense that the wheel self-corrects the initial sideways force, although it may require a few cycles to stabilize. Or it may not stabilize at all. That's what's called a "tankslapper." Tankslappers are bad; *very* bad. They mostly occur at supralegal speeds or when you've done something naughty . . . like sliding the rear wheel out two feet on your 700-pound tourer, then snapping the throttle shut in a panic.

So weaves and wobbles are not good. One more class of handling ills is the "wallow." Wallows are when the mass of the bike moves around on the suspension instead of staying planted in a turn. They occur because motorcycle suspensions, in addition to bumps, must absorb cornering loads. According to Foale and Willoughby, a 45-degree lean angle creates a suspension load 41 percent higher than vertical riding. So, a bike which soaks up bumps neatly when vertical may move around too much when cornering—i.e. wallow.

Fortunately, we have *damping*. Magazine articles assume that we all know what it is, and I think I do. If bikes simply rode on springs, they would bounce up and down repeatedly until all the springs' energy had been dissipated (or we learned how to damp them out with the throttle). *Compression* damping slows the spring's initial reaction to a force (bump, cornering, or braking). *Rebound* damping enables it to return in one smooth motion to the original position. Tell a suspension tuner exactly how fast you'll take a turn, how big the bumps are, and how hard you'll brake, and he'll set up the perfect system . . . for that turn.

A few years ago, when I was off-roading on my 500-pound bike far from home, I completely broke the lower shock mount. Because of the tight design of the swingarm, the shock spring continued to support the weight of the bike—but with no hydraulic assistance. At first the bike felt almost unrideable, but with practice I found that I could still corner with surprising smoothness—provided I used good throttle control.

I reckon it took me about 20 years to learn the most important element of handling. K.S. Carey, an Air Force major from Dayton, Ohio, learned in a weekend. I met Carey at our *Rider* Rally this spring in Richmond, Kentucky, shortly after his test ride on a new BMW R1100R. After a year of riding on a Kawasaki 454 LTD, he was awestruck by the Beemer's "handling" and knew he had to buy one.

A few weeks later Carey joined me and two other guys on 750 sport tourers for a two-day session of continuous corner carving on secluded Appalachian roads. We started slowly, and K.S., who had taken the MSF's Beginning and Experienced RiderCourses, showed he had solid basic skills. But by the middle of the second day, he'd earned the undying respect of the more experienced riders. Diligent, repetitive execution shortened and smoothed his transitions to the point where he was making serious time—*safely*—through the twisties. BMW lost a sale that day.

"I learned it's not the bike," sighed the major. Of course, his humble cruiso-commuter had fresh premium tires and still snug bearings at all the critical connections. So what is handling? I suppose it's rather like pornography, as Supreme Court Justice Potter Stewart described it in his famous 1964 opinion:

"I shall not today attempt further to define the kinds of material . . . but I know it when I see it."

The Six Hippies Ride

August 2003

Back in the early '90s I met an interesting fellow. He had no four-wheel transportation and relied solely on his well-used motorcycles to get through the harsh Pittsburgh winters. He was also the most outspoken and well-known motorcycle safety educator in western Pennsylvania. At first we came in contact at a few random events. Then I enrolled in the Motorcycle Safety Foundation course and he convinced me that after 30 years of limited riding experience I could actually learn to control a bike and even teach others these essential skills.

So it was that Lawrence Grodsky became a mentor to me (and many others) on the road to riding and teaching. I did not know how to repay him for his services but Larry soon made it clear that my mechanical skills could be put to good use in the service of the MSF training bikes as well as his personal fleet. As he went on to form his own unique training program, he often engaged me and others as consultants in his quest to develop and fine tune bike and rider. It is something that I continue to this day.

Tony Capriotti, MSF RiderCoach

My friend, Tony Capriotti, has nine and a half fingers and an insatiable need to know how things work. A machinist and the son of a machinist, he sacrificed half a digit to chain and sprocket research as a junior scientist.

When I first met Tony he rode a Honda FT500 Ascot thumper—a dog's-breath motorcycle if ever there was one . . . except that Tony's was one of the best sorted motorcycles I'd ever seen. He'd done nothing to the engine, which still put out a pathetic 25 horsepower or so. In fact, the Ascot had received no performance-enhancing modifications beyond the addition of a premium aftermarket shock. I remember that it had a slightly customized Corbin seat and a set of adjustable handlebars from a Honda Nighthawk which he'd further customized to get the perfect bend and reach. Tony's a rather small fellow—5 feet, 5 inches—and I remember thinking that I'd never seen a street bike with such attention to personal fit.

One day I loaned Tony my Honda TransAlp, and the next thing I knew, he'd purchased an identical white, blue, and red '89 model. Within days he'd fitted it with Givi luggage (customized for a slimmer profile), lowered it slightly, and added a few other creative touches which made life with the TransAlp more livable. Tony loved that bike, and I inherited some of the trickle-down technology from the little custom parts he fabricated. But alas, after dropping the TransAlp for the second or third time, he concluded that it simply was too tall a bike and switched his attentions to a Honda NX650 thumper. A BMW R850R came and went, but the NX stayed, primarily used as transportation to Tony's job as a math teacher at a school for automotive technicians.

At some point—I think before he sold the BMW—Tony purchased a new Suzuki SV650S, which he fit with a top case for commuting, a custom seat, and suspension upgrades for track days. He claimed that it was the most perfectly suited motorcycle he'd ever ridden, but then one day he brought home a leftover Kawasaki W650, promptly swapping out the handlebars and fitting a small set of Givi panniers. This one, he says, is the most fun bike he's ever had for just getting on and riding.

Oh, and I forgot to mention that he works evenings at the local BMW dealership, where he snagged a killer deal on a pre-owned but unused F650GS. An NX, an SV, a WR and a GS. The man's trying to corner the world market on 650s!

Fortunately, he's not succeeded. Though our average displacement through this year's first month of training rides was 1,198cc, I now find myself breaking bread in rain-soaked western North Carolina with seven good-natured companions, five of them on 650cc or smaller machines. Our voluble hostess, Hylah, bursting through the swinging kitchen door with a tray of delectables, overheard the predictable bike prattle and remarked, "What about the six hippies?" Thus was born, the Tour of the Six Hippies.

Bob Foley, 59, of Seagrove Beach, Florida, rides a pristine red 1990 Honda Hawk GT (a.k.a. NTV650). He's ridden motorcycles for 35 years and owned 20 bikes, the largest an 1,100cc Suzuki and the penultimate, a Honda VFR800. Foley actually bought the Hawk for his wife, hoping it would transform her from around-town scooterist to weekend sport tourer. Mrs. Foley failed to take the bait, but Bob soon discovered it was the machine he'd been searching for all his riding career.

"The reason I was attracted to [the Hawk] was the lightweight, ease of handling, the balance that the V-twin gives you, the seat height—so I can actually put both feet on the ground—just the all-around great handling of the bike."

Linda Graydon, 47, of La Fayette, Georgia, started riding seven years ago on a Yamaha 500 Virago, graduated to a 750 Virago and then a Kawasaki Concours (1,000cc), which she says she handled "OK." She discovered the BMW F650 last year on a tour of the Alps.

"From riding it three days in Europe, I fell in love with it. It's light, I can maneuver it, and it's quick. It's got a lot of pep. The seating position is perfect for me. I like the standard seating position. I feel like I have good control of the bike."

Lawrence Holden, 49, and Jerry Smith, 47, of Poplarville, Mississippi, have been riding buddies since they rode bicycles together in junior high school. They do a lot of touring together, Lawrence on his Yamaha Venture and Jerry on his Electra Glide, but they elected to ride their 650 dual-sports to the Smoky Mountains through 600 miles of the heaviest spring rain in years.

Says Jerry, who owns two Harleys and two 650s (a BMW F650 Dakar model and a Suzuki DR650): "In the mountains the Dakar handles the curves great. I like to be able to go off-road, on gravel roads, and forest service roads. It's got luggage capacity. It's just a lot of fun up here."

Holden, with 32 years experience, has owned nine bikes, three at the present time. His favorite?

"It depends on what I'm doing. If I'm on the highway, I like the Venture; for everything else, I like the KLR. It's light, and it's easy to maneuver. It goes 300 miles on a tank of gas. You can go off-road. If you're just going around town, it's a lot easier to park . . . you can dodge traffic."

Then there's my good friend and co-instructor, Pete Tamblyn, 63 years young, of Alto, Georgia; he's ridden motorcycles since the days of manual spark advance. The 1989 Honda TransAlp he's riding on this trip is 67cc shy of being a real 650, although Honda Europe's current iteration rolls off the Italian assembly line with the Hawk's 647cc motor. Pete owns "about 16 bikes" at the present, including a Honda ST1100, and reckons he's owned about 50 total, the largest being a 1,500cc Kawasaki Vulcan. Is the TransAlp his favorite?

"It is every time I get off it," he quips. When pressed, he names the TransAlp and the Hawk GT before his voice trails off, unable to recall additional contenders.

"My first 650 Triumph was a dual-sport," says Tamblyn. "I rode it to Arizona, flat-tracked on it, commuted on it." Pete's also toured Europe, led Pancho Villa tours of Mexico and Central America, and knows every dirt, gravel, and paved road in the southern highlands.

"When I ride bikes like the TransAlp and Hawk," says Pete, "I feel like I'm cheating."

I didn't mention the guys on our ride who *aren't* riding 650s. There's Luis Santiago, 41, a first-year rider from Cincinnati on a Honda 750 Shadow Ace. Luis, why didn't you buy a 650?

"'Cause I didn't know how good a bike they are," he shrugs. After riding for three days with more experienced riders on lighter machines, would he consider looking into other models?

"I'm definitely into the more sporty looking ones (now). I would certainly try the 650s, if I can get one with a lower seat height."

Ted Panhuis, 58, of Chagrin Falls, Ohio, is a big-bike guy, owner of a BMW R1100RT who has never owned anything smaller than an 850 in six years of riding.

"I like to tour long distance, and I don't think a 650 is ideal for that. I like the protection of the 1100RT."

Though Panhuis is a bit wet behind the ears (his 88-year-old father rides a fully faired Honda 650 Silver Wing scooter) his assessment is correct insofar as bike designers' unwillingness to provide smaller motorcycles with creature comforts. However, 650 engines are completely capable of providing touring smoothness and performance. If you can't out-accelerate 95 percent of today's cars on, say, a Suzuki SV650, then you either weigh 400 pounds or don't know how to shift gears!

There's really no manufacturing obstacle to prevent Suzuki from packaging its wonderful 65-horsepower SV650 motor into a fully featured 400-pound sport or adventure tourer—just the fickle winds of market acceptance. The eclectic mix of singles and twins which carry on the British tradition of the 650 are mellow fellows compared to the headbanger fours in the red-hot 600 supersport class . . . but sometimes it takes an old hippy to show the kids how to rock.

"Looks Like Dirt, Feels Like Dirt . . ."

July 2002

This article is a good example of Larry's calm, thoughtful com-
mentary on motorcycle trends. In mid-2002 when it was pub-
lished, a fair bit of editorial space had been devoted to dual-
purpose motorcycles, and their attractiveness to street riders
wanting to expand their riding options.

I fell victim to the sit-up/ride-anywhere allure of
Kawasaki's 650KLR about that time myself. Some friends had
invited me to join them on a trek to Mexico's Copper Canyon
and I bought a used KLR for the occasion. The trip only lasted
2,000 miles but the KLR remains with me still. If I could own
only one bike and didn't want to travel with a passenger, the
KLR would be my choice. I love its agility, flexibility, and no-
nonsense attitude.

Indeed, many dual-purpose bikes have been sold since then,
some as second bikes and some as primary. In this article,
Larry measures his words carefully, pointing out both the ad-
vantages and restrictions of these versatile machines, and gives
his readers useful advice to help them decide whether to buy
one or not. Evidently, the dual-sport bug had bitten Larry, too.

Dan Kennedy, publisher, Whitehorse Press

If your household is wired to the Speed Channel, then you probably
caught Nicky Hayden's decisive victory in this year's Daytona 200, the
first-ever live broadcast of America's most prestigious motorcycle road
race.

As so frequently happens in the 200-miler, many of the top riders
weren't around at the finish. Miguel and Kurtis gave us some spectacular
dogfights before prematurely pitting their RC51s. From there on in, the
most exciting riders were in the Honda commercials . . . a pair of dust
devils aboard a VTX and a Valkyrie, careening sideways across the
screen as if shot from an underground Nevada test site!

Could this be the direction that Honda—always the innovator—plans to take dual-sporting? An Ariel Sharon-style rejoinder to environmentalists who would banish trail bikes from our western deserts? Nah . . . just good television, I think.

I'm not sure what constitutes a "dual-sport" or "dual-purpose" bike these days, what with slick-shod supermotards and knobby-tired tourers weighing 600 pounds with saddlebags. *DualSport* is actually a registered trademark of Suzuki, whose DR350S and DR-Z400S epitomize go-anywhere motorcycling.

Suzuki DualSports dominate the 50/50 sector because they're so good, and because everyone in the industry knows dual-purpose bikes spend more time on the street than in the dirt. It's just the way things are.

Lord help me, I recently sold *three* motorcycles to pay for the biggest and most expensive dual-purpose bike in the world. It's ugly, it's quirky, and it weighs as much as two DR-Z400Ss! I've logged roughly a thousand miles in my first month of ownership, less than one percent of which have seen me roosting anything looser than the salt with which my state's highway department so generously seasons its paved roads.

So why, oh why, would I sacrifice a century of road-bike development for the right to pound down a dirt road a couple of times a month on a zeppelin of a motorbike as suited to berm-busting as an NFL nose tackle is to dancing on high heels? Well, because dirt style just goes well with asphalt.

Road bike fashion—and make no mistake, motorcycling is a fashion industry—has plotted two major routes on the road back from the oblivious '80s. Call them lean forward and lean back. Lean forward answers the question: "What'll she do?" It's the solution that most any engineer would come up with given the task of making a two-wheel machine negotiate a fixed, paved circuit. Lean back addresses the operator's overall sense of well-being.

"Standard"-style bikes place the rider in an upright position, halfway between the two extremes, in what would seem the perfect compromise for all-around riding. Dirt-style bikes are like standards, but with longer travel suspension to deliver smoother bump absorption and provide greater legroom.

If you ride without regard for curbs or potholes, you might take full measure of a "real" dirt bike's 12 inches of travel (seven more than a typical standard or sport-bike). Otherwise, a modest boost of 2 to 3 inches can provide comfort that you'll feel in town and country, while compromising handling only at the outer limits of aggressive street riding.

To say that dirt-style bikes are merely standards with long suspenders seems a gross exaggeration—but then again, maybe not. Different wheels and suspension components combined with a few off-road styling cues were all that Triumph needed to produce its 900 Tiger in 1995, a bike that shared the same chassis with every motorcycle—three *and* four cylinder—in the first Hinckley collection. This year BMW has performed that trick in reverse—sawing down the second generation F650 to produce the F650CS, a sophisticated urban thumper riding on sporty 17-inch rubber.

Tire sizes are perhaps the most accurate reflection of a bike's intent to conquer rough territory. The narrow 21-inch front, which is standard on virtually every adult-sized dirt bike, doesn't carve asphalt like a sticky, low-profile 17, but it provides maximum gyroscopic stability when rider, terrain, and machine can't all agree on directions. In fact, the 19-inch fronts common to heavyweight adventure bikes tend to steer more like a dirt bike than a street bike with a low center of gravity. The bike "tips" into turns, a condition which hard-core sport riders might find objectionable, but which can actually be quite handy for ordinary street riding.

The dirt-style rider easily counters this falling action by pushing on the opposite end of the purposely wide handlebar. This creates the illusion of "car steering," but it's really the application of countersteering to pick the bike up and out of the turn. Because the tires are typically narrower and less triangulated than performance street tires, they actually respond better to the subtle mid-turn corrections which are so common to street riding, particularly on roads with limited views.

That's another reason why riders with little interest in off-road exploration often fall for the dirt-style motorcycle—superior road view. Cresting a blind hill, the dirt-style rider can stand on the pegs and sometimes spot a hazard several seconds earlier than a lean-forward or lean-back pilot. Such lofty perches do have drawbacks. Wind-blast is one, though most adventure tourers (BMW R1150GS, Suzuki V-Strom DL1000, Aprilia CapoNord, etc.) employ decent wind cutters. Except for the GS, with its miraculous Telelever front suspension, long-travel bikes exacerbate front-end dive under braking, so dirt-style pilots must learn to be smooth and to manage weight transitions.

Then there's the matter of seat height, perhaps the chief deterrent to life in the dirt style. While traditional lowering methods (see "Get Down," *Rider*, January, 2002)can reduce ride height somewhat, it's best to avoid drastic alterations. These bikes are built tall for a reason.

So be flexible. If you can't get both feet flat on the ground, practice so that you can easily—*automatically*—plant one foot solidly. If you're a shorter person considering a taller motorcycle, make sure that it's got perfect carb or fuel-injection manners right off the bottom; you don't want to live with a tall (and heavy) bike that sputters when it's leaned over at walking speeds. Work on clutch control and master the rear brake as a precision low-speed maneuvering device. Take advantage of those wide handlebars and learn to counterbalance. Dirt-style bikes are more "rider active." Mastering their nuances unlocks low- and medium-speed agility that other comparably-sized bikes cannot approach.

Indeed, all is not what it appears to be. In truth, that VTX power cruiser might be a better device for sliding around on a vacant lot (if that's your idea of adventure) . . . at least the fall to earth isn't as far.

If you're serious about riding off-road for the first time or just want practice riding taller dirt-style bikes, get some practical experience through an MSF DirtBike School (877-288-7093), www.dirtbike-school.com, or other formal program. Then, before you choose a surface and a machine to chase the horizon on, imagine how it will feel should that horizon accidentally tilt by 90 degrees. Remember—everything that looks like dirt and feels like dirt . . . is not dirt.

Strange and Wonderful

April 1998

While the philosophers tell us "Know thyself," Larry's advice here is "Know thy bike." Thank goodness shifting is now standardized as "one down, four (or five) up," but beyond that it's anyone's guess. Sure, all of these idiosyncrasies will be immediately learned on your own machine, but till then they can be pretty disconcerting. Turn signals on Harleys, BMWs and metric bikes activate and cancel in different ways. When I climbed aboard a Buell test bike recently I couldn't find the ignition switch—it was tucked into the left side of the fairing. On some bikes it's up under the gas tank, or down below the rider's left haunch.

I tested a scooter recently with CVT (constantly variable transmission) and automatic clutch, but it had the standard lever by each grip. Both were for brakes (which were integrated), but I had to mentally force myself to not whip in that "clutch" lever and possibly send myself flying over the bars. Don't confuse one bike's trait with another's.

My worst incident of unfamiliarity causing a wrong reaction happened in 2006 while riding a big dual-sport in the dirt. I came around a downhill lefthander and started to slide the front tire. My reaction was to grab the front brake lever. While flying head-first through the air I knew A) my riding day was over, and B) I expected to be knocked unconscious. A broken collarbone verified A, but a high-quality helmet prevented so much as a headache. I won't make that mistake again!

Bill Stermer, contributor, Rider *magazine*

For better or for worse, I've been a one-man barometer of the U.S. motorcycle market. I bought my first brand-new bike in 1976, and by 1984 I was on my sixth. Fourteen years later, I was still contemplating number seven.

Contrary to the impressions of many, I get neither the milk nor the cow for free. I purchase and maintain my own bikes just like you, but I do get some nice test rides—several thousand miles sometimes. Over the years, I haven't failed to choose so much as I've brutally and methodically eliminated new candidates. BMWs almost perfectly model the wardrobe of sport and touring I seek: moderate weight, torque, longevity, and a peerless luggage system. You pay more, but you get more—three-year warranty, adjustable ergos, ABS brakes, catcons, injectors, chips. In the end, a bit more than I really want.

When I was studying Spanish I snacked daily on Castilian motorcycle magazines, one of which rated every bike made in five categories (depending upon the style of bike). Honda's ST1100 was the only bike on our planet to score an *Excelente* in every category. But seven hundred pounds for a sport tourer? I have to pass, thanks.

Only one machine in recent years has caused me to lust in my heart, and the chances of it ever docking in my garage were roughly equal to Tyra Banks appearing at Planet Hollywood on Jimmy Carter's arm— Ducati's wickedly impractical 916. I wasn't even looking to buy a new bike when I was blindsided by the 916's newest sibling, the ST2—sort of a Tyra Banks with glasses. It looked, handled, and sounded like a Ducati but came with humane ergos and gorgeously integrated saddlebags.

It idled, carbur-jected, and shifted perfectly, and even did U-turns like a normal motorcycle. According to the documentation, the once-esoteric Desmodromic valves didn't even need checking during the first 6,000 miles. It was as if Italy's finest engineers and stylists had worked their magic, then sent the bike off to Hamamatsu for finishing. I probed and looked for excuses (well, maybe they sent the sidestand to Munich), but before I could find a legitimate one I was sitting across from the loan officer, pen in hand.

So, the industry has officially turned itself around. The last of the balding, middle-aged holdouts has bought himself a new motorcycle. When I bought my first new bike, as a young man, I was picking scabs before I'd made the first payment, thus corroborating the Hurt Report's finding that even experienced riders are at greater risk on new bikes. Today, I need no one to tell me that a new bike doesn't transform me into Zeus on wheels—but I recall several times when simple unfamiliarity put me at peril.

Having limited experience with big touring rigs, I once deigned to answer the age old question "what'll she do" without first addressing the "what about the big trunk on the back" issue. The ensuing speed wobble haunts me some nights like a week-old burrito.

Then there was the time, two years ago, when I decided to firm up the brake lever adjuster (the screw-in type that can actually move the piston) on my recently purchased, secondhand Suzuki DR350. The bike later experienced a total brake failure while wailing down a (fortunately) familiar stretch of twisty road. My Duck's Brembo master cylinder has the same type of adjuster (hot-glued in place), but you can be certain that I'll think long and hard before tampering with it.

Twice, while riding strange machines down busy six-lane sections of Southern California freeways, I've had the puckers induced by the routine task of switching the petcock to reserve. The first was on a Ducati E900 Elefant, the lever of which was somewhere around my left ankle. Not wishing to repeat that experience, I decided one East L.A. evening to make a preemptive switch. After fumbling and fumbling in the dense 80-mph traffic, I finally pulled off into the barrio where I discovered the reason for my difficulty. The Suzuki 600 Bandit's large and convenient plastic lever had shed its Phillips head attachment screw and blown off the bike! My new ST2 has, instead of a petcock, a fuel gauge and a bright yellow warning light. My prediction is that in the coming millennium fuel supply valves will become as rare as kickstarters on street bikes.

That infernal sidestand. The only thing more devious than a self-retracting sidestand is one that stays down when you ride off . . . and I have the X-rays to prove it, another remembrance of a bike I'd not fully familiarized myself with. The spring on the Duck is easily defeatable—and I've thought about doing so—but I've heard of at least three fatal accidents triggered by neglected sidestands. In my mind the electronic switch which cuts off the engine when a gear is engaged and the sidestand simultaneously deployed should be universal.

I have another request for the manufacturers, the ones who make the round black rubber things which go on our wheels. The Ducati is the first new bike I've bought in 14 years, but in that time I've scuffed in maybe a hundred new tires. How about a little buff job at the factory? Until that starts happening, everyone else—won't you please remember that new tires are slippery and must be scuffed in by gradually adding lean angle in turns?

There's no avoiding the fact that strange bikes pose risks that friendly, familiar ones don't. A close friend of mine (coincidentally, the mechanic to whom I'll be entrusting those Desmodromic valves) won several regional racing championships and came within a guy named Schwantz of winning a national title . . . but he crashed two strange bikes one season in his own driveway! Once, during a trouble-shooting session on a Venture Royale, he decided to impress his girlfriend with a big ol' rear brake slide . . . forgetting for the moment that the Yamaha had integrated brakes!

Don't sue Ducati if you drink battery acid and don't know the antidote. It's in the owner's manual; but once, on a tour, we needed an hour just to *find* the battery, because the owner of the new bike had failed to carry the booklet. Whenever I mount an unfamiliar machine, I try to devote 10 or 15 minutes to familiarizing myself with it before I even hit the street. There's no time like the moment for properly adjusting mirrors, levers, and tire pressures. It's funny, but I've seen people spend days polishing their bikes, then ride off with 10 pounds of air pressure in the tires. If it's a brand-new bike, I like to have the mechanic, not the salesperson, hand me the key. He can answer my maintenance questions and make any last-minute adjustments the bike requires.

Before I engage other traffic I want to know how the bike responds, especially in the two most critical areas—braking and steering. Some bikes have mushy yet powerful brakes; others have firm but not particularly strong ones. Some require four fingers, some as few as one. I like to know that I can quickly and easily take the front brake to impending skid, and that I'm not going to lock the rear one in a panic.

Steering response is as varied as braking. Some bikes steer quickly and heavily; others are slow and light. I always spend several minutes practicing U-turns; if a motorcycle has limited steering lock, I don't want to discover it at an embarrassing and potentially dangerous moment.

Every time I've gone on an organized tour involving rental bikes, guys and gals have had to be reminded to cancel their turn signals. So if the machine hails from a nation with a different interpretation of switchgear than mine, I spend a couple of minutes practicing the drill before hitting the road.

When I train new riders on the road, I like to emphasize "no surprises," but strange machines will always present a few. How surprised I was, on my very first ride, to discover that what felt like 55 mph on my old bike is actually 80 on the Ducati. I hope the judge likes pasta.

Encrusiasts

October 2000

What you want in a motorcycle is not always what you get—unless you know what to ask for. Many new riders say "I just want to cruise," and so they choose a cruiser. Perhaps that's the best type of motorcycle on which to start as it makes no pretense of wanting to be quick or corner like lightning. It's usually stylish, low to the ground, offers mellow power and does not challenge the rider to go fast.

Yet there is a potential problem with some cruisers. Riders often gain speed as they gain skill and confidence. Bikes initially purchased for their style and easy riding (which are assets at cruising-around speeds) can become liabilities when that rider begins riding more aggressively and asking more in terms of braking, cornering, and handling. That low seat height, so comforting at first, now may mean that footboards, stands, or exhaust systems drag the pavement in turns. The feet-forward seating position so relaxing at low speeds makes it difficult for the rider to use body positioning to help in high-speed turns. Less sophisticated braking and suspension systems, which contributed to the bike's attractive initial price, now become limiting factors to those who want to ride more aggressively.

At this point it's a good idea to start defining the job you want your motorcycle to do, reading the magazine road tests with a more specific eye, and asking your riding buddies and dealer personnel for their input regarding what type of bike would suit your emerging riding needs better.

Bill Stermer, contributor, Rider *magazine*

When a high-ranking executive parts his lips in this information age, the human larynx generates shock waves like a nuclear reactor generates heat. Ask William Jefferson Clinton or Ray Blank, senior vice president of American Honda's motorcycle division.

Blank, who's never been implicated in any scandal that I'm aware of, gave a provocative response to an interviewer from *Forbes* magazine this past May. Business types beyond the pale of our little two-wheeled colony were taking notice of Harley-Davidson's 1999 vault to the number one position in U.S. motorcycle sales, breaking Honda's three-decade grip on market dominance.

"We cater to the enthusiast," countered the Big Red standard bearer. "We don't attract a rider who buys a motorcycle for driveway jewelry."

Ooh. The words were those of a warrior prince slashing out in defense of a crest he deeply believed in. But when Iron Mike Tyson knocks you down in a closely contested fight, do you jump up and lead with your chin?

On the other hand, maybe some upper-echelon trash-talking is what Honda needs to shake its too-perfect image—at least in this country, where a pony-tailed designer in Navajo jewelry is 10 times more recognizable than a clean-cut five-time GP champion. Anyway, Blank's statement may be fundamentally incorrect, at least according to one market analyst.

"We're in the fashion business, and we need to know that," says Don Brown of DJB Associates, widely recognized as the number one industry analyst and—coincidentally—the go-to guy for Honda *and* Harley. Brown points to the car world for examples which illustrate just how important looks are.

"Look at Volkswagen's new Bug . . . they made a hell of a car. And Chrysler building the PT Cruiser as a statement toward lifestyle and peoples' emotions. They prove you can start with evocative styling themes and build upon a thoroughly modern and competent chassis."

Just yesterday I gave a riding lesson to a gentleman who typified the mature audience today's cruisers attract—a 50-year-old cardiologist who'd been riding about a year on his Honda Shadow Aero 1100. He told me he had another doctor friend who'd considered my course and the MSF Experienced RiderCourse (ERC) but opted out of both because he'd recently commissioned a $3,000 paint job on his Harley and was afraid of dropping it. He did note, however, that Harley Doc had grown frustrated with his too-precious paint job and was considering the purchase of an everyday machine. Kind of like when a woman leaves her expensive jewels in the safe and wears fake ones to the ball. Perhaps American Honda could claw its way back to market supremacy on the talons of this marketing slogan:

Honda. We make beautiful and affordable driveway jewelry. Durable, safe, suitable for everyday use or for that special occasion.

Or perhaps not.

My training tours are about curves (4,000 per weekend) and the synchronization of rider and machine. Fringe, chrome, and anything with the word "thunder" have little place in our curricula, but over this past winter my daily email flowed over with info requests from owners of Vulcans, Viragos, Road Stars, and the like. I confess this made me nervous, because in the past when we had problems, cruiser riders were over represented. But let's define what constitutes a "problem."

1) Fatigue: unpreparedness for long days—often in hot weather—on challenging roads.

2) Difficulty with basic maneuvers: U-turns and stopping on loose or sloped surfaces.

3) Gear problems: self-destructing aftermarket parts, unprotective clothing, poor quality helmets which render radio communications difficult or impossible.

4) Loud motorcycles: sufficiently annoying that others complained about riding behind them.

5) Pokey pace: inability or unwillingness to maintain the speed limit on straight, unchallenging roadways.

6) Heightened anxiety levels: manifested in two extremes: "I'm sorry I'm holding the group up" and "I can keep up with these guys."

If you'd have asked me two years ago, I'd have said that my biggest concern was the accident rate of cruiser/ Harley riders. Over one three-year period all of the mishaps under my watch were visited upon this sector, despite the fact that they represent only 10 to 15 percent of our training tour participants. Maybe these things are cyclical (not one Harley/ cruiser accident to report in '99 or '00); nearly all accidents, I'm convinced, are preventable.

A Harley Road King pilot (also a real-life pilot) left the road with his stereo serenading the animals in the forest. A flatlander who'd lowered his already ground-hugging Fat Boy demurred when he discovered he couldn't execute a right hand bend; he felt that he should have been warned of the need for ground clearance on the Smoky Mountain twisties. What I've learned from these episodes is to assume nothing.

And who knows? Maybe the reminders we've added to our literature help explain why we haven't had a cruiser go down in 24 months.

Feet forward isn't the recipe for winning any competition of speed, but how bad, really, is it? Most (but not all) of today's factory cruisers disdain the old popcorn-sucking slouch, placing the rider in a comfortable, well-supported position with reasonable access to the handlebars. The fact that the rider can't weight the footpegs (or footboards) compromises handling skill somewhat, but this is more noticeable on a multitask parking lot training course than in most day-to-day street encounters.

But which came first? The attitude or the posture? I should keep a logbook of the revealing quotes I get from student riders. Like this from a sport-touring Honda CBR1100XX rider:

"I don't know what it is with me, I just obsess over skill development. I'm never satisfied. Why do you think that is?"

Mr. Safety: "I don't know; what do you do for a living?"

XX Rider: "Oh, I'm a psychologist."

Another rider, a luxury car salesman who'd just bought a new Triumph Sprint ST, offered this lament: "All my riding partners are better than me—faster. Riding with them is really stressful."

His Harley riding associate at the car dealership countered with this: "You should come ride with us (the Harley riders). It's great, we just cruise, get a burger. It's the most relaxing thing in my life." And perhaps the most revealing comment comes from a man who owns a variety of machines, Western and Oriental, feet forward and feet back.

"I don't like my motorcycles too *perfect*," drawled the senior engineer of a certain Midwest motorcycle manufacturer.

I confess I've been less than honest by not revealing the event which provided impetus for this column—a recent training tour which we billed as a "lite" ride. We had four Japanese and American cruisers, and one "master of the universe" BMW K1200LT. With a passenger and luggage, the LT rider faced many of the same handling limitations as the cruiser pilots, plus he'd just come off a Yamaha Royal Star, so the mood of the ride was unmistakably "cruiser."

I've never had a group like them. My assistant, Tony Capriotti, and I just told them what to do—*once*—and they did it. Ease off the brake; don't let go of it—*done*. Stay on the gas if you scrape—*done*.

If motorcycling is, as MSF literature purports, 90 percent mental and 10 percent physical, then the cruiser is perhaps the embodiment of mental motorcycling. With no 911 to dial for first response braking, handling, and acceleration, the cruiser pilot relies on the bedrock values of good planning and solid judgment.

So what's the measure of an enthusiast? Until someone smarter than me comes up with a better answer, I can only say the breadth and depth of his enthusiasm. Wanna see my Royal Star tattoo?

Those Pesky Reminders of the Past

November 2000

In this column calling for self-canceling turn signals, Larry gave a shout-out to my now-defunct TV show called "Bike Week," so I think he'd appreciate this story. For a touring episode, we pulled off a spectacular opening shot. The camera started tight on the host (yours truly) and his bike, then pulled steadily back, first revealing the magnificent Rip Van Winkle bridge and then the entire Hudson River Valley, lit by the setting sun. Sunset was the key factor, dictating that we had just one take before losing the light. We took our one shot and the result was perfect . . . movie quality television . . . except for that damned turn signal winking steadily all the way across the bridge! I'm with you, Larry. We need self-canceling turn signals!

Dave Despain, SpeedTV

Ask me in another year if you want a truly objective answer, but from the honeymoon suite my new Triumph Sprint ST appears to be the perfect motorcycle.

That's not just my opinion either. I'm actually parroting TV personality Dave Despain, whose "Bike Week" adventures often embark from the north Georgia mountains, a peach stone's throw from Triumph America's headquarters. Despain has masterminded over a year's worth of script ideas to keep the Brits from repo-ing his two demo Sprints. For starters, the ST is the most powerful bike I've ever owned, with 100 plus *caballos* and some 65 pounds-feet of torque. So, depending upon your views on free will, it's either the safest or most dangerous global positioning unit on the freeway. It's plush and steers beautifully, Willie Sutton and Hurricane Agnes couldn't permeate its attractive luggage, and the fuel injection is positively seamless. Runs from New York to Vegas on a tank of gas, too.

It may not have quite the finished appearance of, say, a Honda VFR800, but it's the first motorcycle I've ever ridden which makes no apologies—*none*—for arriving without a Japanese passport. In fact, its most frustrating feature comes from the Pacific rim, and I'm referring here to its little green turn-signal indicator.

Go ahead and laugh. Leaving a turn signal on is no laughing matter to me. For years I've been chiding new riders to cancel their signals, and suddenly *I'm* the one who needs reminding. I'll tell you what, though: I ride with all levels of motorcyclists, and there are damned few who unfailingly cancel their blinkers over the course of an eight-hour ride.

Now that manufacturers have supposedly forged a cease-fire in the speed wars, meaning no 200-mph motorcycles in our foreseeable future, magazines might turn their attention to some of the more subtle nuances of performance. How about a giant 12-bike turn-signal shootout? Here's a brief preview of how it might shape up: Yamaha YZF600F: "Good, steady blink but, like the Sprint ST, suffered from the easily overlooked teeny weenie greenie."

Harley-Davidson FLHT. "Self-canceling signals worked every time . . . every time we sat at a stoplight for more than 20 blinks."

BMW R1100RS: "All of our testers loved the ergonomically shaped switches, and the four-way flashers were a big hit. Unfortunately, one tester sprung a tendon in his right wrist trying to cancel the signal while accelerating out of a sharp right hander."

When I started riding, "real" motorcycles had no turn signals, and we bitched loudly when the orange and red orbs defiled the sinewy lines of our favorite models. I still see some of my grizzled compatriots cruising the highways on their old Harleys, Nortons, and Triumphs. They prefer crusty black hides over dandy Andy suits, and they signal coolly, with a finger aimed knee-high cum Miles Davis draining the spit from his trumpet between hot riffs. Often they have a special peg to support their special peg—the one some freakin' cager did a number on.

The first motorcycle I owned which came with blinkers—coincidentally a Triumph ('73 model)—went through a dozen bulbs between Pittsburgh and Denver. They say the 2001 Bonnevilles won't vibrate quite so much.

Who out there can remember the turn-signal beepers which appeared in the late 70s to remind us to cancel after turning? I vividly recall standing on the corner in bike-mad London listening to the endless "*beeeAAApab—beee AAApah—beeeAAApab*" of passing motorcycle messengers. Pity one couldn't hear the damned things above 10 mph.

The one on my sparrowlike 185 Yamaha has been cheeping away for nearly two decades now.

It's often said that there's little which is truly new in motorcycling, and an hour in any of the great motorcycle museums easily supports this theory. Each time a "new" technology sets the motorcycle world abuzz, it's nearly even money that somebody tried it decades earlier. Could be the state of metallurgy or the high cost of production doomed its first coming . . . more often, probably just fickle fashion. Belt drives, hub-center steering, and Desmodromic valves are three examples of innovations deemed "breakthrough" years after someone else had abandoned them. And so I wait still for someone to come up with a self-canceling turn signal that works as well as the set-up on my 1976 Yamaha RD400.

Now *that* was a bike. It was also the first motorcycle I ever owned which had cast wheels and disc brakes front and rear. It sold new for pennies and could wheelie until Wednesday. But enough nostalgia. The thing had turn signals so advanced that a quarter-century later I've yet to sample their equal. You simply thumbed the switch and forgot about it. It incorporated both a time and distance sensor, so it never canceled prematurely while you waited out a traffic signal and only rarely because you were traveling too fast. The system was nothing short of brilliant.

Almost nothing can stop today's manufacturers from delivering the product they want. And because they're businesses, the product they want to deliver is the one you want to buy. I could rant (and probably will in some future column) about the futility of analog speedometers you can't read until you're going fast enough to risk imprisonment . . . but a trick new lap timer will generate lots more interest than a sensibly positioned speedo.

But guess what? Someone at a major manufacturer is on the same page as me (surely a first!). As I write this Senior Editor Ken Freund is tooling around Ventura County on a 2001 Harley Dyna Glide equipped with the most complex self-canceling system offered on a motorcycle to date.

Unlike the previous Harley iterations, this one doesn't pack in early; i.e. when you're stopped at a traffic light or halfway between the time that you signal for and actually arrive at your freeway exit. That's because it now monitors vehicle speed, deceleration, *and* lean angle to prevent premature cancellation.

The system employs a 20-flash countdown utilized as default. The countdown is subsequently placed on hold whenever the vehicle is decelerating or when speed is less than 5 mph. The lean-angle sensor further cuts down on unwanted blinking by canceling after the bike has leaned and subsequently straightened—but only when the speed is 45 mph or less. And, of course, the rider can manually cancel at any time.

About the only situations I can imagine that would "fool" Harley's system would be a low-speed bend or a swerve just before a junction . . . and even then the rider would be guilty of the relatively minor peccadillo of early cancellation. The system is so well thought-out that I'm going to ignore for now the Motor Company's persistent use of separate left and right signaling switches.

Safe riding is the synergistic modeling of tractable and intractable events; a chess game with only seconds permitted between moves. The challenge of the near future is what most riders relish, not pesky ties to the past.

Would I trade my new Triumph's 100 silky horses for the Harley's self-canceling signals? Should I *have* to?

The Roads, Rules, and Risks

Least Likely to Succeed

April 1993

Larry mentions in this article that the Motorcycle Safety Foundation seemed initially skeptical about combining licensing and training, concerned that the separate functions could be corrupted. Time has proved that skepticism correct. This writer has experienced instructors who became too friendly with their students during the several days of training, and could not summon the objectivity necessary to convert from friendly coach to impartial licensing examiner at the conclusion of training. Accordingly, entirely too many students "pass," receiving an unrestricted motorcycle endorsement to ride on the street.

Also, the proficiency of regular DMV license examiners should be in question. Most do not ride. While they may have received the required instruction to administer the motorcycle test, most will not actually do so often enough to become truly proficient. Scoring a brief set of tasks in a parking lot is far from adequate to determine proficiency to ride in the "real world."

Ideally, the examination would be administered by a trained motorcyclist and conducted almost entirely on the street. But that would be much more expensive; are we back to politics?

Ken Murray, owner and lead instructor
Atlanta Motorcycle Schools

Three kicks, four kicks, five. Nothing. Neophyte mechanic though I was, I quickly diagnosed the problem as a blown fuse. I had a spare, but traffic was backed around the block, and the officer was losing patience fast. Odds were that the spare would likewise blow within 50 yards, and then I'd really be cooked.

"Hey, man . . ." called a voice from over my shoulder. It was the guy who'd waited in line ahead of me for the past three hours. "You can use my bike," he chirped, his face flushed with success at having just received a motorcycle license.

I parked my wounded Bonneville and—the world might as well know—earned my license on a Honda C70, automatic clutch . . . *step-through!*

Got a good licensing story? I've got bunches of 'em. Like the time I was recruited right off the street by a gentleman who needed a licensed operator to sit in his car while he waited in line for his test . . . even though he already held valid licenses from France and Nigeria, plus an International Driving Permit recognized by 160 nations.

Whether or not operator exams serve any palpable role in reducing traffic accidents, testing centers are tremendously efficient revenue producers, and you'd best believe the bureaucracies take their little gold mines seriously. A few years ago, when Pennsylvania's motorcycle safety courses began licensing a significant percentage of the state's total, a proposal was put forth to have rider education take over all cycle testing. The examiners' union put the kibosh on that plan, claiming that the 15,000 motorcycle licenses—2.4 percent of their annual test load—would put examiners out of work.

I'm not a "political" person. The basic premise of politics—doing what you know to be wrong so that down the road you may get what might be semi-right—is beyond my grasp. But more and more I'm beginning to grasp the maxim that "everything is politics."

When my state, eight years ago, became the first to link licensing to rider education, the move was met coolly by Motorcycle Safety Foundation (MSF) officials who raised legitimate concerns that the separate objectives of these two entities would be compromised. Today, the Foundation concedes (at least privately) that linkage holds the key to rider education's future health.

MSF has a long-standing interest in licensing. Thirty-seven states currently use MSF-based licensing tools, chief the Alternate MOST (Motorcycle Operator Skill Test). The test is administered thusly: 1) upshift to second, downshift, sharp turn, upshift, downshift, normal stop (front tire in box); 2) offset cone weave, tight U-turn; 3) obstacle turn (swerve); 4) quick stop.

Although variants of the MOST family have proven difficult to administer, the Alternate MOST requires only limited space and equipment and has given a reasonably good account of itself over the last decade. Nonetheless, the Foundation decided about six years ago that it wanted something with more pizzazz.

Who ya gonna call when you want all the bells, whistles, and overblown credentials that money can buy? Right—Washington! Enter the National Public Services Research Institute and its Motorcycle Licensing Skill Test (MLST). MSF took the bait. So did Pennsylvania's newly empowered rider education program, and I gotta admit—I was smitten, too. The premise of the test was spot on: Skip the trifling stuff; identify the behaviors at which riders fail in *accidents* and test those skills. In other words, braking, swerving, and cornering.

There were teething problems. An electronic signaling device performed as if assembled from stockpiled warranty returns on BSA/Triumph electrics. Then, when test sites resorted to hand signals, students instinctively reacted to every perceived twitch, frequently combining quick stops with swerves. In other words, crashing—about one crash for every 50 licenses. A perfect score (never achieved in 2,000 tries at my site) requires cornering at warp speed. Even instructors sometimes crashed while demonstrating the test.

What's more, in practice it became clear that the test (designed by a nonriding Ph.D) didn't really measure the skills it set out to. The worst line through the curve gave the best score. Students sometimes ran off the curve on both their attempts, yet still passed. Braking and swerving were reduced to tests of reflexes, but since the minimum speed was a piddling 12 mph, timid students often approached, chopped the throttle, and executed their "emergency maneuvers" at more like eight mph!

To prove just how bad the MLST was, I recruited a long-legged 26-year-old instructor, and the two of us took turns attacking the course under tightly controlled conditions—i.e., with no engine. In fact, we used none of the primary controls—no clutch, no throttle, no shifter, and neither brake. We just ran and pushed, leaped onto the footpeg and coasted through the timing zones. On the timed turns, even my tired old legs cracked the 12-mph minimum speed. Swerves were a snap—we both aced those. "Quick stops" posed the toughest challenge, but we met it and passed the test by leaping off "at speed" and halting the mighty 125s with only our boots!

"The power of accurate observation," said George Bernard Shaw, "is commonly called 'cynicism' by those who have not got it." I've gotten a lot of mileage out of that quote, but I didn't conduct my "experiment" to be cynical. I did it to prove a point, and having proved it, I spent last summer trying to develop something better.

MSF has contributed its MOST, MOST II, and Alternate MOST. As a working title I think I'll simply call my exam "Larry's Easily Administered Skill Test." The LEAST requires 3 1/2 minutes per person, can be administered by one examiner, and tests the critical skills of cornering, braking, and swerving. But unlike the MLST, there is no performance "bonus;" examinees are expected to meet minimum objectives and nothing more.

But meet them they must, because the LEAST carries automatic "death penalties" for major errors such as running off the curve or stopping beyond the standard. And since education stresses the importance of searching and predicting, there are no "panic" reactions; the rider has roughly one-half second to interpret his signal before initiating a response.

I never knew before how much work goes into developing a skill test. Though my basic idea has remained unchanged, it has required continual experimentation. Swerving, for example, was most difficult to quantify. Both the MOST and MLST gave the exam taker great license to "cheat," so each week I juggled the dimensions, speed requirements, and point values, then recruited fresh volunteers to test them on. After each session I wrote tiny rule changes to avert every conceivable misinterpretation.

When the time came to show my test to my state's coordinator and chief instructors, I learned that my work was just beginning. I took their criticisms and suggestions and honed the system even more. A plan was set forth to train examiners and to pilot test the exam for an entire year. Having been seduced once by the MLST, I conceded the necessity of moving cautiously.

It never got that far, though. Despite the unanimous backing of the state's administrators, my test failed to win approval of the Department of Transportation. Technically, they never looked at it. In reviewing the accident statistics of the previous year, they found that accidents had "leveled off." They had more important matters to debate.

Budget, I think.

California 101

May 2003

"The Grodster" was an excellent riding companion, even better at the dinner table. The man had a wit about him that was truly exceptional, although he understood that some dullards "did not quite get it." No matter, as he also knew that one can't entertain all of the people all of the time. Out here in California we would pull into some roadside café where the help was usually Mexican, and he would order with his best Castilian Spanish—much to the amusement of these locals who speak a very different Hispanic dialect.

He was a realist, not only in his evaluation of human nature, but also with his students' skills, which is why he enjoyed his on-the-road schools so much; he could see the progress. Except with me . . . no progress there. When he was visiting us, we would roll through the ranchlands at a pleasant rate of speed, with my constant cutting of corners, and his constant reprimands. But I did learn, albeit slowly, and I do less corner-cutting these days, thanks to Larry.

Clement Salvadori, contributor, Rider *magazine; author of* 101 Road Tales *and* Motorcycle Journeys through California and Baja

"Reckon this'll be awright," I growled in my best Sam Elliott imitation, imagining my voice to be as big and coarse as the desert night. Like a moth to a flame I'd been drawn to the neon red "café" sign, and I swung the door open with high expectations—none of them faintly gastronomical.

So, imagine our surprise when the waiter uncorked his Parisian accent and delivered *salade nicoise,* shepherd's pie with fresh venison, and *profiteroles* for dessert! Over a glass of good merlot I chatted with newfound friends—two fellow Pennsylvanians and an ex-New Yorker now hailing from tony Newport Beach. The meal stretched to two hours, and I scarcely noticed when the piano player drifted in off the street (*"Damn,* they have a good sound system here!"), transporting me back to a cherished memory—a stop on Duke Ellington's final concert tour.

It was a dinner to die for, and that part sucked—that fate had chosen a deadly high-speed pile-up to back us into Independence, California, and the Still Life Café. U.S. 395, cradled between the snowy Sierras and the chocolatey crenellation preceding Death Valley, is like Lyle Lovett's *Road to Ensenada* " . . . plenty wide and fast." Not wide enough, though. Not at night, when headlights boring through the thin desert air at 100 yards look little different from beams a half-mile beyond. Not when motorists think that all you need is enough horsepower to shrink what once took weeks by stagecoach into a commute of a few hours.

Do people drive and ride faster in California than in other parts of the country? My supposition is that they do. According to the U.S. Census Bureau, 96.7 percent of the state's population is "urbanized," a rate second only to New Jersey, which has five times California's population density. Their habitudes dictated by ocean on one side and mountains on the other, Californians regularly find themselves living—and driving—in parallel universes. Would that not make the perpendicular connectors (i.e. mountain roads) the thread by which Californian life is held together? Heaven or hell, depending upon your mood and circumstances.

There's an age-old debate in the enduro world over who meets the tougher riding challenge: eastern woods riders, or western desert racers. The former claim that their tight, technical trails demand greater skill and cunning, that deserts are for lugs who can do little more than twist a throttle. The latter liken woods riding to mud-wrestling, a comically tedious game demanding little power or courage.

I've long theorized that there's a similar, albeit subtle, dichotomy between street riders in the east and west. Track schools on both coasts have convinced me that street riders on the west wing do ride faster. A 12-month season no doubt sharpens their skills, but I also think that California roads attenuate a rider's sense of speed. I remember once leaving Willow Springs Raceway and subsequently realizing that I was rolling faster across the desert than I had on the track! A scary realization . . . and yet the big landscape made lesser speeds feel unnaturally slow.

My latest California excursion actually began with a breakfast in Los Angeles with Edelweiss Bike Travel's Werner Wachter. Wachter opined that the skill levels of American riders are "all over the map" (I think those were his words). Since Edelweiss runs several "touring centers" (fixed locations from which riders can enjoy a variety of day trips), in places like France, Arizona, and Montana, we discussed which rider skills might be honed at which centers. I candidly remarked that the limited training I'd offered in the Mountain states had left me with too little to comment on—what with their lack of driveways, intersections, and traffic.

Climbing Highway 33 into Los Padres National Forest (the *Rider* staff's favorite backyard game), it was as if we'd rented the road for the afternoon. Nevertheless, I warily regarded the abundance of turnouts on my right—many of them at the entry points to left bends from whence oncoming drivers could potentially sweep across our path. Think that drivers only turn left in front of motorcyclists in the *city?*

In the arrow-straight Cuyama Valley (still on Highway 33) I spotted a sheriff's car . . . but not before its driver spotted me. I slowed down to 70, trying not to appear too furtive but mindful of a costly 40 minutes spent in the penalty box outside of Mendocino last summer. California's finest, compared to the constabulary in my part of the world, takes a keener interest in life beyond the freeway. The lawman tailed me for about a mile at short range, grew bored, passed, and disappeared at what I'd estimate at 115 mph.

Highway 166 was another story. I was *glad* to see cops on this rapid two-lane corridor. With heavy truck traffic and hemmed-in drivers itching to pass, I found myself frequently riding next to the shoulder so as to "present" myself to the numerous tailgaters. California—even 150 miles out of L.A. is definitely not Montana, I concluded.

Highway 58, the route described by Mr. Salvadori in his February *Road Tales* column, was an absolute treat —except for the low-lying sun, the searing rays of which penetrated dark glasses. We affixed strips of electrical tape to our visors, though Clem, who mapped out some terrific back roads for us the next morning, carries a little shade which attaches via suction cups. He went to Harvard, you know.

Highway 1, an expressway in the Morro Bay area, can serve up wind gusts unknown to many eastern riders. A column of mine once drew some flak for implying that more speed is an effective antidote to potent wind. It is on paper—where wind doesn't gust or suddenly change directions.

Just off the coast, below Paso Robles, lie some vineyards, which—

while not so famous as those of the Napa/Sonoma region—are just as scenic. We rode over blind hills and past live oak trees, not so dense as the eastern hardwood forests, but big enough to hide a driveway. Overall, a riding challenge much like you'd encounter between the major eastern cities and the Appalachian ridges.

Nacimiento-Ferguson Road is another story. Guidebooks recommend more than an hour to negotiate the 17-mile "back way" to Big Sur Highway! Steep, narrow, and slimy with mud and pine needles, nearly every left bend on its descent to the ocean is negatively banked. Its builders surely held the conviction that one plunge into the abyss is worse than a hundred collisions with the mountainside. Perhaps, on a 270-pound dual-sport, I could have slid the bike around those weird-ass hairpins, but with 900-plus pounds of motorcycle, cargo, and human weight, our pace reflected my painfully mortal skills.

How many states have a *fog* season? We scampered through the redwoods on more drizzly Salvadori roads before dropping into the San Joaquin Valley, the freeways of which are notorious for chain-reaction collisions, particularly in the winter months. Last January, a 54-year-old motorcyclist was killed by a speeding Dodge Ram while stopped in the soup. It's been suggested (though not proven) that California riders who split lanes may be safer than those who sit patiently and defenselessly in stalled traffic.

While technically neither legal nor illegal, lane splitting is a skilled discipline. Most motocommuters ply the gap between the two lanes farthest to the left. The time savings in stop and go traffic is remarkable, but savvy riders content themselves with the HOV lane once its flow reaches about 30 mph.

I saw not one pistol brandished in the fury of rush-hour traffic. Although a local friend insists that "using a turn signal in L.A. is a sign of weakness," I think that many SoCal drivers have met the enemy and admitted that "he is us." On every mountain pass, from south to north, California drivers politely used the turnouts upon sighting our advancing Suzuki V-Strom in their mirrors.

I won't go so far as to say California drivers are better than those in other parts of the country, but I think that motorcyclists who live and ride in the Golden State receive a daily education that riders anywhere would find invaluable. And, as sadly witnessed out in the desert on U.S. 395, they need it.

Without Rancor

July 2000

Most of us have gripes about the clueless road users who just don't seem to get it. Imagine riding in a locale where you share breath-taking scenery and invitingly sinuous roads with alert drivers who share your motorcycling passion. Noticing you in their mirrors, they invite you to pass with a friendly wave, adjusting their lane position if necessary so there's room—at least for the paint. In this nirvana, feathers aren't ruffled even if you lane-split to the front of the pack at stop lights or road construction delays (and why not?). The only rule seems to be "play nice!" Close your little eyes and click your Alpinstars three times; you're in Spain!

Pete Tamblyn

A turnkey European motorcycle tour is one of the great motorcycling experiences. But don't take my word for it . . . or look at my photos for that matter (there aren't any). Let's talk safety. Specifically, safety in Spain.

The Iberian Peninsula was for me the last unexplored corner of Europe when I arrived there two years ago to ride the Spanish-built Honda Deauville. I returned early this spring at the invitation of Scott Moreno, a native New Yorker and Madrid resident for the last 10 years, who operates Iberian Moto Tours. Moreno wasn't looking for a review of one of his tours, but rather instruction. Together we concocted a "spring training" ride in the Andalucia region of southern Spain.

Spain had surprised me the first time—greener and more environmentally diverse than I'd imagined. It's the most mountainous nation in Europe—great for honing cornering skills—but I privately questioned the validity of my methods in a foreign land with its own traffic patterns and driving ethos. A glance at the guest list revealed a preponderance of flatlanders—several of them cruiser devotees. How would they adapt to sinewy mountain passes and *autopistas* where the slow lane moves at 85 mph?

Pretty well, it turned out, though the new environment demanded a pretty steep learning curve. Some in our group had never even seen motorcycles split lanes, and though Beemers with bags won't challenge a sport scooter for guerrilla commuting honors, our gang quickly grew enamored of their new-found freedom.

To their credit, our group built speed gradually over the six riding days. I wouldn't claim that it was my instruction, but perhaps the supplicating act of signing onto a "training" ride contributed to the fact that not one bike went down . . . something no previous packaged tour I'd attended could claim. It was amusing to watch the same rider—who had cruised out of Seville the first morning neck-and-neck with 50cc scooters plying the shoulder—bend his R1100RT into 80-mph-plus sweepers on the steep multilane ring road around Malaga on day number four.

Ah, but he and the others drew my wildest invective on the ultimate day of the tour. Moreno, who captured the moment on film when we stopped at the café, said that the sight of me charging the entire eight-rider group with my flailing clipboard and marker was the highlight of his trip. I dunno, I had a different perspective. Here's my version:

Cruising the *autopista*, rider one pulled out to overtake a slower vehicle. Because we were "in transit" between scenic routes, the tour had pretty much compacted into a phalanx of eight bikes. I was the last in line and waited until all but the rider in front of me had gone around to change lanes. Now I was the only rider left in the passing lane. Everyone, I felt, had taken too long to overtake—had been too "paradelike"—but it took more than that to set me off. Over the hill a BMW 8-series sedan appeared in my mirror, and he was *moving!* With all the other riders doddering close together in the right lane, there was no way to safely change lanes, so I accelerated (on a new BMW 1150GS—*mucho* torque) up to maybe 115 mph and proceeded to blow past the group.

Without consulting his mirror, a "gentlemanly" member of our party migrated into the left lane in deference to a semi lumbering up an entrance ramp on the right. I squeezed by our guy—both of us in the left lane—at least 40 mph in excess of his speed. I don't know about the driver of the big sedan; he must have had *very* good brakes.

The whole event lasted maybe five seconds and wasn't nearly as harrowing as it might sound, but I nevertheless seized the moment to vent.

"This is *Europe!*" I screamed over the clattering espressos and *cortados.* "If you want to overtake—do so and get the *hell* out of the way! Otherwise, stay out of the passing lane!"

I tried to sound menacing, which isn't easy when your charges are giggling and snapping your photo. Actually, I think that's pretty good advice (overtaking, not giggling) on either side of the Atlantic, and it irks me to no end when I hear that a motorcyclist received a ticket for accelerating into an open pocket while a tailgating driver gets off scot-free.

The Spanish do drive quickly, but surprisingly free of *machismo* or any sort of attitude. The speed limit on the super highways (some of them marvels of engineering, unfurling through the mountainous landscape) is 120 kph (74 mph). When drivers spot the Guardia Civil cruising the slow lane at the posted limit, they routinely slow down to 140 and go around. Civil indeed.

When I first visited Spain, I expected drivers to behave more like the Italians—weaving, gesticulating, sounding horns at the slightest provocation. That's simply not the case. Unlike the British or Germans, whose matrixes balance upon elaborate rules and regulations, the whole thing seems to sit atop a foundation of common sense. At an informal riders meeting, I asked Moreno to explain the rules for rotaries or "roundabouts" as the British call them. "I really don't think there are any," he shrugged.

To be sure, Spanish motorcyclists can be a bold lot. Reigning 500 GP champion Alex Criville is a national hero on the scale of Michael Jordan, and *motito*-mounted teens do their best to emulate him. But the lesson of the 50cc scooter—*seize your opening and then get out of the way*—seems to stay with those who matriculate to both four-wheelers and proper motorbikes. The Spanish are masters of what an acquaintance calls "flow technology"—the subtle art of easing on and off the gas so that others can make progress as well as you.

American drivers, by contrast, appear to navigate with blinders, oblivious to the needs of parallel traffic until they must jam on their brakes in angry response. Nearly all of the cars in Spain have manual transmissions, which pays a pleasant dividend in the absence of telephone chat. Should one be tempted to try, there's a fine of about $100.

Curiously, Spain had the highest traffic fatality rate in western Europe during the Franco era—10 times that of the United States. Economic prosperity has vastly improved the road conditions, the caliber of vehicles . . . perhaps the desire to live. Many of the mountain roads began life

2,000 years ago as Roman footpaths, and to fans of technical riding, they're a real treat. At the other extreme are the *autopistas,* and in between lie a marvelous network of swoopy, modern two-lane roads. My gal, MaryAnn, and I borrowed the GS for four days following the tour, and because we had to cover ground, we logged some big miles on those routes.

The region surrounding the cliffside town of Cuenca (home to the casas *colgandas* or "hanging houses") could have doubled for Zion National Park. Banked over, descending a particularly swoopy section, I peered much farther into the distance than I'm able on my native Appalachian roads. That's when I spotted a suspension bridge not quite as large as West Virginia's famous New River Gorge span but painted bright orange and purple—a fusion of art and engineering that lent a measure of contrast and safety to the mesmerizing desert conduit.

I suppose the Alps will always be the top foreign destination for American riders, and I certainly wouldn't turn down an assignment to go review a tour there. But after two visits, my view is that *España* has more types of riding (even dirt roads). Superior weather is a given. Though traffic in the major cities can be nightmarish, elsewhere it's surprisingly light. "Where are all the people?" asked one tour member.

Most Americans will probably find the language easier to slip into than French, German, or Italian. If you understand "Hasta la vista, baby," you probably recognize more Spanish than you realize. Our two languages are fraught with cognates—words that have the same meaning in both tongues.

The word "rancor"—*rencor* in Spanish—is one of these, though I never had use for it in two weeks; never encountered a drop of it on Spanish roads. Someone recently posed the question, "Imagine if people exhibited the same anti-social behavior in other public places that they do on the highway—standing in line at the bank for example?"

In Spain, the way one behaves on *la ruta* and in *el banco* are *iqual.*

Safe Talk

May 2005

Larry was a minimalist. Same was true of his views on motorcycle communications. While he embraced the value of coaching students via radios, LG and I would depart a tour's concluding ceremonies in silence, in tune with our riding in favor of being tuned in to a common frequency. Fortunately, while we enjoyed conversation elsewhere, we both preferred a more private ride. So, winding our way toward the right side of the map with the sun settling at our backs, we would enjoy a spirited ride through the countryside, free to generate our own internal dialogue. We rode together, but we rode alone.

Communication? Minimalist. Anything more would have been disruptive. We picked up needed information from the environment. No pointing out road kill. No hand gestures. More was communicated by pace and position than anything else. If I was leading and Larry dropped back, I would know my pace was faster than he cared to travel, so I would simply adjust my speed. Apparently, if he slowed even more, eventually pulled to the shoulder of the road and threw his arms in the air, then that clearly meant he wanted us to exit earlier while there was still fuel in his tank.

Eric Trow, senior instructor
Stayin' Safe Motorcycle Training

For some, a squeeze of the thigh is the deepest form of communication, but others will ask, "Can you hear me now?"

Some years ago, at one of our Rider Rallies, I sat in on a seminar in which a manufacturer's rep told the following story:

A man stormed into the parts department of a large dealership and angrily slammed a box down on the counter.

"Can I help you, sir?" asked the parts manager, aware that the man was in a volatile state.

"You'd better—you sold me a *dee*-fective communications system!"

"Well sir, what exactly seems to be the problem?" the parts manager inquired as calmly as possible.

"I'll tell you what the problem is," snapped the angry customer, "I can't hear a word my wife says!"

"Ohhh," replied the parts manager, his face suddenly alight with recognition. "You bought the deluxe model!"

Whether or not you laugh at Henny Youngman-style humor, this tale illustrates an oft overlooked component of the communications process—intent. Since I rely on bike-to-bike communicators in my work—training riders on the street—many people assume that I'm a proponent of these systems and ask me for my equipment recommendations. Those folks are usually surprised when I reply with something like:

"Well, personally, I'd rather ride in silence"

No offense to all of you whose road rhythms are rooted in Vivaldi or U2, or for whom Monument Valley would seem barren without the shared perspectives of a close companion. My headset is a work tool, and while I enjoy my job, like you, I also enjoy getting off work. When my co-instructors and I finish a ride, we're usually pretty talked out. Besides, conversation between speeding motorcycles never struck me as very natural. Unlike cell phones, which are full duplex, two-way radios are only half duplex, meaning that parties must take turns speaking. Now that's a novel communications idea, but if you use a VOX system (Voice-Operated eXchange) as we do, then the sensitivity must be finely tuned, lest one rider's signals permanently block out the other's. Recreational users, who merely wish to communicate route instructions and other basics, might be better served with push to talk (PTT).

I am blessed to have a lovely riding companion who enjoys the view from both ends of a motorcycle seat, and she tolerates aural infusions even less than I. In fact, if she didn't find internet forums nearly as offensive as intercoms, I'd suspect her of being the blogger I recently copied on a discussion of the wireless Bluetooth helmets unveiled at last fall's Intermot show.

"Call me a Luddite," scoffed the blogger, "but I prefer a squeeze of the thigh for communication. I like the fact that you can't talk on a motorcycle, for me it is part of the experience"

One might argue that running out of gas is also part of the experience. This would not be a balanced piece if I didn't admit that I did so last fall, returning from a training ride in West Virginia—with our radios safely stowed in the panniers. My partner, Eric Trow, was in the lead (with a half-tank of fuel), and if wishing could make it so, he would have disembarked at the Elkins exit, but having no way to communicate my need I simply hoped for the best. Alas my best was not good enough, though thankfullly it brought me within half a mile of some low-octane, above-ground swill that half the county was probably sipping from brown jugs.

Chances are that you readers are as divided as red states and blue over this issue, so let's move on to the real question. Does communicating with another person (on a bike-to-bike, cell phone, or intercom) make you a more dangerous rider?

I doubt anyone's keeping those stats, but with roughly 160 million passenger vehicles and 160 million cell phones in the United States (take cheer—there must be 90 million Americans who at this moment aren't driving and talking on the phone!), there is plenty of four-wheeled data out there for anyone who wants to take the time to examine it.

As long ago as 1997, researchers were documenting the risks of driving and phoning. In February of that year, the *New England Journal of Medicine* published a paper by Donald A. Redelmeier, M.D. and Robert J. Tibshirani, Ph.D., which studied 699 drivers who made 26,798 cellular phone calls over a 14-month period. While engaged in those calls, the drivers were involved in accidents at a rate four times the average— about the same risk factor as drunk driving!

In another study undertaken early this year, the University of Utah's David Strayer examined an interesting subset of the motoring world— 18- to 25-year-olds. Strayer put his youthful subjects in a driving simulator and engaged them in hands-free cellular conversation with an assistant. When called upon to brake, the phone users were 18 percent slower than the control group. In fact, their performance was equivalent to that of 65- to 74-year-olds who were not talking on the phone. "Instant aging" was the way Strayer referred to the effects.

What, you may be asking, makes talking on a phone any different from talking to a passenger in (or on) the same vehicle? We don't know. One study showed that a single passenger doubles a teen driver's risk of a fatal crash—a second passenger quintuples it! However, another study revealed that elderly drivers are significantly less likely to be involved in a crash when accompanied by passengers in the car. I'd hypothesize that it comes down to who the passenger is and what they're discussing.

For similar reasons, when I started using radios eight years ago, I made a pledge to limit my commentary to only those matters directly related to road safety. On those rare occasions when we've remained on air after "punching out," we've found it remarkably easy to descend into pointless, attention-robbing banter. On the other hand, bound by my instructor/pupil contract, I've learned to successfully guide a rider's eye up the road and to prioritize the activities which are most likely to provoke an accident. Occasionally, I'm able to reorient a rider whom I suspect is headed for trouble. Come to think of it, I probably have as much data as some of the researchers I've cited—about a quarter-million radio-controlled miles. In those miles I've watched two riders I was coaching blow turns and crash—in both cases, less than a minute after I'd cautioned them (unsuccessfully) to slow down!

Most of today's luxury-touring bikes are already equipped with rider-to-passenger intercoms, and I predict the Bluetooth technology, still considered too expensive for the U.S. market, to be unstoppable. Sure, some will prefer a squeeze of the thigh, but to many more, a cozy helmet that promises clear communications without wires or buttons will seem too good to be true. And it won't be long afterward until all of the sport-bikers are connected to all of their friends with unlimited weekend minutes. Maybe when that happens I'll need to design a course on talking safely . . . not that it's ever been my strong suit.

Where the Geritol Meets the Road

March 2002

There is a dark side to any sport, avocation, or other pursuit in which risk is inherently linked to the chosen activity. For motorcycling, it is a crash that results in a fatality. These accidents are oftentimes dispassionately reported as raw statistics that cannot tell the whole story behind the numbers. That's why it takes someone with a keen analytical mind to decipher the data and accurately interpret the information. The following column by Larry is a case in point. In it, he expertly sums up a Los Angeles Times *article about the continuing rise of motorcycle-related fatalities, particularly for riders over 35 years of age who ride large-displacement bikes. But instead of just reporting the facts, Larry—ever the teacher—offers advice on how to be a safer rider in hopes of reversing the rising trend of motorcycle fatalities. His thoughts on how reaction times of an older, more experienced re-entry rider compare to those of a younger novice offer a unique perspective into this disturbing trend.*

Unfortunately, the statistics Larry wrote about have changed little since March 2002. Motorcycles still comprise about 2-3 percent of all registered motor vehicles and account for over 10 percent of all motor vehicle crash fatalities. For this reason, the article is just as relevant today as it was when it was first penned. Herein lies the underlying message in both the following article and one that can be taken from Larry's own tragic accident: No matter how much experience or training you have, you are always at risk while riding a motorcycle—regardless of your age or the displacement of your bike.

Bill Shaw, freelance motojournalist;
contributor, Motorcycle Consumer News;
editor, Iron Butt Magazine; *MSF RiderCoach,*
and instructor, Stayin' Safe Motorcycle Training

With the average age of U.S. riders having crept up to 38 and change, a sizable percentage got a wake-up call last year when the mainstream media caught wind of what was, perhaps, an inevitable trend: Annual motorcycle fatalities among "older" riders more than doubled during the '90s.

The fallout began on March 25th with a piquant and widely circulated *Los Angeles Times* article citing the rise and fall of motorcycle fatality rates along the baby boomer divide (age 35). By May 18th the damage control team at the American Motorcyclist Association felt obliged to issue a news release; it pointed out that while the mean age of fatally injured motorcyclists had risen by 7.2 years, the mean age of motorcycle *owners* had risen by 11.2. As the summer riding season hit full swing, media outlets across the country slipped readers another downer—two consecutive years of rising motorcycle fatalities. Finally, on September 24th, with rumbling hawgs and howling crotch rockets fading off the public's radar screen, Secretary of Transportation Norman Mineta released some final bad news—motorcycle fatalities in 2000 (the most recent year studied) had risen for the third straight year.

That these stories became as big as they did has to be due in large measure to the obsessive fear of aging with which baby boomers have, rightly or wrongly, been stereotyped. And to new-wave journalism. If it's true that everyone in Los Angeles has a screenplay in the works, then *Times* Staff Writer Ricardo Alonso-Zaldivar's 2,000-word piece puts him ahead of most. How's this for plot twists:

- Che Guevara's Andean motorbike adventures
- Celluloid flashbacks from *The Wild One* and *Easy Rider*
- California street-racer narratives
- NHTSA fatality stats
- An interview with the coordinator of a Daytona Beach trauma center where more than 1,000 riders had their blood pressures checked during Bike Week 2001.

All that, and the provocative title, *A Deadly Side to the Baby Boomers' Thrill Ride.*

Flash forward to August, when I dodged the worst of a blistering California heatwave for a superlative ride across the Sierras aboard a new Ducati ST4s. My destination, Reno, Nevada, was the site of the National Association of State Motorcycle Safety Administrators (SMSA) annual conference. Among the featured speakers was Umesh Shankar, a

NHTSA mathematician, who presented findings from the June Technical Report, "Recent Trends In Fatal Motorcycle Crashes." Herewith a quick summary of its conclusions:

- More motorcycles, more vehicle miles
- More riders over age 40
- Larger engine sizes
- More fatalities on rural roads
- Majority of fatalities on undivided roads
- Speeding a major factor, especially among under 30s
- Intoxication continues to be a major problem
- Many operators—particularly under 30s—improperly licensed

The gathered, most of whom were not merely safety professionals, but enthusiasts on the demographic hot seat, all but lynched the messenger Shankar. Where, they wanted to know, was the exposure data? There really was none, but if NHTSA had been snoozing, they should have done so where I took my Friday afternoon siesta, at a brookside idyll high atop Sonora Pass. When I emerged from my slumber, I took 15 minutes to fiddle with the Ducati's idle—long enough to count 40 motorcycles go by.

From my roadside perch I easily ascertained that all 40 rode large displacement motorcycles; if they weren't all Harleys, then they at least looked like them. Naturally I didn't do an ID search on each rider, but from what I could see of them, nearly all had passed 35 summers or more.

Now contrast that with a four-hour interstate trip which I regularly make back east. In good riding weather I rarely see more than a half-dozen bikes. On the street corner where I live—within walking distance of three college campuses—I probably see one or two bikes per hour, and only about half are "youngsters" under 35. Despite what we might think of the motorcycle's utility, people are riding them for recreation, and for most, that means riding on two-lane country roads. At least that's my unofficial finding. The latest International Common Methodology for In-Depth Motorcycle Crash Investigations calls for more thorough 24-hour/365-day traffic censuses. Also, while poking holes in the NHTSA data, it's hard to ignore its three-tiered displacement based grouping—a system which treats a Ducati 996 the same as a Suzuki 650 Savage; a Yamaha V-Max the same as a Honda Gold Wing.

NHTSA's data does acknowledge small but steady yearly increases in the aggregate miles traveled by American motorcyclists—9.8 billion in

1995 up to 10.6 for 1999, the last year studied. How, I wondered, does the agency obtain this tally? My search led me to the Federal Highway Administration (FHWA), where I received the following reply from Highway Engineer Paul Svercl:

"Oh, we go out there and individually survey *every* motorcyclist in the United States," said Svercl. "It's obvious we spent *billions*," he added, as I felt a slight tug on my femur. A bureaucrat with a sense of humor.

"The truth is we hardly spent anything!" he admitted when I suggested that they really had no exposure data. The government's Vehicle Miles Traveled (VMT) figure derives in part from the Motorcycle Industry Council (MIC) survey, but is, in Svercl's words, "a general estimate."

Accurate mileage estimates shouldn't be all that difficult to obtain. Most states require annual safety inspections, so noting the mileage is a simple formality. Sure, the margin of error will always be influenced by uninspected bikes, shared usage, and even broken speedo cables, but it shouldn't be that difficult to search a national database and determine that John Smith, age 41, has three motorcycles on which he accumulated 8,564 miles last year. Why, the same database could generate a reminder to John's nephew that he's been riding three years without a proper license (like 15 percent of all fatal crash victims, according to NHTSA).

There are ways to confront a perceived crisis. The first, and most obvious, is to enlist the services of those with the greatest firsthand knowledge. The International Common Methodology calls for "motorcycle-qualified investigators"—people who can not merely regurgitate data, but who can interpret its hidden subtleties.

But "experts" can sometimes be the brick wall at the end of the tunnel. After World War II, Japan lacked the collective motorcycling expertise of the British, but when they looked to the West they saw "experts" whose dated ideas were cemented by stubborn management and a crippled infrastructure.

So we shouldn't assume that information is invalid simply because it was gathered and/or analyzed by people who don't ride. Secretary Mineta's September report noted several traffic safety milestones, including the fact that the highway death rate among children dropped to the lowest level since record-keeping began in 1975. Making cars so much safer for children took the combined efforts of designers, manufacturers, educators, and legislators. Surely in that chain there are minds who could look at motorcycling and see things that we haven't.

Motorcycle accidents and fatalities are up for riders over 35 and for operators of large-displacement cycles. That's a fact. The idea that the faculties for accident avoidance should suddenly desert healthy riders who hit their mid- or late 30s sounds far-fetched, to say the least, but that doesn't mean that the negative stats can be explained by market demographics alone.

Older riders, "mature riders"—whatever you wish to call them—tend to fall into three categories: lifelong enthusiast, re-entry, and "late bloomer." Three years out, it may be difficult or impossible to tell the latter two types from their more experienced riding mates, but invisible factors can still play a role. *One*—most lifelong riders started out on relatively small bikes, taking incremental steps to today's bigger machines. *Two*—even limited experience during the formative years rapidly establishes neuro-motor connections which the brain stores almost indefinitely. So an older novice might have more total miles, yet have to think about actions that the re-entry rider does instinctively.

The feds like to study fatalities, an accident type which, thankfully, I've never witnessed. Dropped motorcycles and bikes ridden into a ditch account for nearly all the accidents I've observed while training over the years. In both scenarios, machinery too big and heavy for the rider often figures prominently, sometimes causing spills and other times aggravating the injuries (I can think of two guys who got up without so much as a lost button, only to later discover that they'd broken foot bones underneath their massive machines).

Since the dawn of the automotive age, generations have grappled with the issue of when to take Gramp's car keys; the graying of America's motorcyclists took a lot of us by surprise. But for most of us, the keys to riding safely are still keeping fit, riding an appropriate bike, and getting sufficient practice (and training) to maintain critical skills.

On the Horns of a Dilemma

September 2002

I ride a lot—frequently at night. During my rides, I've seen plenty of roadside deer. I used to go blasting down country roads on the way home in the evening and would freak myself out thinking about what would happen if a deer would be in my path. Strangely, it didn't slow me down.

My only actual impact with a deer occurred when I was driving a car. I never saw it coming nor knew what happened—just a sudden whack! It was on a night when I was supposed to be riding, mapping out a route that had to go to press the next day. I needed 10ths on the odometer for accuracy; my old BMW didn't have them, so I took the car.

I'm a fatalist; I believe that when my time is up, it's up—slipping in the bathtub, getting struck by a deer whether I'm going fast or slow—who knows? Fate was responsible for an opening to participate in one of Larry's training tours. I recall his piercing stare as he asked me over dinner, "So, what have you done to make the world a better place?" I still don't have an answer. He had so much to give and helped so many people. He was so safety conscious, so the haunting question is, why him and not me? Fate?

Elsie Smith, Design Solutions Plus,
participant, Stayin' Safe Motorcycle Training

One of life's enduring mysteries for me was why a so-called "dual-purpose" bike should have an engine as wide as a logging road and weigh in at nearly 600 pounds. But no longer; not as of two days ago. The reason, I now know, is: so that when you look back in your mirror at 60 mph, the 200-pounder lying hooves-up in the ditch isn't wearing your Aerostich suit.

I've had close encounters with deer before. Most anyone who has ridden extensively in the Mid-Atlantic or Appalachian regions has tested their bike's brakes against *Odocoileus virginianus* (a.k.a. white-tailed deer). On a couple of occasions I've outrun menacin' venison that elected to sprint diagonally across the road. Maybe, had I been riding a Yamaha R1 this time . . . . Ah, but no excuses are needed for the brawny R1150GS, the motto of which henceforth shall be "the buck stops here."

What happened, exactly? Accident victims, I've learned, make poor accident investigators, and I literally did not know what hit me at the time. My recollection is of a blurry amorphous brown bursting forth from the green wall on my left, then coming alive as if Tinkerbell had suddenly taken her wand to it.

Behind the surrealism lies an explanation in fifth-grade arithmetic. People typically under-report distances of vehicles which violate their right-of-way; they use figures like "50 feet" to describe events that evolve half a block away. But the hardwoods and dense underbrush along U.S. Route 22, near Antrim, Ohio, surely came within two or three yards of the tarmac. Adult white-tails can sprint up to 36 mph—that's 53 feet per second.

"I can't believe that you—*Mr. Safety*—didn't just hammer those ABS brakes, knowing that you could stop on a dime!" a friend of mine ribbed me the following morning when I described the scene. Even covering the brakes, I don't think I could have stirred a piston nesting in its caliper before we collided. It's possible that I countersteered enough to avoid an ugly entanglement with the front wheel, but good fortune measured in hundredths of a second is probably a sounder explanation. The best research shows that experts need a full second to effect a significant change of direction . . . but just the width of the front tire could have made all the difference.

I know I gave it throttle, because when I felt the thump on my left leg the bike began to weave from side to side, and that was the most like a dirt bike that the GS has ever felt during our three-month relationship. Only when I saw the deer crumple in my right mirror (his momentum had carried him the rest of the way across the highway) did I understand what had happened. A mile up the road, where I caught up to my riding partner, I realized that I'd lost my left saddlebag, which took us 15 minutes to locate in the dense brush. The deer, which I'd expected to find dead or near death, was gone. Since there was no blood on the bike and only a few hairs trapped in the lid of the saddlebag, I'm going to guess he merely had his bell rung.

One can hardly count the ways in which I lucked out. For starters, there's the time of year—late spring, just before male deer grow their new antlers. Any other season, and I might have been gored in the leg or abdomen. A split-second later, and I might have been cast into the air with the spring pollen. In my youth I used to ride flat-out on straightaways whether they were forested or not, and I still snatch a few quick passes—sometimes overtaking multiple vehicles—on a typical ride. The odds are good, but the stakes are high.

Everyone knows that the odds of colliding with a deer keep growing shorter, particularly in metropolitan areas. In the woods where I played daily as a boy, we tormented all manner of birds, reptiles, and amphibians, but no mammals larger than a groundhog. Today, when we ride our mountain bikes in the park, we see deer almost nightly. On a recent ride, we shined our Night Riders up under a bridge at one of the busiest intersections in the city and froze *seven* pairs of vitreous marbles in their tracks!

The Erie Insurance Group, with 2.5 million customers, reported in a 1998 release that one out of every 100 Pennsylvania vehicles will have a deer collision claim. In some counties the rate is as high as one in 20 (divide that by the number of vehicles the average person will own in a lifetime). Since 80 percent of all deer accidents occur between dusk and dawn on two-lane roads, the single most effective action we can take is to limit night riding. What about deer whistles? Like rabbits' feet and St. Christopher medals, they're weightless, painless add-ons . . . but there's no bona fide proof of their effectiveness.

Both the Erie Insurance study and another by the Fairfax County (VA) police department indicate that about half of all deer collisions occur during the rutting season—October through December. Cold-weather riding fans note: Erie reports a *500 percent* increase in deer collisions on the opening days of doe and buck seasons!

As motorcyclists, most of us would rank property loss as a far lower concern than personal injury, but it's smart to ask your insurance company where they stand on deer collision claims. Some regard them as "chargeable" (i.e. they're factored into future premiums along with other accidents and tickets), while others don't. In fact, it's whispered in some riding circles that the way to keep your record clean after a crash is to indicate the presence of an animal in the road. It's a game where suspicions run high on both sides, so I paid for a new saddlebag out of pocket, rather than risk a surprise rate increase.

Avoidance, without question, is the best policy, and that means aggressive braking in the vast majority of cases. If a deer charges from the side, you may be able to adjust position and accelerate out of harm's way, but never try to swerve around a confused deer, even if a full stop doesn't appear possible. They're completely unpredictable and can change direction much more quickly than you can. Stay on the brakes, and worst case, you'll collide at reduced speed; with luck he'll scamper off while you're scrubbing off speed.

Smaller beasts warrant wilier tactics. Dogs want to chase, not ram, and every MSF grad knows that the best strategy is to sucker'em in, downshift, then motor away. If it's a groundhog or smaller, I try to go *through* it, upright, and on the gas. I figure it's their obligation to get out of my way—which they usually do—and the last thing I want is to slide out trying to avoid some gushy little rodent.

I just happened to be at the right speed and angle, in the right moment, and on the right motorcycle to blast that big buck back to where he belonged. And if the law of averages is to be trusted, I'm good for my next 99 bikes!

Braking

Braking Techniques

December 1988

Recognizing when and how to brake may be one of motorcycling's most complex tasks, Larry examines and questions accepted wisdom (and myth) surrounding the correct use of brakes. He concludes by describing a drill of his own designed to give most riders a foundation for mastering the front brake (use of the rear comes later).

Pete Tamblyn

I hope you never have an accident—but if you do it's even money that you'll have bungled the braking. So, I've been thinking a lot about braking, and my conclusion is that it's more difficult than jumping over Datsuns.

Jumping's easy, a simple matter of generating just enough thrust and then hanging on for the ride (landing is another matter). Braking, on the other hand, requires constant and precise monitoring of two independent systems, each having its own properties and vastly different potential. Not enough of one, your nose is imbedded in a Peterbilt. Too much of the other, you're on the ground. And of course, all the while you're monitoring these systems, you're observing your surroundings and maintaining your balance.

Motorcycle manufacturers know braking is tough. They read the same reports as safety instructors and magazine editors. And they study each other's products, which is why Old World eccentric Moto-Guzzi has inspired two of the Big Four to create integrated braking systems of their own. Certain safety experts believe that such systems, which relegate a portion of the front brake's operation to the foot pedal, do not adequately address the problem; they call for a complete one-control system like the one common to all of the world's billion or so autos.

The Motorcycle Safety Foundation, resigned to the inevitability of skidding rear wheels, devotes a 10-minute drill to controlling skids. In fact, it's only in the last two years that the MSF stopped teaching "deliberate" rear wheel lock-up as part of the quick-stop process. The rationale for so radical an approach was that, given the rapid transference of weight to the front wheel, a modestly applied rear brake would eventually lock up in mid-stop, destroying the rider's concentration and possibly inducing a high-side.

With 10 minutes of training, nearly anyone can control a rear-wheel skid; all you do is keep it locked and steer in the direction of the skid. But controlling the direction of the bike with the rear wheel skidding is more difficult—in fact it's impossible. That's why road-racing guru Keith Code takes the opposite approach to rear wheel braking—abstinence.

MSF graduates recite from rote that 70 percent of a bike's stopping power comes from the front brake. That means that 30 percent must come from the rear. How can you simply ignore 30 percent of your capacity to stop the bike? Well, you're not ignoring it; you're simply reassigning it. The harder you squeeze the front brake, the more rapid the forward transfer of weight. In an emergency stop the action is so sudden as to render the rear brake impotent.

Let me address a pair of front-brake myths:

1) "If you squeeze too hard, you'll go over the handlebars." It's been done. Code watched it happen to a student on his outrigger-equipped braking-enhancement bike. To do this on your bike, you must have a) powerful dual, disc brakes, b) a sticky front tire, heated by repeated hard stops, c) above average gymnastic ability, and d) the will to push yourself into the annals of motorcycling folklore. You're more likely to hit the lottery for $30 million than to loop your bike with the front brake.

2) "If you lock your front brake, you'll crash immediately." Wrong. Locking the front wheel creates an immediate loss of steering control. You've experienced that condition thousands of times crossing speed bumps and railroad tracks, but your momentum carried you through until gravity brought your front wheel back to the pavement. When you skid the front tire, though, you've only your own skills to get the wheel rolling again.

A recent go 'round on Code's outrigger-equipped emergency-braking bike shed some illumination on the dark question of front-wheel lock-up. Dave Messimer, an instructor in Code's California Superbike School, performed a series of stops at 30 mph—the median pre-crash speed in the Hurt Report. With the brake held past the point of lock-up, the tire laid down a black streak, arrow-straight and 20 feet long before the bike fell over on its outrigger. Each repetition at that speed netted nearly identical results—a straight skid of 20 feet—more than half a second in duration.

Messimer's experience handling a bike at its ragged edge undoubtedly helped yield the consistent results. While he sat there, unruffled, a lesser rider might have tugged at the bars or stuck a foot out, capsizing the cycle.

Of course, the object is to stop quickly without skidding, and that can only be achieved through practice. I recommend starting at a speed of five mph to get used to the plunging action of the front forks.

Don't up the speed until you can bottom the forks and keep your feet on the pegs until the forks have fully rebounded. An errant foot can be enough to spill the bike when braking at the limits of traction. Gradually build speed to 35 mph—even if it takes weeks to gain the confidence. Don't quit until you can consistently stop in under 50 feet.

Short, smooth stops are characterized by a firm squeeze (do not grab) followed by a gradual release as the speed is reduced. Learn to recognize the faint chirp or squeal that signals impending skid. Two fingers are enough—if yours are long and strong enough, and if the lever hasn't so much travel that it's trapping your unused fingers against the grip.

Let the tape measure—not a guess—be your final arbiter.

Still Bringing Up the Rear

March 1996

Larry explained to his students that the front brake is the stop-ping brake; the rear is the control brake. In addition to ex-pounding on the differences between the two systems, in this column he describes when only the rear brake is preferable, fo-cusing on a drill or two to illustrate how to improve your con-trol through discreet use of the right toe.

Pete Tamblyn

At a party the other day I listened to a former Air Force pilot recount his brush with death in a B52 bomber. It was his first flight since be-coming certified on the craft, and his hydraulics had gone south. Step by step he went through his emergency procedures—each to no avail. Ground control couldn't help, and to make matters worse, he was running low on fuel. As a last resort, he was connected to a mysterious guru code-named "Fred Boeing" who literally taught him to rewire the system in mid-air!

Wouldn't it be nice if we motorcyclists could call on a "Harry Honda" whose magical formulae would rescue us whenever we got in over our heads? Then again, most motorcyclists prefer their own ways of doing things.

In the early '70s the Motorcycle Safety Foundation provided the first large-scale effort to educate American riders on the fine points of motor-cycling, free of myth and hubris. All the research of the day cited braking skills as the area most in need of attention. Rooted in the days of me-chanical drum brakes and rutted dirt roads, American riders needed to be led to the front brake and forced to squeeze it.

Observing the multitude of riders who slammed the rear brake dur-ing panic stops, the Foundation adopted a policy of having them *deliber-ately* lock it. The rationale was that this would eliminate the element of surprise and free the rider to concentrate on modulating the more criti-cal front brake. Plus, riders who locked, then released the rear brake could go over the high side if the drive wheel stepped out far enough, then suddenly regained traction.

Subsequent MSF courses would still include rear-wheel skids, but with the emphasis on controlling inadvertent ones. By the mid-'80s, close to a million motorcyclists had taken MSF courses, but even as the message "both brakes every time" was finally reaching mass audiences, traction technology was once again clouding the issue. It was probably only moments after the first "stoppie" that riders began questioning why we even use the back brake. After all—what good is a brake if there's no wheel on the pavement?

MSF materials state that 70 percent of a bike's stopping force comes from its front brake and 30 percent from its rear. This is probably a reasonable average, but the exact ratio is a product of several factors: motorcycle length and weight, rapidity of braking, coefficient of friction (pad/rotor and tire/road) and, of course, rider technique. In my experience, laying off the rear brake during all-out 60 mph braking lengthens minimum stopping distances by 15 to 20 percent for long, heavy machines. For shorter, lighter-weight bikes, distances are virtually unaffected.

So—does such a small contribution justify the increased risk of skids and high sides?

Eight years ago, while touring Norway on a Euro-spec Honda VF400F, I had occasion to test some of these theories. While turning left with my sidestand down, I made the acquaintance of a guard rail and spent the rest of my trip with my right (braking) foot in a cast. Whereas the 400 was short, light, and amply endowed with front wheel braking, I scarcely noticed any loss of stopping power . . . but I felt strangely unsmooth navigating the precipitous Norge roads.

Two years later, fully mended, I was back in Europe with an alpine tour group, under strict orders not to use the rear brake. Locking the rear wheel on the steep downhill stretches, we'd been warned, was the leading cause of accidents. Over dinner, many tour guests remarked how they didn't miss their rear brakes at all, but I kept quiet. I'd disobeyed. Maybe there was something wrong with me, I worried, because I felt insecure without my rear brake.

So, apparently, did road-racer Mick Doohan. After the Aussie superstar crushed his right foot a few years ago, he had a special rear brake control rigged to his handlebar, and it helped him to reclaim the 500cc world championship this past season. Grand prix racers, with their ability to yank the back wheel off the ground almost at will, don't need the back brake for stopping power, but many rely upon it for fine control. In fact, a race-bike's volatility is what makes the rear brake such a useful tool. A racer might have 100 percent of his weight on the front wheel before a turn's entry, and then 100 percent on the rear wheel upon exit. "Trail braking," gently easing off the brakes in a turn, allows him to smoothly return weight to the rear without upsetting the suspension.

Steep mountain roads can present a similar challenge for street riders. On downhill sections, use of the rear brake helps to correct the heavy front wheel bias which makes the bike difficult to turn. Approaching uphill turns, dragging the rear brake may enable you to hold the throttle open and thus avoid the disconcerting nose dive which accompanies sudden roll-off.

Lower speeds exacerbate every type of chassis reaction, so dragging the rear brake has a stabilizing effect during U-turns and other low-speed maneuvers. It also eliminates much of the annoying driveline lash which occurs during throttle transitions on both chain- and shaft-driven bikes.

Entering a turn too hot is a condition everyone encounters sooner or later. Front-wheel braking is dangerous at steep lean angles, and even throttle roll-off will cause chassis pitch, so what do you do? There are several things: 1) turn your head even more sharply than your desired path of travel; 2) press harder on the inside handgrip; 3) maintain constant throttle; and 4) apply slight rear brake pressure. You can practice the technique by riding in circles on a parking lot, particularly if the parking lot is sloped. Try to maintain a steady speed by adding (downhill) and releasing (uphill) pressure.

Each of these techniques, while having little effect on the rate of deceleration, enhances control by enabling you to roll the throttle with confidence. To take the concept one step further, you can use the rear brake as a clutch to smooth out the power delivery. Though I personally prefer bikes with a strong midrange and a fair amount of flywheel effect, I find myself using the rear brake to keep the engine at optimum power when I ride the twisties on less-forgiving models.

By now, you must think my bike is detectable from three miles by the stench of burning brakes, but the truth is I've *never* worn out a set of rear brake pads or shoes. My last bike went nearly 70,000 miles on the original back pads, and my current ride has over 50,000 on them. Just because you use your right foot doesn't mean that you operate the brake pedal like your automobile's. In your car, braking pressure is modulated with the upper leg, but on a motorcycle, a tiny amount of ankle flex is all that's required. Cruiser bikes, with their in-your-face brake pedals, demand the most restraint. To avoid lock-up, I recommend that you only contact the pedal with part of your big toe.

And remember—the harder you brake with your front wheel, the *lighter* your pressure must be on the rear. When longer stops are necessary, such as on wet roads, the weight transference is less dramatic. Apply slightly less front and a little more rear brake in inclement weather. If your bike has integrated brakes, you'll require heavier pedal pressure during hard stops (to maximize the effectiveness of the second front disk), but normal stops should differ little from conventional brake applications. As for ABS, there's no art, but the correct emergency technique—slamming both brakes on while upright—takes practice in order to override your natural instincts.

If motorcycle training were as sophisticated as flight training, everyone who bought a new bike with ABS or integrated brakes would become certified on that system before soloing in traffic. We're still bringing up the rear in rider education . . . 'cause it's still a pretty useful control.

Student Teachers

December 1996

During the first few years as Larry started to get busy, many of the MSF instructors he asked to assist him declined. By default, and to my great advantage, I became Larry's assistant. This gave me more time to pick Larry's mind about the finer points of our sport.

When Larry asked me to help him with his first six-student tour, he didn't mention my demonstrating the drills. I told him that I wasn't sure I was comfortable doing the drills on my big bike so he agreed to do them. That's why he heard me telling one of the students, "I learn from watching you guys." It's similar to watching a golf swing. If you are a student of the golf game you can spot problems with 90% of the duffers out there. If you're a student of our sport you know when someone's doing things right and when they're not.

Frank Swaney, early assistant instructor
Stayin' Safe Motorcycle Training

Back in August of '93 a news release in this magazine announced the inauguration of Stayin' Safe Motorcycle Training, my free-market attempt to combine small group tours with cycle safety training. The timing couldn't have been more crucial, coinciding with my first-ever column on group riding.

Miraculously, folks still phoned for information. They still signed up for lessons and tours, even after reading the lurid crash details of various group rides I'd participated in over the years. Maybe they were naive, but apparently they bought the argument that I'd learned and could teach others from my experiences. My MSF classes had become remarkably accident-free, but after 13 years I felt I needed more of a challenge; I wanted to see if my theories about accident prevention worked on the street.

Well, in the first two years, we took nary a single soil sample. We were very lucky. Then reality came knocking. Business increased, riders of varied backgrounds and abilities participated, and there appeared the inevitable mishaps—three of them in an estimated one million corners. Fortunately, each rider got up and rode off with nothing worse than minor abrasions and maybe a bruised ego. Tour guides, group ride organizers, and riding school operators tell me the record is still phenomenal, considering the number of miles and the challenging mountain roads we cover. So I'll reiterate: *v-e-r-r-y lucky.*

When I was in need of assistance, fate delivered a most able and patient aide, my friend Frank Swaney. Swaney seemed an unlikely candidate for a safety course when he signed up as a student in '94—a dedicated sport tourer who knew the best roads in three states, and a road racer working on his expert license. I thought he was just patronizing me when he said that the two-day course had changed his approach to street riding, but then I overheard him saying something more revealing to a recent student.

"I learn more from watching you guys than from doing drills myself."

Those words started me thinking of all I'd learned from my students during the last four years. Usually it's by observation, but sometimes a pupil simply comes forward with the information I need.

"Pressure, not motion," is the way John Gelm, a flight instructor for a major airline, explained the modulation of hand controls on the company's flight simulator. It made me realize how misleading the term "lever" can be when applied to a motorcycle's clutch and front brake controls. Pictures and words are fine, but they cannot convey the sense of touch so crucial to smooth riding. Now I accurately demonstrate *and* evaluate braking touch with a simple hand squeeze.

I don't see enough young sport-bike riders in my courses, but I have Payte Baldwin, a Honda CBR600 owner from Irvine, Texas, to thank for this comment: "The way you come off the brakes is nearly as important as the way you apply them." It's true. Now, no matter how short on time I am, I always finish braking seminars with a drill in which students practice properly easing off the brakes to avoid lockup and stabilize the chassis for cornering.

About those soil testers: One was a near expert, one an intermediate, and one a novice rider. The skilled rider was, by his own admission, "being a butthead." The early pace was slow for him, so he began dropping back and playing catch-up. He became so engrossed in this game that he barely noticed a pickup truck encroaching on the centerline. When he finally woke up and saw the pickup, he swerved into a roadside ditch.

A ditch also claimed the intermediate. I've known this rider since he began his first MSF training, and I know he wouldn't have made the mistake two years earlier. He was riding with two fairly equal partners and had just assumed the lead position for the first time. Immediately he set a pace faster than he was accustomed to and quickly found himself too close to the edge on a debris-littered left-hander. I thought he'd save it, but then he froze and the next thing we knew we were scraping clumps of mud off his new BMW. No damage.

Accident number three was simply a rookie mistake. Running wide in a steep, downhill right-hander, the rider instinctively grabbed his front brake. He went down fast but at least he hadn't far to fall. In fact, had he been wearing full protective gear—not just denim and summer touring gloves—he probably would have escaped without a scratch.

Ironically, he was the only one among four doctor buddies who wore a full-face helmet. Earlier I'd pointed out that roughly one-fourth of gonged helmets hit face down, but it was hollow data compared to my "student teacher's" experience . . . he had a silver dollar-size chunk of fiberglass missing from his Shoei's chin bar!

Three accidents hardly make a statistically significant sampling. I can live with that deficiency. However, they bolster my suspicion (as did one controlled study) that, while inexperienced riders are overrepresented in accidents, *skill* level isn't so highly correlated to accident likelihood. Wobblers, after all, tend to compensate by holding speeds down and avoiding risky situations.

Minimizing training accidents requires no voodoo on my part. People *pay* me to tell them what to do. I know I'd eat better, exercise more, and be the picture of health if I suspended free will and hired someone to manage *my* body 24 hours per day.

What accident warning signs do I look for? More than anything else—panic braking. I begin each tour by copying a popular racetrack exercise . . . no brakes, or "swooping." There's no better way to size up a corner than to approach it as if you have no brakes. Even with practice, a smooth brake/lean/roll transition is less than automatic for most riders. I've watched too many students' brake lights flash at the last instant, a condition that causes sudden loading of the front wheel (especially going downhill). Often there's an equally sudden rearward transfer when they release the brakes . . . all this when you want the chassis to be its most stable.

The way you come off the brakes is nearly as important as the way you apply them. I thought about my wise student's words and about all the components of braking I'd emphasized.

Pressure, not motion. I thought about that one, too, and about the various studies I'd read documenting the time intervals skilled riders need to execute routine tasks—far more than average riders usually suspect. I added it up and saw that it took one full second to roll-off the throttle and establish minimal braking pressure. Expert riders, I'd observed, eliminate sudden nosedive by performing these two functions together. Then, depending on how much speed reduction is required, it takes *at least* a full second of moderate brake pressure. Finally you've got to come off the brakes, and here again, smooth riders roll the throttle on while simultaneously easing off the front brake. Another of my students contributed the phrase "cam braking" to describe the necessary finger action on the lever.

Add them up and you've got three seconds . . . *minimum.* Three and half to be on the safe side. When I see brake lights popping like flashbulbs, I get nervous. A rider who makes it through a turn on less than three seconds of setup braking almost certainly could have entered with no braking at all. So that's become the rule—three seconds or nothing. It's probably instilled more confidence and composure than any single item in my on-road agenda, and it's the aggregate contribution of hundreds of student riders.

A prophet once said: "When the student is ready, the teacher will appear." Fortunately for me, a new teacher arrives almost daily.

Stopping on a Curve

August 1989

It's your favorite "Sunday Morning Road." You've just eased off the brakes, re-opened the throttle slightly, and flicked it in with authority; the only thing that could make this right-hander any better would be if it weren't blind.

And then you see it—a dead brontosaurus sprawled across both lanes and you've got to stop right now! *Sooner or later, most of us encounter such a situation, at least in our minds . . . or in this column. Larry insists that neither training nor testing address this issue well, and offers his suggestions.*

Pete Tamblyn

Sad to say, no matter how careful you are, no matter how skillful or well-trained, there's an accident out there with your name on it. If statistics are to be believed, it's due to arrive around your four-millionth motorcycling mile, but like my long-lost Uncle Isadore, it could show up tomorrow or never. Accidents are like that; all you can do is be cautious and wear clean underwear.

Personally, I've yet to see the unpreventable motorcycle accident, but I'm not so naive as to think I can handle every situation on the highway. Recently, a friend described to me a ride during which he and his wife were rounding a curve on a lovely mountain road, only to be assailed, not by an errant automobile, an animal, or even a nasty road spill but—get this—a giant wall of water!

It was a flash flood, and if you were to ask me what you do when confronted with such a hazard, I'm afraid my reply would be pretty unsatisfying. Of course the number of accidents triggered by broken dams, UFO landings, or even tire blowouts pale in comparison to those occasioned by rider error or inexperience. I'll hark back to the December '88 column "Braking Techniques," in which we discussed the mysteries of braking. In it, we encountered the problems associated with bringing even state-of-the-art motorcycles to smooth, non-skidding stops in relatively short distances. We noted that with all we know about bikes, there is still disagreement among experts on how this goal is best accomplished. And that was only *straight-line* braking. So think of how weight transference and changing traction conspire against a motorcycle in a turn, and then think of how you would instruct a novice to perform an emergency stop in mid-corner.

The Motorcycle Operator Skill Test (MOST) is a sophisticated, electronically monitored licensing tool developed for NHTSA by the National Public Services Research Institute (NPSRI), in league with MSF. It was determined in 1975 that urgent steps were needed to reduce the high accident rate among novice riders, so the MOST undertook the considerable challenge of evaluating nine separate skills, starting with low criticality ones (e.g. starting on a hill) and culminating with the most challenging: stopping quickly on a curve.

The MOST is effectively dead now, a victim of high administrative costs and mediocre field test results, but a streamlined version, the Alternate MOST (ALMOST), is employed by over half of the nation's licensing agencies . . . *without* a quick stop on a curve. NPSRI's A.J. McKnight, in recommending the elimination of the last exercise, noted that "in addition to simplifying instrumentation, (it would) overcome the biggest threat to safety in administration of the MOST."

McKnight's paper further stated that "over half of the accidents (during testing) occur in Exercise 9." Reporting off the record, a safety official who participated in the field test quipped, "They were *all* going down in that one!"

As a license examiner, I can tell you that few things mess up your schedule like having to hail an ambulance. But as a safety instructor, I don't feel very good about ignoring an accident-avoidance skill. Neither, apparently, does MSF, because they include not one, but two stopping-on-a-curve exercises in their novice and experienced rider courses. The first of these exercises is a "normal" stop, and the objective reads: "You will ride around a curve bringing the motorcycle to a smooth, controlled stop at a designated point." Among the evaluation points, probably the most critical is, "Gradually apply both brakes with increasing pressure as the bike straightens up." Leaning, of course, consumes traction—traction which could be put to use for stopping—hence the directive to increase brake pressure as the bike straightens.

When the concept is reintroduced later in both courses, the new objective reads, "You will ride around a curve, bringing the motorcycle to a *rapid* stop on instructor's command." (The adjective "smooth" is added for the benefit of experienced riders.) The source of this rapid stop is likewise the cause of more confusion than probably anything MSF teaches. See, in this exercise, which was based on the results of a 1985 study by Neil Tolhurst, then of Northern Illinois University, students are instructed to completely straighten the motorcycle, square the handlebars and then apply the brakes; in other words, convert to a straight-line-braking situation.

Let's talk about the advantages of this technique. The shortest stop, whether it be in a straight line or on a curve, is achieved at impending skid; that is when both brakes are applied maximally, just short of lockup. Impending skid is easiest to identify when the bike is going straight, which also happens to be the only time when 100 percent of traction may be spent on braking. Tolhurst's study indicated that the more quickly riders returned their bikes to vertical, the faster they got them stopped.

Now the disadvantage is that unlike driving ranges—where stops are practiced at 10 to 15 mph with no vehicular traffic—real roads seldom permit total separation of cornering and braking. At 45 mph, leaned over, say 35 degrees, your motorcycle will sail over the center line or off the road if you straighten fully before starting to brake. Therefore MSF adds the caveat, "If road and traffic conditions permit. . . ."

Buried deep within the volumes of commentary in the MSF library is another annotation: "Any delay in the onset of braking while straightening the motorcycle would negate any advantage in reduced distances." In other words, total straight-line conversion is merely a training device—not a real-world technique—but I'm not sure that distinction always filters down to the student level. Anyway, the permit-holding neophyte who hits the streets on eight hours of closed-course training has about as much chance of successfully executing an emergency blind-turn stop as leapfrogging a flash flood. There are no miracles in the MSF or any other instructional package.

While nothing will make this advanced skill easy to learn, I'd like to see MSF move toward demystifying it. For instance, its discussion of "the two methods of stopping in a curve," to my way of thinking, clouds the issue. The technique for "emergency" stopping in a curve doesn't really differ from the "normal" stop. It's the *rate* (of transition from leaned to vertical) that changes.

MSF courses allot 30 minutes to these two exercises. Students spend most of their time waiting in line while others take their turns. But mastery of braking technique requires hours of diligent practice. I suggest that you spend as many as it takes to perfect your *smooth* stops before you even attempt to stop quickly on a curve. When you're ready, go ahead and try the MSF training exercise, fully straightening the machine before braking. From there learn to apply progressively harder braking as you quickly straighten, setting imaginary boundaries to correspond with those of a real road. Remember: a panic stop is not a skill; if you're even a little out of shape, you've gotten ahead of your learning curve.

There's no substitute for practice time when learning a difficult technique. But sensible speeds and sound street strategies will lessen the likelihood that you'll need to use this one. As for the wall of water, I don't know—does flood insurance cover you on a motorcycle?

The Toughest Skill in Motorcycling

August 2002

Larry proposes that the toughest skill in motorcycling is down-shifting while aggressively braking. Some might argue that teaching this technique is the toughest skill in motorcycling! Whichever, the dauntless Mr. Safety gives it his best shot.

Pete Tamblyn

Were it not for my lack of talent and courage, I would surely attempt the signature move of 18-year-old X Games super hero, Travis Pastrana—the back flip! Ditto the 100-mph leaps into the heart of African darkness which Dakar aces like Fabrizio Meoni take aboard their twin-cylinder Molotov cocktails. But could any skill in motorcycling be more difficult and daring than going wheel to wheel on a 200-horsepower GP bike, both ends sliding, dragging your elbow on the curb? Sadly, I'll never know.

I may not be qualified to decide what is the toughest skill in motorcycling, but I can tell you there's a task which nearly every street rider attempts on a daily basis, yet which damned few execute with precision and smoothness. That's braking and down-shifting simultaneously.

When I taught the old MSF curriculum, that was exercise number 11—a six-pack of novice riders revolving around three ovals (small, smaller, and smallest) while a few yards away six more rookies circled the wagons in a succession of tight 90-degree turns. Some instructors called it a four-ring circus; "sausage making" tended to be my metaphor of choice.

But what are you going to do? Riding a motorcycle—a proper motorcycle with gears and separate brakes—demands the mastery of five delicate primary controls, and sometimes you've gotta work them all in unison. Some trainers say roll the ball out; let the kids play, so to speak, and they'll eventually—perhaps on their own—figure things out.

Call me Mr. Negative. I think that people will not figure it out, because I've seen so few do it with any real finesse. My first advice to you, Mr. and Mrs. Everyday Street Rider, is don't bother to attempt it.

Not unless you have a lot of time and distance. I've heard enough tales of corner entry panic (and its consequences) to last me a lifetime . . . but I've yet to hear of a rider who braked on time but then crashed because they didn't downshift before a turn. On a racetrack, you might hear the boys wring three, even four quick downshifts, before a bend, all the while squeezing enough front brake to nearly loft the back tire off the ground. But seriously, does your favorite road have a 135-mph straightaway leading to a hairpin turn? Neither does mine. Few are the corners in my world that demand more than a single downshift.

What I use to deal with that downshift is a trick that Reg Pridmore taught me several years back—finish the downshift before you even touch the brakes. Even if you're running at redline (which is seldom the most effective part of the powerband on public roads), you can still smoothly downshift before braking. That's because you'll need to roll out of the throttle no matter what. With a five- or six-speed gearbox you shed enough speed during roll-off to come down a gear without overrevving the engine.

Are you blipping the throttle on your downshift? If you've been riding more than a year (let's say 4,000 to 5,000 miles) you should be. If you're not sure, look at the tachometer needle as you release the clutch. It shouldn't move. If the needle rises, you've failed to match engine speed to road speed, and that places more strain on the entire drivetrain while increasing the risk of rear wheel lock-up. Here's a quick lesson on "blipping."

It doesn't have to be done quickly. On a straight, empty section of road, while holding the throttle open slightly—revs roughly one third of redline—lightly "preload" the shifter (i.e. press down only enough to take up the freeplay). Now roll the throttle on at the same moment you start to apply clutch pressure. Easily and deliberately, but don't be shy with the throttle: "brrROOOmmm!" You'll scarcely need any more downward pressure on the shift lever; it should practically slip into gear by itself. When it does, back off the throttle and release the clutch.

Does the tach needle move? Keep practicing and surely the timing will improve. As it does, the action will likely become quicker (though a slow-revving cruiser will always take more time than a free-revving sport-bike). You can ease the clutch out, but the true measure of timing and smoothness is the ability to simply let go of it. Match the engine and wheel speed and there's no need for the clutch plates to dance the lambada.

Now, having dispatched that attention-robbing downshift, you're free to concentrate on braking. Again, that means leaving yourself plenty of time, and believe me when I say that the average rider brakes too late for optimum smoothness (often in situations where an earlier roll-off would have been quite sufficient to set entry speed).

If you're on the brakes now and not satisfied with a single downshift before the turn, you're going to need considerably more skill. At this level, you'll start to appreciate the benefits of two-fingered braking (a technique that is both rider- and bike-specific). Good racers are quite skilled at working fingers one and two about the lever in a rotational motion while twisting the throttle with the thumb and remaining fingers. Keith Code used to train riders with what he called a "smoothometer," a hydraulic pressure gauge which measured changes in braking force as the throttle was rolled on and off (blipping). Keep in mind that the racetrack offers long intervals in which to modulate brake pressure and to shift gears—a real boon to smoothness.

You can practice for years and still not claim ownership of this highly sophisticated task, but here's a partial shortcut: If you insist upon squeezing off another downshift before the corner, you can ease off the front brake while continuing to apply pressure on the rear (this is actually a good way to smooth the weight shift from front wheel to rear). If you're a skilled downshifter, you can do the deed while lightly applying the rear brake. Finally you ease off the rear brake to complete the skill sequence.

These things take time and distance. Riders who spend enough years around this sport usually recognize that they lack either the space or the talent to wing a revvy supersport-bike up and down the gearbox on a public road while using more than a fraction of the bike's stop-and-go potential. To make a joyful sound in one or two gears, to feel the promise of brakes that are so willing, and to graze a footpeg feeler every now and again . . . that's nirvana to most real-world riders.

Let me render an opinion on one other subject—what's known in British police parlance as a "box" downshift—coming down more than one gear at a time between clutch releases. It's a simplified way to downshift two, three, even five gears while riding the brakes and, thanks to the advent of "slipper" clutches, many racers have added it to their repertoires.

The box downshift may be a legitimate skill, but I say do so at your own peril. One downshift too many on, say, an 1800cc V-twin could make for major wheel lock-up and who-knows-what driveline calamities. Now, if you're coming to a full stop, by all means hold the clutch in and row the shifter, but the only time I allow myself a true box shift (two or more consecutive downshifts preceding a clutch release) is when I'm slowing down to parking lot speeds.

Want to master the toughest skill in street riding? Find a long down-hill straightaway, give yourself lots of time and distance, and keep practicing. Wanna ride like Pastrana, Meoni, or reigning 500 GP champion, Valentino Rossi? Look in the mailbox.

Your sponsors will explain your next move.

Cornering

Steering 101

September 2000

Larry, and his dad, have some good advice to address how one makes a two-wheeler go in the intended direction. This column is aptly named, as it condenses a plethora of skills into a single, basic read.

Pete Tamblyn

"Son, when assessing the response lag between steering torque and roll-angle amplitudes, a higher phase angle indicates a greater delay between input and output values and thus, an unmaneuverable bike." Thus my father might have begun his instruction on how to ride a two-wheeler, but it was to be another 35 years before the Technical University of Aachen, Germany, would publish Tilo Schweers' paper, *Objective Assessment of Motorcycle Maneuverability*. What he did say—"Pedal faster!" and "Look where you want to go!"—was probably better suited to my six-year-old attention span.

At what point does information become too much information? Looking back on my 20 years of teaching motorcycle riding, I'm sure that I've crossed over the line on a few occasions. Reflecting upon the columns which I've authored over the past 12 years, it's more a question of how much information before I embarrass myself. Not that I'm a total fraud, but in the area of motorcycle handling dynamics, I'm no Erik Buell.

Actually, I can relate to Mr. Buell because his motorcycles employ one of my favorite features: handlebars. Now, technically, every motorcycle fixes some metal appendages upon the steering axis and adorns them with levers and switches, but you've got to admire the unpretentious candor of an old-fashioned tubular bar. Handlebars must be the most misunderstood and unrespected part of the motorcycle. In my 30 years of riding, I've had tires deflate, engines seize, clutch cables snap, and even brakes turn to worthless mush. I've lived to tell about them all, but I can't imagine what I'd do if my handlebars suddenly snapped off.

MSF, how is it that you don't recognize the handlebars as one of the five "primary" controls? Why, you don't even call it a control, period! When your free VIP bikes arrive in Irvine to usher in the next riding season, just you hang onto the fork tubes for a quick run down the PCH and over the Ortega Highway!

To be fair, some years back the curriculum folk at the Foundation recognized that the swerve exercise taught in the waning moments of the course was a rather tardy introduction to the concept of countersteering. They rightly installed the mantra "push left—go left; push right—go right" at the baptism of their 15-hour course.

How fast must you be going to countersteer? When I started teaching, our chief instructor told us "10 to 15 mph," which I figure makes for some tough choices when you slow to take a corner in tight traffic at, say, 12.

I don't think the curriculum ever did mention a specific speed, but my range cards, for as far back as I can remember, have said "lean and turn handlebars" to make a sharp turn . . . something I respectfully disagree with. You see, handlebars left to their own devices will turn in by themselves when the motorcycle (or bicycle) leans. Things that make it lean are countersteering, gyroscopic precession, body steering, road camber, and plain old gravity-induced instability.

Now I'm no Schweers or Buell, but give me a motorcycle and I can clearly demonstrate that it will countersteer at *any* speed at which the wheels remain functioning gyros, and how bodily inputs and throttle affect the direction of travel. New riders would be safer, I believe, and many experienced ones would be more skilled, if they simply understood the guiding (pun intended) principles of motorcycle steering.

MSF courses emphasize the use of throttle to stabilize the machine coming out of both low- and high-speed turns, but I find that no more than half of experienced riders can correctly predict which direction the motorcycle path will diverge upon the application of power. (The answer is "toward the outside," at least until the rear tire breaks loose, dirt-track style, redirecting the front wheel toward the inside . . . rather beyond the handling envelope of the average street rider).

Back to countersteering: A forward push on a hand grip will *always* result in the motorcycle leaning in the direction of the push—push right, go right; push left, go left. When we think we're "turning the handlebar" or "carsteering," we're actually recovering from a controlled fall by pushing on the opposite hand grip. Once you relax your grip on the handlebar you'll see exactly how the bike responds to your input.

There is a technique, used by mountain bike riders and enduro motorcyclists, whereby the handlebars are rapidly turned in order to thread them between tightly spaced trees. It's used at very low speeds, when the rider is balancing the cycle, and even then he must quickly abort the maneuver in order to prevent the motorcycle from leaning in the direction of the initial input.

One of the great lessons of riding off-road is that one should use the handlebars only when one has to. I like to take new riders on the back of my bike before they've conceived too many notions of bike handling. I show them how lightly I hold ("touch" is a better word) the handlebars and invite them to try to steer the motorcycle by shifting their body weight.

Yes, they *can* make the bike turn with just body weight shifts. You don't need to countersteer to make a bike lean. You need countersteering when you *need* countersteering (you can quote me, but make sure you use proper footnotes). Anyway, about the time that the student is working up a pretty good rhythm, flopping the bike side to side at about 15 mph, handlebars tucking in of their own volition, I clamp down on the bar ends and block any further rotation of the steering axis. The bike refuses to lean, no matter how big or forceful the student.

Rider rigidity, especially in the arms, I'm certain is a leading cause of running wide in turns. This can be demonstrated in another way. Walking the bike toward a sharp turn with the engine off, I tilt the bike with just the grab rail, tank, or seat; the front wheel tacks in and turns naturally in the direction of the lean. Afterward, I grasp the handlebars and lean the bike, but no matter the lean angle the bike cannot, will not, turn. It just continues straight.

During that ride on the back, a gradual increase in speed drives home how futile body steering alone can become. A firm, forward push on a hand grip clearly effects a much more rapid and forceful change of direction. Pushing *down* on a hand grip has no effect, although a sharply angled bar might create the illusion of downward pressure. At 100 mph, a 180-pound man could probably stand on the right hand grip, and a 100-pound woman could still make it go left by pushing on the left hand grip.

Mind you, I only do that in my advanced course, and if you have to ask, you can't afford it. But a last word on body steering. You don't jettison every vestige of it simply because speed and bike size command a forceful push on the handlebar. When you see racers hanging off, they're doing it to make subtle steering changes and to increase the effective lean angle and thereby avoid dragging hard parts on the pavement. When you see sport-bike riders doing it in the canyons, they're doing it to imitate roadracers, but also—probably unconsciously—to place their centers of mass out there over their ultrawide tire footprints.

There's room for differing styles of riding on the track or the street, and every good engineering team records subjective as well as objective findings. But remembering a few basics could help you put your bike where you want it when you want it:

1) Don't grip the handlebars; rest your hands on them.

2) Use your lower body to initiate turns at low speeds.

3) If you want to change directions rapidly, push forward, not down . . . no matter the velocity.

4) Use throttle to help steer the bike to the outside. At low speeds, a little clutch and/or rear brake pressure is a better antidote for a too fast/too wide trajectory than is chopping the throttle.

And, as my father said, "Look where you want to go!

A Touch of Class

October 1989

My first encounter with "Groddy" was back in the late 1980s at Grattan Raceway in Michigan. It wasn't exactly a stellar experience—I recall the need to pull him off the track and express to him that it was "only a matter of time before we'll have to pick you up." I even had picked out the particular corner (turn 12) that didn't seem to favour his particular riding style and I told him to stop being a "point and shoot artist." Just one session later, old Groddy didn't disappoint old Priddy . . .

But he brushed off the grass and went home in one piece. He later documented some of his feelings about CLASS (below). I knew then and there that he was okay.

Larry strived very hard to get his safety message across to those of us listening and went on to express many of the smooth throttle, clutch, brakes, and body steering techniques. I like to think he mastered some of these from his association with me and my CLASS schools. His special way of dishing out subtleties when it came to control and techniques are sorely missed. Groddy was a good bloke in both his educational written presentation and in his love for the sport of motorcycle riding.

Okay Larry, take your earplugs out now. I'll see you someday at the end of that bloody long straightaway of this thing we call life.

Cheers. Your mate,

Reg Pridmore, CLASS Motorcycle School

Ask an insurance executive to name the biggest risk in motorcycling and he'll say "speed." Ask a motorcyclist and he'll tell you "cars." The venue for California's Leading Advanced Safety School (CLASS) makes clear its proprietor's orientation. Reg Pridmore runs his safety course where there are no cars—on a racetrack.

There are a number of "schools" these days that, for a fee, will let you flaunt your hormones on a racetrack. CLASS is the one where the instructors wear bow ties on their tuxedo-trim leathers. It's also the only one that bills itself as a racetrack school for safe *street* riding.

For many, the notion of using a racetrack to teach safety takes a willing suspension of logic, but Pridmore, three-time AMA Superbike Champion in the '70s, adamantly insists that his is a street riding school. After all, half of the accidents on the street are single vehicle mishaps where the rider simply loses control and runs off a curve.

Only a fool would suggest that high speeds aren't inherently dangerous. But speed doesn't kill; *misapplication* does. Off hand, we'd probably define a speed of 35 mph as "low," but apply that to a curve marked 15— on a mountain road with no guardrail—and I say you're looking at a dangerously high speed.

Anyway, in a Pridmore school you're likely to hear the word "smooth" 10 times for every "fast." In the session I attended, at Michigan's Grattan Raceway, machinery and riders spanned the motorcycling spectrum. From Hurricane to FLXR and club racer to club colors, participants went as fast or as unfast as they felt comfortable. Students reported their top speed on the straightaway at anywhere from 130 mph down to 80, with nary a spill or a collision all day.

"You have a nice, relaxed day ahead," says Pridmore, beginning the session. "There's a cooler over there with plenty of Gatorade® and cold sodas. Feel free to pull off the track any time you feel like taking a break." Sounds like an innocuous comment, but Pridmore is a master psychologist, and for he who is patient, it's the first step toward a revelation; i.e. "you have to go slow to go fast."

Using the "ladder of progression," the student is encouraged to gradually build toward his personal limits; if he *does* in his enthusiasm skip a rung, the grassy periphery of the track is a far more forgiving milieu than a phalanx of speeding four-wheelers.

Following the initial briefing, the next rung on the ladder is a small group tour of the track, courtesy of instructors like Stuart Beatson, 1984 Battle of the Twins champion, and Pridmore's own son, Jason—1994 World Champion. The emphasis is on learning the correct line, with smooth transition between throttle, brakes, and shifting. There's a debriefing session, and then it's back on the track, governed by three simple rules: no racing, no lap timing, and no passing on the inside.

The eight-hour program is remarkably free of "nuts and bolts" theories which might overload the typical student. "You can't learn it in one day," says Jason. "In the next two weeks, you'll learn a lot of things that won't sink in today." At 19 he's a bright and shining testimonial to his father's educational philosophy, as poised and timely in his classroom contributions as when he's skimming his knee across Grattan's "sugarbowl."

CLASS's emphasis is on one-to-one coaching, which the instructors accomplish by leading, following, or simply sitting in the grass, taking notes. For many students, the day's highlight is a three-lap junket on Reggie Pridmore's pillion. Prior to this experience, I'd been astonished by the ability of the CLASS instructors to pass me on the straightaway with their "slow" BMWs.

One lap with Pridmore—a lap in which he leaned no farther and braked no harder than I—instantly revealed the "trick!" Two words— throttle control—sum up the magic with which Pridmore floats through the esses. He *r-r-rolls* it on and *r-r-rolls* it off, never fumbling with harsh or tentative settings. In contrast to my own technique (described by Pridmore as "squirting from turn to turn"), the BMW smoothly builds momentum through the last three turns, providing the impetus for its strong rush down the straightaway.

All well and good for getting around a given racetrack on a given day. But Pridmore had made a larger promise to his students. "You're going to learn a lot about *yourself*," he had told us at the onset. An early *sortie* into the grass had taught me the necessity of taking the ladder one rung at a time, but I believe CLASS taught me more about *teaching* than it did about riding.

I was coming off a bad teaching experience. I'd spent Monday through Friday teaching a basic riding course to a group of permit-holders, and though most had some street riding experience, four of them failed the end-of-course license examination, an event which heavily occupied my thoughts during the 500-mile ride to Grattan on Saturday.

Now since the only thing that's assumed in a novice course is the ability to ride a bicycle, I normally beg the indulgence of the more experienced students, as I bring the total beginners up to speed on basic control.

WRONG! It didn't take two weeks for CLASS's most important lesson to sink in. The truth bowled me over like a hot wind as I ambled down straight, flat Interstate 96 at 60 mph; my semi-experienced students had failed, not because they couldn't corner, swerve, and stop, the skills measured by our electronic timing device, but because they lacked the smooth throttle operation to stabilize their speeds! When it was time to react to signal lights, their concentration had already been spent on throttle jockeying. "Sometimes," says Pridmore, "you've got to take two steps back before you can move forward."

So, what would I tell someone contemplating CLASS, as a means of sharpening their skills? As a safety instructor, I'd note that 40 percent of our class members were MSF certified instructors, and that every effort was made to relate the objectives to street riding, but that the best place to learn street strategies remains an MSF or CSC course.

As a motorcyclist I'd say you haven't lived until you've experienced the sensation of riding unencumbered by speed limits and unseen hazards. As a writer, I'd tell you that 75 percent of the attendees were repeat students, that the course fee includes test rides on all of the new BMWs, and that the class roster included a policeman (sirens, flashers *et al.*), a 346-pound Gold Wing rider (who rode on the back with Pridmore), and a charter member of the Warlocks, Detroit, Michigan.

Will I be able to go faster now? Sure—on a racetrack; on the street, I was already going too fast. Did it make me a safer street rider? No class can do that; only discipline and honest self-evaluation can achieve that goal.

To assess the value of going 125 mph under the tutelage of a man in a leather tuxedo, I'm forced to invoke the phrase book of my grandfather, the late, great, Ellis A. (for Action) Kopelman: "The purpose of an education is not to learn. The purpose of an education is to learn *how* to learn."

Grandpa, meet Rego.

Wheel of Fortune

December 1993

Alan Robinson, the person most responsible for the existence of the Pennsylvania Motorcycle Safety Program, was not afraid to try new teaching techniques. An instructor can talk about gyroscopic precession, push right/go right, or any other "method" of turning a motorcycle and get blank stares in return.

Using the Bicycle Wheel Gyroscope to let someone feel the reaction to steering input is a much better teaching method than talking about the counter-intuitive "push right/go right."

By the way, Larry dubbed the wheel "the Cleavage Maker."

Chris Freed, MSF instructor

There's what you know and then there's what you *know*. Most people who have been riding motorcycles for years can respond effectively to all sorts of situations, but the catalog of techniques they can accurately explain is considerably more limited.

There's nothing wrong with doing things intuitively, but it's better to be able to explain them. Earlier this week I was on a dual-sport ride with two gentlemen who had more than 80 years of combined dirt-riding experience, most of it in the Southwest deserts. Because I had almost no desert experience, I was having difficulty in the sandier sections, so I asked Derek, a 61-year-old trials expert, for some advice.

"Just take it easy, up to the apex," said Derek, "and then when the bike is pointed where you want it, well, you can do what you wish with the throttle."

I followed behind Derek for a few miles, keeping a close watch on his back tire. The sand spewing off of it was a virtual computer print-out of his throttle activity, and soon I was taking the turns much more smoothly and with less effort. But you know what? His advice was almost exactly what I tell my students when I teach them to corner on pavement. I knew the answer all along, but I didn't *know* it. I needed an illustration.

All you need to know to steer a motorcycle is "push left/go left; push right/go right," but it's useful to have a rudimentary understanding of gyroscopic precession. Basically, the front wheel spins on its axle—which is just a derivative of the word *axis*. However, since it's a gyroscope, it can rotate on another axis—the one you look down on when you spin a top (or turn the handlebar). Any force delivered in this perpendicular axis causes the gyro to roll on a third axis: clockwise rotation causes roll to the left; counterclockwise rotation roll to the right. This roll (or lean) is what initiates the turn.

Most of us recognize this process as "countersteering," but some instructors, fearful that the notion of bass-ackward steering might cause irreparable psychic damage, endeavor to soften the blow with an exhortation to "push *down* on the appropriate handlebar."

Well, I hate to shake up anyone's fragile psyche, but Santa Claus is a part-time Macy's employee, babies aren't delivered by the stork, and pushing down on your handlebar only wears your gloves out. Don't believe me? Just make a fist and try pushing down on the left bar as you hold the throttle at a steady 60 mph: it doesn't do *anything*. You could probably set your cruise control and stand on the handgrip (if you do, take photos and mail them to me in care of *Rider's* legal department).

My friend and associate, Chris Freed, knows a good deal more about physics than I do, and several years ago he decided it would be useful to demonstrate gyroscopic precession with a bicycle wheel mounted on an axle. Now, whenever we arrive at the point where students are ready to learn where turns come from, out comes the wheel (kind of like an anatomically correct Barbie and Ken), and each student gets the opportunity to experience the phenomenon by pushing laterally on the axle. Even before any torque is applied in the perpendicular axis, the gravity-defying magic of the gyro can be clearly elucidated by balancing the whole assembly on the tip of an index finger!

By countersteering first on the bicycle wheel, students can expedite their progress toward aggressive swerving, a crucial hazard-avoidance technique. However, the wheel's usefulness and appeal has proven even greater than we'd anticipated, and it's been known to pop out of the shed on numerous other occasions.

For example, one of the earliest and most important lessons in the MSF curriculum is the relationship between stability and maneuverability. It's simple: The faster a motorcycle goes, the more it wants to go straight. In other words, stability increases . . . but maneuverability *de*creases.

You knew that, but maybe you didn't *know* it. Conceptually, it's a major step toward riding a motorcycle smoothly and maturely. Young novices rarely take long to progress past the wobbly stage; their eagerness to twist the throttle makes the motorcycle inherently stable. However, there comes a time in every ride when you want to make the motorcycle *less* stable. Enter the wonderful wheel.

I like to start at one end of our 250-foot range and give the ol' wheel a good fling. It typically tracks arrow straight for a hundred feet or so. "This," I tell my students, "is how much skill it takes to ride fast." Then, as the wheel approaches the midpoint of the range, something starts to happen. It loses speed and begins to tilt—a little at first, then farther and farther until it's turning in small circles. "What's going to happen soon?" I ask the students.

"It's going to fall," one quickly volunteers.

"So, then—if that's your motorcycle, what must you do?"

"Give it throttle!" Exactly. Throttle will restabilize the motorcycle. Simple, yet I'd forgotten my own lesson when I found myself in a new environment. It took Derek's wisdom and guidance to persuade me to destabilize the front wheel a little in order to turn it.

I generally give that demonstration about the time that we introduce sharp turns. Often students—the stronger ones in particular—can negotiate these turns with scarcely any speed reduction. When this happens, I must caution them to brake more and let the front wheel "flop" into the turn—like the bicycle wheel in the final moments before it topples over—then restabilize, using clutch and throttle. In this way, they're able to do a true 90-degree turn—the value of which may not be readily apparent.

"You'd never make a turn this sharp in the real world, would you?" is a comment I'm accustomed to hearing. Perhaps *you* wouldn't, but *I* would, and here is an example. Say I want to make a left-hand turn onto a cross street, and a car on the adjoining street is waiting at a stop sign to turn left. Maybe the driver's creeping out for a better view, or perhaps the sun is in his eyes. In either case, a "normal" turn will take me too close to a potential collision. I need a larger space cushion. So I keep to the right— delay my turn—simultaneously brake and squeeze the clutch in to make a very sharp turn—out of striking distance of the turning car.

Here's another lesson of the wheel: Sometimes, even at high speeds, our gyros aren't as stable as we'd like. This has less to do with physics than with the surfaces we ask them to track over and the ambiguous signals we sometimes send through our controls. But the wheel is wise. I launch it—this time with a deliberate twist. It wobbles, even hops across the range, but then—miracle of miracles—it straightens and tracks beautifully again. This is what happens after you've crossed a patch of gravel or some nasty bumps—even after a locked front brake—if you relax and let the wheels roll.

High-speed stability can effectively mask skill deficiencies, but lower speeds will eventually uncover them. There's a left turn near my friend's house that I've made hundreds of times, usually on big touring bikes or sport tourers. It's well paved, slightly off camber, and has a big, slippery crosswalk painted over it. I feel like a wuss, because I creep through it, almost vertical, while I know there are guys who could flick it right through. I could, too, on my featherweight dual-sport with its 21-inch front gyro. But I'm deathly afraid of losing my front end on the paint, and I don't trust myself to keep the back wheel spinning if it starts to slide.

Perhaps I need more desert practice . . . on the boss's Gold Wing!

The Theory of the Left Bend

December 2002

I met Larry for the first and only time at a motorcycle safety conference in 2003. I was taken by his friendliness and honesty as we spent a couple of special hours discussing our thoughts on riding skills and motojournalism.

Larry wrote from experience, reflection, and love for the sport of motorcycling and was a great influence on me as I was learning to be a motojournalist. He impressed me with his insight and ability to unravel some of the most illusive aspects of motorcycle riding. Larry regularly questioned subjects nobody else thought to question and in the process, unearthed some interesting theories.

The two articles he penned entitled "The Theory of the Left Bend" and "The Theory of the Right Bend" represent just how insightful he could be. Larry sheds light on the perceptions and physical factors that influence a rider's comfort level when cornering.

Larry observed over many thousands of miles how riders handled the particular characteristics of left and right-hand turns. "The Theory of the Left Bend" article reveals the nuances inherent with left-hand turns and how the particular characteristics of left-handers can erode confidence and compromise control.

Larry also knew that in contrast, many beginner motorcycle students learning to ride in a parking lot struggle more with right hand turns. In "The Theory of the Right Bend," Larry analyzes the reasons why right hand turns give many riders fits when riding at parking lot speeds.

Ken Condon, "Proficient Motorcycling" columnist,
Motorcycle Consumer News; *MSF RiderCoach;*
chief instructor, Tony's Track Days (www.tonystrackdays.com);
expert level roadracer; and author of Riding in the Zone.

Well, for starters, I put no stock in the notion that it's the Coriolis effect. Yeah, that's the business about the water swirling counterclockwise around the sink in this, our northern hemisphere, then straightening out as Johnny nears the equator and reversing directions on the other side. There's no geophysical component in the execution of left- or right-hand turns, but whatever the reason, it's a fact that left-hand turns are easier. An Austrian researcher presenting at MSF's international conference in Florida two years ago produced evidence that street riders steer 20 percent harder to the left than they do to the right. I don't find that at all surprising. What do we tell people when we introduce them to countersteering?

Push left, go left; push right, go right.

Well, just place your open left palm against a wall or a desk, elbow bent and forearm nearly parallel to the ground. Push forward and feel how directly the power flows from your chest and shoulder (the major muscle groups). Now ball your other hand in a fist, and repeat the gesture on the right side while simultaneously rotating your wrist backward. See how much energy is diverted? If you attempted a bench press with one arm thusly handicapped, it's likely the barbell would end up on either the floor or your larynx.

Of course, not all turns require high levels of countersteering force. On a lower speed turn, one may simply shift body weight and allow the front wheel to "tuck in." For some bikes, especially supersport models with low clip-on handlebars, throttle control gets very tough to come by with that right fist squeezed between handlebar and gas tank. Plus, if you're like me, you feel more secure when dragging the "control brake" (i.e. rear) during low-speed maneuvers. This you can accomplish in either direction, but psychologically, it's much more comforting to know that you can "dab" at the bottom of the arc . . . an unavailable luxury when you are banked way over on the right, your foot working the brake pedal.

So, why not conclude that left turns—high speed or low—are just plain easier than right ones, put this page down and all go for a nice ride? Well, for the same reason that rats outside the laboratory can smoke all the cigarettes and drink all the diet soda they desire and never develop cancer. The "real world," or in our case, the street, is different than the laboratory. What makes our world different from parking lots and test tracks is that we have completely different surfaces for left and right turns.

In countries like ours, where automobiles arrive at the showrooms with their steering wheels on the left side, the left turn wraps around the outside of the right. Every road. Every turn. So in any given corner, the left turn has a greater radius (easier, no?) than the right, and on average a longer view.

Does the evidence that left turns are easier ever stop mounting?

YES. The greater radius is only easier if it's as constant as whatever it's being compared to. Any fiddling you have to do with the steering negates the advantage, and because left turns are longer but not wider, the chances of finding a perfect (circular) arc through them is less.

In addition to being longer, left handers are narrower. Not in the eye of the engineer who designed the road, but from the seat of the motor-cycle which travels it. Where do you set up for a bend? On the outside, typically—close to the center line for a right turn and toward the shoulder for a left. Which side would you rather err on? Most riders can take it right to the paint line, knowing that they can turn in whenever a car appears in the oncoming lane. If they kiss the line, no big deal. However, kissing the shoulder *is* a big deal, so many riders turn it in earlier on left-ies than they would on righties. I call it "edge fear," but it's no phobia—it's a rational policy based upon the need for self-preservation.

The downside of turning in early is that it increases the likelihood that a correction will follow once rider radar determines that a path too close to that of oncoming traffic is imminent. No sooner have you banked to the left, than you have to straighten and head toward the shoulder. The result, frequently, is not an arc at all, but a wobbly series of weak, defensive steering inputs.

Everything stated thus far could apply to a road which is table top flat. Most aren't. Take a look at your bike's tires and you'll find, almost certainly, that the left edge shows more wear than the right. That could be because you corner harder to the left, but more likely it's due to the shape of the roads you ride on. Because most roads are crowned for better drainage, you spend more time riding upon one side of the tires. Just picture a severely crowned road with two motorcycles approaching one another. They're traveling in opposite directions, but they're *both* riding on the left sides of their tires.

Now on steep roads, drainage takes care of itself, so highway departments can bank most turns the way we like them. But where the terrain levels off (like in farm country), the crown creates a right bend which is positively banked and a left turn which is off camber. Flick the bike into the right turn and odds are it will go where you want. The same thrust to the left will not only send you across the center line, it will carry you over a hump (which coincidentally is on the same side of your bike as the protruding center and sidestands).

I've seen riders who ignore all of these negative stimuli, as well as the debris along the shoulder. They ride the outside, firm in the belief that one "... can always lean it over a little more." I don't necessarily share that roseate view. The way I coach riders to maximize the slimmer ribbon available going left is what I call the "power boost." It goes as follows:

1) Slow Down: As long as you're not wobbling, you're technically not going too slowly.

2) Position close to the shoulder: If you've handled number 1, then you're less likely to panic as you near the edge.

3) Settle your suspension by rolling-on gently: Yes, this will propel you *toward* the edge (did I mention number 1?)

4) Countersteer: Keep the power *on* as you do this.

When you think about it, the combination of steps numbers 3 and 4 is tantamount to steering in both directions at the same time. Their net is an arc that doesn't necessarily follow a perfect circle, but which is nicely curved and safely distances the bike from hazards on both sides. The key is to maintain the two steering forces (throttle and counter) in proportion to one another.

As with any technique, it gets smoother and quicker with practice, but in my view it's worth sacrificing entry speed to set the bike up for the special needs of a left bend. Without a doubt, left turns are easier in a parking lot, but over the past 10 years I've observed on the order of half a million rider miles on mountain roads. Five million curves probably. The number of serious errors (which would be anything that makes me cringe) I've watched on left bends has outnumbered right-turn mistakes by a five-to-one margin.

Next month—the theory of the right bend.

The Theory of the Right Bend

January 2003

They're not the same. They should be, but they're not. Last month we examined left turns, pointing out why they're easier for most riders to negotiate at parking-lot speeds, and referencing research which found riders steered 20 percent harder in that direction . . . on *closed courses.*

Then we dissected the left turn on *real* roads and concluded that negative camber (due to road crown), unfriendly shoulders, and oncoming traffic actually made them more challenging. If you're reading this in Sydney or Newcastle on Tyne, put on your reverse-world glasses or just skip ahead to next month's column.

Right turns are easier. I base this on 10 years of experience watching all levels of riders negotiate mountain roads. When riders end up in the rough it's the right-side ditch by a factor of about three. In part, we can attribute this to the right bend's paved runoff area—a.k.a. the oncoming lane. Mercifully, the sight of a head-on collision has eluded me thus far.

Runoff room alone does not explain the lower error/accident rate on right turns. The motorcycle just plain prefers it. If a rider has a basic understanding of cornering lines, countersteering, and throttle control, he or she can setup near the centerline, flick the bike in and most of the time it'll come out where it's supposed to without much fiddling. That's principally due to the positive camber which most right bends enjoy. Reason two is that the centerline is a more forgiving turn entry point than is the shoulder. Reason three also has to do with the shoulder: get too close on a left turn, and you need to add lean angle (difficult and scary); too close on the right turn . . . just roll on more gas.

Ride an oval dirt track and you'll only make left turns. Ride on freeways with cloverleafs and you'll do nothing but rights. Almost anywhere else, you'll negotiate them in near equal number—often in combination. The "model" for cornering efficiency is the "racer's line," sometimes known as "outside/inside/outside." Simply put, it's the most direct pathway through the turn, and on paper it works every time . . . so long as there are no traffic hazards and the turn begins and ends with a straightaway.

I think where a lot of riders go wrong is with their almost religious adherence to the "late apex" or "delayed apex," two terms which have lost their geometrical relevance as they devolve into synonyms for riding the outside of the bend. Mind you, I'm all for *setting up* on the outside. While I make it a point to keep my bike's rubber off the yellow paint (that's what makes us *street* riders), I see nothing wrong with hanging a mirror or saddlebag over there—in the absence of oncoming traffic, of course. Occasionally I'm asked if I'm not made nervous by the proximity of oncoming cars rounding the bend, to which I reply with a resounding *yes.* That's precisely why I position the bike where I'll get the earliest view of them.

Once the pavement starts to arc, however, I don't want to crowd that centerline any longer. Exactly how far away I position the bike depends upon the severity of the bend and the limitations of sight, but there's only one justification for staying wide on the right turn—increased view past the obstruction on the right. There are, however, a number of good arguments against the wide line:

- Proximity to oncoming traffic
- Greater distance to be traveled (meaning higher velocity required to get through in the same time)
- Greater need for mid-turn steering correction once the view opens up
- Difficulty of adding lean angle when faced with above elements
- Increased risk of scraping when lean angle added
- Weaker drive off the bend and onto the straightaway
- Poor position for a subsequent left bend

Add up these risk factors in a logical order and it becomes even easier to see why there are more incidents involving left bends. Riders miscalculate their right turns or get spooked by oncoming vehicles, and before they can fully recover, they're headed toward a severe left turn, poorly positioned and carrying too much speed.

Of course each of the above risk factors can be mitigated by simply lowering speed, prior to and within the turn. Is your goal to go through corners as fast as you can or as safely? Most riders strive for a happy compromise—a safe execution that pushes their tiltmeter far enough to send a pleasant tingle through their systems. When riders panic in curves, I'll bet that short sight lines sound more alarms than do steep lean angles.

How far ahead should you see? That's a subject for another column, but too few riders truly know where to look in a bend. They try—especially in right turns—to see past a given obstruction and fail to recognize indicators that the curve is either opening or tightening. Those indicators are typically on the *opposite* side of the road. The rider who cranes his or her neck for the ultimate glimpse past the trees or rocks on the right frequently fails to recognize that the opposing verge—a guardrail, for example—is actually straightening out. If so there's an awfully good chance that it's fixing to double back into a left turn.

So what you have are two tactics for getting down the road in pretty much the same amount of time. You can "read" the road, choosing economical lines which trace the clues left by the landscape, or you can use what Reg Pridmore calls a "looky loo" line. In the latter, the rider clings to the outside, shredding every stitch from the veil enshrouding the turn's apex, then he swoops across the lane and into position for a left turn which he or she attacks in the same fashion.

The cornerstone of the former approach to the right bend is knowing when to say when. Most hazards on the shoulder of a right bend are easy to deal with. Usually you just straighten a bit and go around them. If it's a fast-moving vehicle, at least it lacks a "forward motion" component. If you spot it at four seconds, then you've got four seconds to respond . . . but if your sight line reaches four seconds to the *outside* verge, then you're lucky to have two seconds, since oncoming drivers are invading at roughly the same speed. Avoidance typically requires leaning harder at higher speed.

In my opinion nearly all experienced riders hang to the outside longer than necessary on right bends. I was never more aware of this than the other day, as I followed behind a student who rode *much* faster than me through a series of switchback bends. He went in deeper, leaning harder in both directions, and I didn't try to keep up. Amazingly, I didn't have to; he never put any ground on my bike! Often, he stayed on the outside until startled by an oncoming car, then he'd correct so violently that he'd nearly clip the right shoulder—necessitating another violent thrust to the left. Had we taken odometer readings, I'll bet his would have shown 10 percent more mileage than mine!

If all this comes across as a bit too theoretical, then just contemplate the following when you next encounter a blind right turn: 1) There's a car coming around the bend with a wheel or two in your lane. 2) The exit of said right turn will become the entrance to a subsequent *left* turn. You can't go wrong by guessing wrong . . . unless you're on the wrong bleedin' side of the road, mate!

Brakes? Perhaps . . .

September 2003

The late Larry Grodsky noted in the following column that "top experts" don't agree on braking technique for turns. For street riders, I advise braking when approaching turns as part of your cornering technique. At least ease on a little front brake as you roll off the gas to decelerate, so that you're no stranger to braking as part of cornering.

My logic is based primarily on how humans react to sudden surprises. When we are suddenly faced with a hazard—say a stalled truck just around the curve—we tend to react immediately, and think about it later. The survival reactions we take are based on habits, or what some folks call "muscle memory."

In other words, when you round a blind corner to discover three bikes sliding in circles, or a pickup truck making a U turn, you will resort to habits. If you are in the habit of smooth throttle-brake transitions, you're likely to go smoothly from throttle to front brake and pull off a successful stop in a curve without thinking about it.

Larry once confided in me that he couldn't understand why so many of his students would fail to slow for hazardous turns even after he had warned them of a specific nasty corner. They would still ride into it too fast and crash. I suggest that the mistake is not so much in students failing to understand the hazards, but rather instructors allowing students to get into the risky habit of controlling speed only with the throttle.

David L. Hough, author of Proficient Motorcycling, More Proficient Motorcycling, *and* Street Strategies

On the street corners of Mexico, wherever men gather to admire the fulsome beauty of the fairer sex, the most traffic-stopping *señoritas* can evoke this bittersweet lament: *"Tantas curvas* (So many curves) . . . *y yo sin frenos!* (. . . and me with no brakes!)."

Mexico has some seriously steep roads. I once cooked two sets of front brake pads on a 10,000-mile journey along its jagged spine—an experience which may have helped to shape my earlier training methods. Time was when I'd start a training tour with a series of morning cornering drills, march the troops down the road just long enough to let the asphalt get *really* hot, then stop for 90 minutes of braking drills on a steaming parking lot.

Those intense practice sessions would noticeably sharpen the average student's parking-lot braking. The problem was that we'd get back on the road and ride for miles before many riders would ever test their new-found skills on steep terrain. A sizable contingent, I observed, considered it to be a sign of skill to ride a challenging section of road without touching their brakes.

David Hough, author of *Proficient Motorcycling*, one of the most widely respected books on safe street riding, takes an entirely different view. He says you should brake for *every* turn short of a Freeway sweeper. Why? To get in the habit, says Hough.

"First, you should be prepared to brake hard for a turn that you discover is tighter than expected. Second, if a hazard comes into view only as you lean over, you should be prepared to use both brakes to the limit of tire traction. If front braking is part of your cornering habits, your survival reaction will be to brake harder on the front, which helps avoid a rear-wheel slideout."

That's a fair amount to digest in one paragraph. It also sounds like a lot of braking "practice" should you be negotiating a road such as the Blue Ridge Parkway, where I frequently conduct training. A narrow, shoulderless two-laner, the BRP's a far cry from the average freeway, yet reasonably skilled riders routinely negotiate its entire 469-mile length at 5-10 mph over its posted 45-mph limit while their brake pucks sleep unmolested in the calipers.

Now start your descent down any of the dozens of twisty roads which cross the BRP and you'll soon confront a more challenging array of radii and inclines. I'll use U.S. 60, dropping into Buena Vista, Virginia, as an example. There are perhaps three dozen curves on the five-mile descent, only two for which I would normally brake. Quite honestly, many of my students don't carry sufficient speed to require braking even for those two.

I want to believe Hough's analogy. In theory, its application would eliminate the number one problem we encounter descending U.S. 60 and other mountain roads: students who've been lulled into complacency by a series of lesser bends, then suddenly hit their brakes at the entry of a steeper, more severe one. Grazing the lever just enough to take the free play out would at least smooth out the response and reduce the chances of lockup or loss of control.

My problem with the Hough approach is that braking—*effective* braking—takes time. The longer the straightaway, the more time the rider has to modulate pressure, settling weight on the front tire and smoothly returning it to the rear for optimal cornering. Sandwich all that activity into a short gap between turns and smoothness has to suffer. British "pursuit" trainer Mike Waite takes a different approach. During two fall days under the ex-police motorcycle instructor's tutelage, I heard not a word devoted to braking technique. All emphasis was placed on rolling off the throttle when the "visual point" (the convergence of features paralleling the two sides of the road) approaches and then rolling it on at the moment said visual point begins to recede. A brake light was almost universally assailed as a dropped visual point.

Perhaps Waite's and Hough's ideological differences stem from their geographic disparity; the former hailing from the rolling terrain of southwest England, the latter from the Pacific Northwest, where roads sometimes climb to over 10,000 feet. And maybe *my* equivocation comes from training 80–90 percent of the time at elevations between 500 and 3,000 feet.

I do like this visual point though, and so—with or without benefit of brakes—I've endeavored to slow students early and get them back on their throttle by the time the visual point starts to "go away." I just think that riding on the street, not knowing what's around the bend much of the time, it makes good sense to get all of the difficult stuff out of the way early. I've never claimed it's the fastest way to get around a corner—just the most efficient for the majority of street riding situations.

If faster lap times are what you're after, then few writers can explain the drill better than Nick Ienatsch, whose new book, *Sport Riding Techniques,* also contains some astute observations on safe street riding. A long-time motojournalist, two-time AMA 250GP national champion, and now chief instructor at Freddie Spencer's High Performance Riding School, Ienatsch preaches a low-aggression, high-safety margin approach to street riding, which he calls "The Pace." So it comes as a bit of a surprise that he advocates "trail braking"—carrying the brakes to the apex of the turn—as a means of mitigating mid-corner surprises.

"Those who use their brakes in a straight line and then let go of them to steer their bikes are deciding very early in the corner what speed they need," Ienatsch maintains. I wouldn't argue the factuality of that statement, but I doubt many street riders can muster that level of control—particularly on unfamiliar roads.

So, if top riding experts can't agree on how to brake for a corner, what should you do? I say first get your throttle control down. Do so by tenderfooting it to each and every turn entry until you can comfortably throttle through even the downhill bends. Throttle /brake/ throttle transitions are a much trickier proposition (only a small percentage of the street riders I've observed exhibit even adequate technique). Practicing this important skill will require either a long (traffic-free) straightaway or a grade of eight percent or better. Braking from 45 mph to 40 on a modest slope might teach you to manage driveline lash, but higher levels of control demand the ability to significantly weight (and unweight) the front tire. And—again—that takes time.

For most motorcyclists, the situation is seldom *tantas curvas* and no *frenos*; it's usually too much straightway speed and too little processing time. Suddenly events are outside the rider's comfort envelope and a quick reach for the brakes seems the only answer.

Braking skills, unfortunately, aren't a substitute for judgment, but remember this—the mere act of leaning the motorcycle will scrub off *some* speed—(fewer wheel rotations per engine revolutions as the tire leans onto its smaller inner diameter). A rider who tips the bike into the turn without tensing up and clenching the bars will regain composure sooner than a rider who hits the brakes and upsets the chassis at the turn entry.

All of this puts me in mind of the old parable about the—um—pair a' bulls, gazing down from the hilltop at a meadow full of comely heifers.

"Let's run down there and please a few of those cows!" said the younger bull, excitedly.

"Let's walk down," sighed the elder bull, " . . . and please them all."

An Ass No More

October 2003

*This column illustrates Larry's unwillingness to set aside unre-
solved issues. It was penned as a follow-up to the preceding
"Brakes? Perhaps . . ." in which Larry admitted being puzzled
by various theories regarding the correct method for setting
turn entry speed.*

*After digesting several conflicting approaches, copying none
as the superior line of reason, Larry answers his own question.*

Pete Tamblyn

Everything I know about journalism can be summed up in three sen-
tences that I learned in my tenth-grade communications class: *Tell
the people what you're going to tell them. Tell them. Then tell them what
you've told them.*

And so I drag my angst-ridden butt back to the keyboard this month,
knowing that my last epistle, "Brakes? Perhaps . . ." failed to pass the
sophomore journalism litmus test. You may recall that I struggled to reconcile my wishy-washy corner entry strategy with those of two highly
placed authorities on street riding: Nick Ienatsch, chief instructor at
Freddie Spencer's High Performance Riding School and author of the recently published *Sport Riding Techniques,* and David Hough, author of
the *Proficient Motorcycling* series. Ienatsch, a decorated racer, extolled
the benefits of trail braking (carrying the brakes past the turn entry),
while Hough advocated braking for every corner short of a freeway
sweeper.

OK, but a day after hitting my computer's "send" button, while riding
a student on the back of my bike down twisty Ohio Route 260 in the
Wayne National Forest, I had an epiphany. Heading opposite to my usual
northbound direction, we came upon a downhill straightaway—unchar-
acteristically steep and long by Ohio standards—which culminated in a
tight, 90-degree left turn. I warned the student to lean back a bit, as I was
going to give a braking exhibition—which I did, shedding a good 40
mph for the bend. I suspect that the student, a reentry rider and a

flatlander, had never before experienced such hard braking for a corner; I *know* that for me it was a singularly eye-opening moment.

As we returned to the picnic grove where the rest of our group was relaxing, I formatted the syllabic substance of my awakening: *Late braking demands an early commitment.*

I know, it doesn't sound so brilliant, but I felt like I'd tripped the floodlights on Plato's Cave, though as philosophical metaphors go "Buridan's Ass"—the pathetic beast which starved to death, unable to choose between two equidistant bundles of hay—would be more fitting. No longer would I be an ass, unable to choose. Brakes? Perhaps . . . would become Brakes—Yes! or Brakes—No! and would do so at the exit of the *preceding* bend.

A couple of distinctions must be made. One, late braking, as executed by accomplished racers or experienced road riders on familiar routes, is part of a complete corner strategy, and in no way related to the last-second stab which street riders often make when they've suddenly realized that a corner is sharper than they'd imagined. Two, when I say "Brakes— No!" I'm not suggesting that riders disregard their survival instincts and just dive in. What I'm saying is that once riders have made an early decision not to brake, they can take their time and sneak up on a turn; what Ienatsch refers (not sympathetically) to as " . . . deciding very early in the corner what speed they need." It's a pacifist's approach to sport riding. Its practitioners sometimes enjoy corner exit speeds rivaling those of their disc rotor-melting brethren, but they refuse to be goaded into battle with their sight line.

"Brakes—Yes!" comes with a tacit manifesto: You must actually *know how* to use your brakes. I'm not being flip. The median pre-crash speed identified in the Hurt Report was between 25 and 30 mph. MSF's Experienced RiderCourse (ERC) will give you controlled stopping practice at 25 mph, so if you head to the local K-Mart for half an hour per week, by the end of the season, you'll be ace on the most important of accident avoidance skills.

That's great for intersections (where most collisions take place), but the number of back road corners that call for hard braking from 25–30 mph is a percentage of zero. The number which call for even modest braking at that speed is nearly as slim. Street riders often ask me what they'll get from a track school, and this is the answer: *brake modulation practice.* You may hit 130 mph, depending upon your equipment and your *cojones,* but you will brake hard and often from speeds of 60 mph and above. Guaranteed.

Most tracks deploy braking markers on the back ends of the straightaways to help racers gauge their initiation points. Unfortunately, most street riders—and I've worked with thousands of them—can't judge their stopping distances at speeds over 30 mph. If you painted a line on a runway and asked 100 riders to stabilize their speeds at 60 mph, delay their braking as late as they dare, and then stop right at the line, you'd get a real mishmash of results. Some would start twice as soon as they had to, while others would sail past the line. Many would lock the back brake . . . or worse.

Now I'll tell you something. I'm not God's gift to motorcycling. I couldn't scuff Nick Ienatsch's knee sliders with a Sears Craftsman orbital sander. But I'll bet I could come reasonably close to matching his best 60-mph stops for distance and accuracy. You could, too, if you practiced as much as I do.

The other thing that most street riders lack—but would develop with enough track practice—is a smooth throttle/brake/throttle transition. I'm often appalled to see how many experienced riders simply grab at the front brake lever and then just let go when they're done with it—no sense of "touch." MSF courses—novice or experienced—can't help much here. Just rolling the throttle on and off at 25 mph is a challenge to one's parking-lot smoothness. If you want to develop velvety transitions but don't want to pay track fees, then find yourself a deserted section of highway where you can make five- to seven-second brake applications.

Back to the two strategies. The Brakes—No! approach demands that one keep the visual point (in a blind turn, the confluence of features verging the left and right sides of the road) at a comfortable distance: *roll off* the throttle as soon as the visual point grows nearer; *roll-on* as it recedes. The Brakes—Yes! guy also keeps the visual point at a comfortable distance, but he doesn't mind holding the throttle open as the scenery rushes toward him; "comfort" for him means being able to stop short of it, even in a curve. The result, therefore, can be trail braking—i.e. hard braking on the straightaway, lighter pressure as the bike bends into the corner, then a smooth transition back into the throttle for the drive out.

I'm not sure my nerves would ever permit me to take responsibility for strange riders who dive into blind, wooded turns with their blinders on. Someday . . . who knows? I may stumble onto a breakthrough training method which universally empowers riders to perfect their braking in mere hours. Then maybe we'll see riders braking to set up for a high percentage of corners. Until then, I think we'll be sneaking up on the majority of them. The crucible is the level of speed one is willing to carry down the straightaway.

So don't be an ass, unable to make a choice. If you want braking to be part of your cornering repertoire, learn to brake well and start looking for your initiation point as soon as you depart the previous bend. If you want to rely on engine braking, you should *still* learn how to brake well, but your attention coming out of corner A has to be focused on conserving your margin of reserve for corner B.

And folks, I believe I've now told you what I've told you.

Legally Blind

January 1998

Assignment: Apply maximum braking to a full stop within your sight line in a curve. Piece of cake you say? Don't try this at home (It's harder on the carpet than a new puppy), but if you've got some favorite blind curves, cautious practice is the preferred approach. Additional advice is to examine your turn entry speed.

Pete Tamblyn

It was 2 a.m. and the other tour members had long since snuggled up to their feather beds in the glitzy Italian lakeside hotel. In the hotel bar the tour operator, an egocentric man whose impresario talents were exceeded only by his appetite for other people's funds, was plying me with scotch in an attempt to make me utter eight little words: "This is the best tour of my life."

Having no small ego myself, I opted to continue absorbing his verbal and chemical beating. "Where have you ever ridden roads like these?" he demanded. "There are no other roads like these in the world!"

"Yeah, these are all right," I allowed, " . . . but we have better roads than these in *Ohio!*"

Okay, there are no fifteenth-century castles on Lake Erie, no 14,000-foot-high glaciers overlooking Columbus, and Cleveland's Black Forest cheesecake may not attract gourmets from around the globe, but head down the Ohio River and hang a right on just about any secondary road, and you'll be rewarded with what must be motorcycling's best-kept secret. No tour buses. No traffic lights. In fact, no traffic of any kind save the occasional goober, who inevitably turns off onto some dirt road within a mile.

The twisties of southeastern Ohio, however, are quite different from most mountain riding. Since the terrain is not particularly steep, there aren't a lot of heavy braking opportunities, nor many hairpin turns. These Appalachian foothills rise and fall more like roller coasters, and taking them fast is like riding with your eyes shut.

How far ahead should you be able to see? The textbook answer is 12 seconds, and you can do that on the backroads of southeastern Ohio . . . if you're willing to get off your motorcycle and push it. An altogether less demanding environment is the Blue Ridge Parkway in Virginia and North Carolina. Surely one of the most over-engineered roads in the nation, it further minimizes surprises with a 45-mph speed limit and federal rangers who aren't above impounding your vehicle. Still, there are plenty of blind turns, especially right-handers, so I recently asked three of my students what the minimum sight line was after we'd cruised the scenic byway for some 20 minutes.

"Don't know," responded one of the students. "Haven't a clue," said another. Just as I'd have predicted, but without deliberation, the third flatly replied, "Four seconds." Exactly the right answer.

If there was anyone who'd come up with the correct answer, it would be Ron, a high school teacher and former MSF instructor with a cool and analytical approach to motorcycling. "Do you think you could stop within that distance?" I asked Ron. He shrugged his shoulders, and it was then that I realized I'd found the perfect subject for an experiment I'd long wished to conduct.

I explained the conditions to Ron, and he willingly agreed to them. I would ride up the road to an undisclosed point and place a six-inch traffic cone along the side of the road. When he saw the cone, Ron would attempt to stop at or before it. It was understood this was not to be a "panic" stop; he would brake with authority, but not risk a skid or loss of control in an all-out attempt to stop short of the cone. I knew I could trust Ron, because he's a skilled yet conservative rider.

About two minutes after I set the cone, I heard the rumble of Ron's new BMW R110GS approaching the blind turn. When he spotted the cone, Ron straightened and applied the brakes, coming to a smooth stop exactly at the cone. Afterward, he reported that he felt he had "a little" left in reserve.

The only thing Ron didn't do textbook perfectly was put his left foot down when he stopped . . . and when he put his right foot out, he discovered that the banked surface was a bit farther away than he'd anticipated. I rushed to his side, but the two of us couldn't prevent the 600 pounds of loaded machine from toppling over. Together we picked up the fallen bike and wheeled it onto the grass, when another twin cylinder rumble arose in the distance.

Unbeknownst to either of us, Ron's wife, Joyce, had decided to join in the experiment. A less seasoned rider, she nonetheless brought her Yamaha 535 Virago to a halt within her four-second sight line . . . and then *she* put her right foot out! You can guess the rest. The bounds of ethical research, I'm afraid, may force me to abandon this particular line of investigation. However, even two short repetitions seem to have shed some light on the subject.

MSF curricula, in addition to recommending a 12-second visual lead, discuss a four-second zone—that which demands one's immediate attention. Another way of looking at it would be that the 12-second zone is what you think about, and the immediate four seconds is what you actually do. Ron and Joyce's experience, riding at the speed limit on a well-engineered two-lane highway, gives credence to the theoretical four-second response zone. The reality, unfortunately, is not such a simple equation.

When we did a braking study several years ago, we found that the best riders needed 50 feet to respond to a signal and stop the motorcycle at 30 mph. Of course, they were expecting the signal, and of the 50 feet almost half was covered during the reaction time between signal and braking. At 30 mph it takes 1.14 seconds to cover 50 feet.

It's generally accepted that, as speed rises, stopping distances increase exponentially. The rider who stops in 30 feet at 30 mph, for example, will need 120 feet at 60 mph. Okay, to that 120 feet add .5 seconds reaction time (another 44 feet); total stopping distance, 164 feet. That equates to a "response envelope" of 1.9 seconds, nearly double that for 30 mph. Follow this line of reasoning up the scale and you find that the response zone (measured in seconds) rises in almost direct proportion to the speed. The only thing that keeps it from being a perfectly linear equation is the reaction time (throttle to the brakes) which is more a product of throttle position than speed.

All of the aforementioned theory is based on straight-line braking. But if it carries over to the Blue Ridge Parkway, the rider who takes curves at 90 mph (doable on modern sport-bikes) would have a visual lead of two seconds and a response envelope of nearly eight! Put another way, the closest point by which he can stop is four times the distance of the farthest point he can see. However arbitrary these figures, it's apparent that riding fast on the street takes more nerve than skill. Of course, any real racer could've told you that without a calculator.

But back in Ohio (and by the way, contrary to what some magazines have written, there are other roads even better than Route 555), the constant ups and downs make the equation all the more complex. While apexing a turn you may be able to see an object six seconds ahead . . . and yet be blind to a surface hazard one second or less in front of you.

When we ride in southeastern Ohio, we buy a little extra time by standing on the footpegs, dirtbike style; and crest hills mid-lane, because we really can't predict whether the danger is a car passing (on our left) or pulling out of a driveway (on our right).

The reality is, there's no magic bullet. Even if you can see 12 seconds ahead and stop in four, a deer could jump out of the bushes a half second in front of you. But I think that anyone who rides mountain roads owes it to himself to try a Ron and Joyce; when you spot a driveway while rounding blind curve on an unfamiliar road, don't just ask yourself if you could stop short—give it a shot. Should you lose control and crash, your response was just the tip of your iceberg of foolishness. And should your skills survive the test, please—get both feet down before you congratulate yourself.

Street Strategies—Stayin' Safe

Home Base

December 2005

Few concepts were more important to Larry than "Put the bike where they can't touch you." The essence of safe lane position- ing begins with an understanding of the home base *concept— where the bike should be when there are no other consider- ations. Elsewhere, Larry admonishes riders to emulate the common housefly. Here, we're encouraged to move like a snake. What's next? Anything but a groundhog. . . .*

Pete Tamblyn

There's no single lane position that's best for all riding situations, but there's one that's always worth returning to.

My friend Bob, a resident of Brussels who has given me shelter on many a European journey, minced no words when he made the follow- ing observation: "Larry, for someone who travels so much, you're really not very good at it"

I would take issue with that statement. I don't think I've traveled so much at all. Certainly not compared to Clem Salvadori, who has visited a hundred countries on a motorcycle. With all that worldly experience, I suppose Clem never loses his passport, misses a flight, or stumbles tip- sily through the door marked *Damen*.

Truly, what makes Clem a better traveler is the ease with which he connects to faraway places, though no one I've ever known appears quite so content under his own roof. Those restless souls who call the highway their home are more likely found on Nashville song sheets, I think, than on real roads. Most of us feel the gravity of a place we call home, and if we can't be there, we try to establish a home base.

I can still remember one of my earliest motorcycle conversations. I was hitchhiking (probably with a helmet under my arm after my bike had broken down), and the older driver, a veteran motorcyclist, was in- terrogating me on my riding knowledge.

"Do you know what part of the road yer supposed to ride in?" He didn't wait for an answer. "It's not the middle of yer lane. A lot of people think it is, but it's not. It's the *left* wheel track. Did you know that?"

I did. Vaguely. Maybe I'd figured it out on my own or perhaps from watching other riders. I understood that I got a better view most of the time from the left wheel track and that truckers could see me better in their mirrors. I'd heard horror stories about grease in midlane and intuitively knew that the part along the shoulder was where the mopeds and bicyclists rolled. So yes, when the driver picked me up hitchhiking, I think I'd already decided that the left wheel track was my "home base."

Since I was blessed to learn about motorcycling in an area chock full of serpentine roads, I quickly learned that the left wheel track position gave the best view prior to entering a right curve, though not so for the left hander. My home base was a lot like my parents' home or my home on campus—a place I often looked forward to returning to, but one from which circumstances prevented me from spending all of my time.

For many riders, home base is the middle of their lane. That's the best position in which to crest a blind hill and often the best compromise position when sandwiched by hazards. But those are reasons to visit, not to move in. The reason why people make the middle of their lane their home base is usually distrust of oncoming traffic—a healthy aversion, actually, and I don't relish head-on collisions any more than the next guy. But motorcycle accident studies, the Hurt Report to name but one, show us that the chances of crashing into a parallel vehicle are slim compared to the odds of colliding with something traveling perpendicularly. Why do you think the fastest roads (interstate highways) have the lowest accident rates?

Now, mentally exit the interstate, and you see that there are driveways, cross streets, and tertiary roads almost everywhere, but the ones that cough up the most collisions are the ones on the right side. That's because we're closer to them and have less time to react. So if I see driveways on the left and driveways on the right, I'm going to position my motorcycle just as close to the center stripe as I can, even if that means hanging a mirror or a saddlebag over the centerline. I'd stay there all day, if I could, but it's seldom long before I'm looking into the eyes of someone piloting a vehicle much larger than mine, so I never challenge oncoming drivers. I move right and create at least as much space as that which passes between the dual-track vehicles. If there's even the possibility that other vehicles are hidden in the slipstream, I move way right, to ensure that a shadow vehicle doesn't pull into my pathway to overtake or turn left.

You may think I do a lot of moving about within my lane, and you'd be right. But I tell my students to be like a snake rather than a waterbug. If you're looking well up the road, anticipating where risk can invade your path, then you can move to and from the home-base position in a series of graceful and fluid movements.

Even if I could, I wouldn't want to be the world's most efficient traveler. Sometimes the fondest travel memories lurk behind the "wrong" door, but stumbling blindly from one junction to another is not a recipe for continued success on a motorcycle. One lesson my feckless travels have taught me is to always carry the sleeping bag—my two-pound bundle of home away from home. And that's how I feel about negotiating traffic. Though I may not always be able to position my bike in total safety, my little piece of home is never more than a few seconds away. Where's yours?

Gypsy Lanes

May 1991

Writing and publishing research papers can be a funny business. You labor in solitude for dozens of hours trying to get a paper just right and then you send it out into the world and wait to see what others think of it. A lot of my papers seem to have landed with a thud. I had more than my normal nervousness at a motorcycle safety conference in Orlando in 1990 when I presented my paper about choosing a lane position to maximize your odds of avoiding a collision, because it was all mathematics and reconstruction of hypothetical crash situations, not the analysis of data from the Hurt study that was more customary for me.

Larry grabbed me and pulled me aside as soon as that morning's session ended and asked me a lot of questions about the paper as it clearly piqued his interest. I had read his columns before, but what was immediately obvious in our first conversation were the things that made Larry so good: his curiosity, intelligence, and his dedication to making motorcycling as safe as it is fun. It wasn't something he dabbled at as a way to pay the bills; it was his calling and he never lost his enthusiasm for it. I saw Larry in Denver in 1997 and again at the motorcycle safety conference in Long Beach in March, 2006. He still had tons of questions, the same interest and curiosity, the same desire to push ahead in motorcycle safety. I wish you could bottle that kind of caring and enthusiasm, or buy it or transplant it, but you just can't. Losing Larry is a loss for us all.

James Ouellet, motorcycle accident analyst
Los Angeles, California

Before there was MTV and Madonna, there was burlesque and its great star, Gypsy Rose Lee. What made her stand apart from the toothsome competition was not bawdiness, but brains, and the fact that she never actually took it all completely off. There are a couple of lessons to be learned here from the legendary Ms. Lee: one, always keep something in reserve; and two, never underestimate the power of a good illusion.

Most all disciplines have their gypsies, people who dance to the downbeat, throw a good curve, and would sooner laugh at life than wrestle with it. In motorcycle safety that could describe James Ouellet, a name found on a lot of important research—usually behind that of the famed Dr. Harry Hurt.

Ouellet, whose Hawaiian shirts and youthful good looks smack of an itinerant tennis pro more than a research scientist, bent the needle on the laugh meter with his presentation at last fall's MSF International Motorcycle Safety Conference in Orlando, Florida. But the premise of Ouellet's *Lane Positioning For Collision Avoidance*—that lane positioning might be a more effective weapon against motorcycle accidents than braking and swerving—raised a few hackles along with the chuckles. Not that anyone was arguing that riders should deliberately expose themselves . . . but was he implying that emergency skills are the stuff of *illusion,* like tassels and fake fur?

The hypothesis has roots in experimental psychology but draws most of its sustenance from the dark soil of accident investigation. According to Ouellet, it is an elementary principle that, "while moderate stress may improve the performance of well-learned behaviors . . . high levels of stress lead to a marked deterioration of performance." His mathematical reconstructions of typical collision situations might be summarized by the tried and true formula, an ounce of prevention is worth a pound of cure.

The representation 28.35 gr. Verhinderung = .45359 kg. Heilung . . . doesn't have quite the same ring, but the umbrage taken by a top German delegate was more likely a defense of his nation's skills-heavy curricula. The Germans can be justifiably proud of their training record, but Ouellet's paper nevertheless poses legitimate questions about the effectiveness of current educational schemes, and possibly even the design of future motorcycles. Of the two principal evasive tactics, he confines his discussion to only one—braking. Swerving he dismisses as too time consuming (up to four seconds according to two separate laboratory studies), and apt to put the rider in the vortex of a whole new accident scenario.

So proceeds Ouellet's discussion, confined now to direct comparisons of braking vs. lane positioning. It's further simplified by limiting analysis to only the two most common collision situations: an oncoming car turning left, and one crossing the motorcyclist's path perpendicularly. In each case, the researcher plots a so-called "window of risk"—that portion of the bike's path in which the motorcyclist is vulnerable to encroachment by the car.

To the front and rear of this window are risk-free zones, dubbed "A" and "F," from which the rider will escape collision—if only by inches— simply by maintaining his speed. Inside the window are various subzones: "E," where rear-only braking is sufficient to avoid collision; "D," where both brakes are necessary; "C," where collision is unavoidable. At the window's leading edge is the ironic zone "B"—the period when the rider could clear the intersection by maintaining speed, but by braking, delays arrival long enough to be struck by the car.

For all instances of left-turning cars, zone C—collision unavoidable— is reduced by moving to the right. In fact, at the three bike speeds analyzed (25, 30 and 35 mph), there is *no* zone C for the right portion of the right-hand lane . . . provided the driver turns from a stop. Lowering speed shortens the window of risk, but even at 35 mph, zone C shrinks from 90 feet down to zero in the course of repositioning a lane and a half to the right.

When confronted by a car approaching perpendicularly from the right, reducing the at-risk zone involves moving to the far *left*. The principle remains the same, however: "faced with a potential right-of-way threat, the rider should move laterally away from the threat." How could such a statement possibly be construed as controversial? After all, Ouellet's conclusion squares perfectly with the street strategies professed by the MSF in its films and literature. Indeed, the author stressed when delivering his paper, that instructors should not yet change anything about their teaching methods.

The controversy surrounds the implied effectiveness of evasive skills. Citing data culled from the Hurt Report, Ouellet writes that " . . . as many as 40 percent of those who braked in order to avoid a collision lost control and fell to the pavement." He goes on to state that " . . . for about 61 percent of the zone in which braking could avoid a collision, unskilled, rear-only braking would be sufficient to avoid an impact." Here things get a little prickly, for what self-respecting motorcycle instructor would ever tell a student that braking technique doesn't really matter?

Of course it matters; 61 percent is not perfection—far from it. But let's say the bike has integrated brakes. The "correct" technique for operating integrated brakes is using both front and rear controls in concert—just as you do with a conventional braking system. Or *is* it? If rear-only braking is effective for 61 percent of zone E, surely the addition of one front disk would take you well into the 90th percentile . . . not bad, considering that the likelihood of front wheel lock-up would be greatly reduced by laying off the second disk. Now if you were to couple that 90th percentile efficiency with an anti-lock system, you'd have a margin of error that looks pretty darned good . . . even if the rider himself looks awful.

The potential for wedding anti-lock and integrated braking technologies should provide plenty of fodder for future columns. Let's not lose sight of the initial premise, i.e. risk can be severely curbed by stressing lane positioning. The point is that MSF and other curriculum designers have to start stressing it *more*. Presently there's not a single item on MSF's course-ending exam that requires students to evaluate the factor of lane position.

And while a workbook exercise diagramming the dreaded left-turn invasion exhorts students to " . . . move to the right portion of your lane," that position, at 30 mph, would still expose the rider to a 40-foot path of "unavoidable collision" according to Ouellet's calculations. Yet that drawing shows two more lanes (occupied by cars), both of which could place the risk completely within the manageable zone. The strategy is correct, but the emphasis has to be shifted so that riders plan early to maximize their space cushions.

Part and parcel to the MSF credo is the belief that motorcycling is 90 percent mental and 10 percent physical. That philosophy has been borne out repeatedly by accident studies adjusted for age and experience. You can have the sharpest skills, and the best protective gear, but without the necessary space around you, you're riding naked. And Gypsy Rose Lee would tell you that's a dumb act.

21st Century Junctions

June 2002

Larry was a wordsmith of the first order. His deft and speedy writing style made reading his columns not only informative, but entertaining as well. He could recognize a potential problem, present his observations in a clear and intelligible format, and then offer a strategy on how best to minimize the risk.

He was frequently inspired by an unusual occurrence during a training session, as when his planned (and scenic) training route was detoured through a congested urban morass. "21st Century Junctions" relates how this became an opportunity to illustrate the hazards that vans and SUVs create at intersections, thus introducing readers to the concept of vehicular "eclipses." In typical Grodsky fashion, he then offers a strategy on how to best deal with this situation.

Many factors contribute to the frequency of motorcycle accidents, but intersections are inarguably the most dangerous. As Larry's article aptly points out, today's roads, combining faster-flowing traffic, multiple intersections and larger vehicles, create multiple hazards. Riders who fail to anticipate and prepare to react to these dangers risk grave consequences.

Bill Shaw, freelance motojournalist; contributor, Motorcycle Consumer News; editor, Iron Butt Magazine; *instructor, Stayin' Safe Motorcycle Training; and MSF RiderCoach*

The smart people at Harley-Davidson, when faced with the challenge of molding the Motorcycle Safety Foundations' acclaimed rider training in their own image (Riders Edge), knew that beginning riders would pose questions that a classroom and a parking lot simply couldn't answer. So they added time to visit the dealer showroom and service department. Who says that education and clever marketing can't complement one another?

Now ask anyone who's even contemplating the purchase of a street bike where most accidents occur, and they'll tell you "at intersections." So, why don't safety courses include a visit to the crucible of motor vehicle operation?

Well, some do, actually. When I traveled to London three years ago, I tagged along with a group of neophyte street riders on their first three days of instruction. On day two, they spent an hour circulating one block of an old Dickensian neighborhood as their instructor coached from the street corner—first on left turns, then on right. Day three was more perverse—a lesson on one of the busiest roundabouts; in central London.

Those Brits are clever, but my first exposure to "intersection education" actually came as a high school junior. My drivers ed teacher dispatched a group of us to a busy inner-city corner, ostensibly to count infractions by those who "knew" how to drive. I'm not sure what, exactly, I learned that day about safe driving. What I recall is that the teacher said the city would lose most of its shopping revenue if police cited all of the infractions that we tallied.

One of the most frequent violations—one we've all been guilty of—was stopping beyond the painted lines. And lots of turn signal peccadilloes. I'm sure there were drivers who imparted their own interpretation to the concept of "yellow" lights, but one couldn't build up enough speed there to justify the term "running" a red light.

Back then most of us lived in clearly defined residential environments: A) urban, B) suburban, or C) rural/small town. Population shifts, we've been led to believe, have deposited the majority of us in the "B" group—suburban—but that's not altogether true. In the last half-decade, the percentage of Americans living in cities has actually risen above that of suburbanites . . . sort of.

Many cities have annexed suburban territory, while others, particularly in the Sunbelt, have turned from the traditional downtown nucleus toward a more "free range" development, with homes and businesses linked by new, multilane boulevards. So, too, has the face of small town life changed. The distance-shrinking Interstate highway system and the powerful pull of national retail chains now ensure that few Americans—even in the most rural areas—go a week without navigating what author William Kowinski calls "Mall Condo Continuum."

I spend most weekends, April through October, leading training tours in various corridors of the Appalachian region. Up until very recently, I prided myself on designing routes that were chock-full of twisties and relatively traffic-free. My thinking's undergone an evolution of sorts in the last three years, but it took a tour gone awry to make an overdue change to my routing and my curriculum.

One of my routes includes a lovely afternoon ride through "Walton Country," in the foothills of the Blue Ridge Mountains, but a series of un-planned events put us nearly two hours behind schedule. The only way to make up the time was to burrow through Charlottesville, Virginia, a city of roughly a quarter million, on busy U.S. 29—Mall Condo incar-nate. Half an hour of *nasty* Saturday afternoon shopping traffic . . . and the best classroom a motorcycle safety instructor could ask for. At least with respect to the modern intersection.

Approximately two dozen times we witnessed what appeared to be the identical junction: a pair of left-turn lanes facing another pair of left-turn lanes—almost always, it seemed, full of vans and SUVs blocking the sight lines of both north and southbound drivers. By the time we reached Interstate 64 en route to the Blue Ridge Parkway, I was confident that each of my students appreciated the potential harm from those "eclipses" in the left-turn lanes.

But what about the danger on the right? A hot topic around the coun-try these days is red light running. Many municipalities have installed cameras to crack down on violators, but no camera, unfortunately, can cut down on *legal* red light running—i.e. drivers who turn right on red in full compliance with the law. So, after pointing out maybe a half-dozen consecutive junctions with eclipses to the left, I turned my commentary to the situation on the right, where nearly as many van and SUV drivers, patiently awaiting the change of the signal, obscured the ingress of other drivers turning right and into our southbound path.

So what you have is at least four significant ways in which these mod-ern junctions differ from the urban intersections of my youth. One is the proliferation of the left-turn lane (which sometimes is and sometimes isn't controlled by a separate signal). Two is the exponential increase of visually obstructive vans and SUVs. Three is the legalization of right turns on red. Four is the longer distances and hence higher speeds which drivers attain between intersections—often exceeding what we not so long ago referred to as our "national speed limit."

If you're fortunate to catch a series of green lights on a road such as U.S. 29, and if you're driving something like a Ford Expedition, chances are excellent that drivers aiming across your path will afford you the respect that you so richly deserve. If not, you've got ABS brakes, a V-8 engine block, an airbag, and even a seat belt between you and a big hurt. But if you're on your motorcycle, you've mostly got your wits.

Clearly the best strategy is to put the bike where they can't get to you. With a generous space cushion, I'm in and out of there at least as fast as the flow of traffic—usually faster. But the busier the intersection, the less chance you'll have to position at one extreme or the other. A lot of riders don't realize that just because everyone else is going 45 mph doesn't mean that it's your safest speed. If the guy turning right from behind the van doesn't see you—and if you've got fast-moving traffic on your left— then you'd better be able to stop before he enters your path. The beauty of matching safe speed and position is that it confers upon you an advantage that few four-wheelers possess—the ability to *accelerate* out of danger at the appropriate moment.

I spent my last week poring over videotape that we've collected over the last year and a half. I organized it into about two dozen clips of varying lengths, ones which I felt best represented the range of situations which motorcyclists would encounter in day-to-day riding. And then I stumbled upon a clip of two successive traffic lights on a multilane road—a complete safety course in 52 seconds. I think I'll call it 21st Century Junctions.

Good Sports and Bad Sports

April 2004

This column is a fine example of Larry's ability to get past the emotional name-calling that often surrounds contentious issues. Given that SUVs (and other larger vehicles) are in fact a part of the riding environment, how does this affect motorcycles, and how should riders respond?

Pete Tamblyn

W e Americans can tolerate a little hanky panky, and we don't blame you if your father was a Nazi . . . but don't ever tell us what to drive!

They've been called rude, selfish, and aggressive, branded unChristian, accused of poisoning the very air our children breathe—linked to global warming and Al-Qaida terrorists. It's hard to imagine a group of individuals with a more repugnant public image . . . and it's nearly even money that you're one of them.

Last year 51 percent of the new vehicles sold in the United States were in the light truck category, but let's not speak euphemistically. You know what we're really talking about here—SUVs—the machines we love to hate nearly as much as we love to drive them. Syndicated columnist Arianna Huffington drew a battle line through our ambivalence last year by initiating the Detroit Project, a self-described "grassroots campaign to prod Detroit automakers to build cars that will get Americans to work in the morning without sending us to war in the afternoon." Huffington, despite her slight height advantage, was subsequently trounced by the Hummer-driving Terminator in California's gubernatorial recall burlesque.

But hey—they don't pay me to do political commentary. This is a safety column, and lord knows SUVs generate enough heat to light a fiery debate on this subject as well. On the one side, you have SUV advocates who maintain that sport utes are twice as protective as the average passenger car in a front, rear, or side collision. Detractors point to SUVs' greater rollover rate and claim that they are leading us into a highway arms race, as consumers seek assurance that their vehicle will prevail in the inevitable collision.

What does this mean to us, as motorcyclists? Well, I doubt anybody chooses to ride a motorcycle out of a belief that he will vanquish *anyone* in a highway fracas (although speeding motorcycles can, in fact, rip through a driver or passenger door). The rollover issue, frankly, I'd rather not take up. I've yet to hear of an SUV rolling *onto* a motorcyclist . . . and if safetycrats start to ban vehicles because they roll over, whose do you think will be the first to go?!

Personally, I don't really care whether or not Jesus *would* drive a Cadillac Escalade. He *doesn't;* ordinary mortals do. If it's a busy mom, driving five kids to soccer and dance recital, then her vehicle is consuming less fuel and emitting fewer greenhouse gas particles per capita than I am on my motorbike. What I care about is her state of mind and my ability to see and be seen in her shadow.

The former is yet another sensitive area. I can urge you to watch out for drunks between 2 and 3 a.m. without offending that half of the motoring public which is passing soberly through the night, but it's dicey to discuss "aggressive SUV drivers" without the entire breed feeling incriminated. Surveys have shown that on average sport ute owners drive more aggressively—a closer following distance is one example cited. Some attribute this to a sense of "invulnerability" which comes from driving a heavier, more powerful vehicle with a superior road view. But make no mistake, automakers invest a great deal of time and money learning about the personality traits of their various markets.

For example, market researchers tell us that mini-van and SUV buyers are nearly indistinguishable, demographically speaking. But while they share the same age, income, and family status, their personality profiles are worlds apart.

"Minivan people want to be in control in terms of safety, being able to park and maneuver in traffic, being able to get elderly people in and out," said Fred J. Schaafsma, a vehicle development engineer for General Motors, in an article posted by the *New York Times* News Service. "SUV owners want to be more like 'I'm in control of the people around me.'"

The same article cited a study by Auto Pacific Inc., a California auto market research firm, in which SUV buyers reported that they drove faster than average, placed a lower value on road courtesy, and were more likely to agree with the statement "I'm a great driver."

But enough controversy. Let's talk about something upon which we all can agree. Ninety percent of the input upon which we base our riding decisions is visual, and both minivans and SUVs pose serious limitations upon our abilities to see and be seen. When the Hurt Report was published more than 20 years ago, the majority of collisions could be boiled down to two scenarios: 1) car driver turning left in violation of the motorcyclist's right-of-way; 2) car driver invading the motorcyclist's pathway perpendicularly from the right. I think it's safe to say that, had they *seen* the motorcyclist, most would *not* have driven into him.

Nearly all of today's thoroughfares flow more traffic than in the Hurt Report days, but the rise in obstructive vehicles (not just mini-vans and SUVs—how many delivery trucks has UPS added since 1980?) is especially problematic. It's pretty hard to proceed through a modern urban intersection without having your line-of-sight eclipsed by a large vehicle. The textbook example is the SUV (or series of large vehicles) queued up to your left, waiting to make their left turn while blocking the view of oncoming drivers who wish to take the same action . . . across your path.

The situation is just as precarious on our right side, where a stopped van or SUV can impede the view of other drivers who would turn right or shoot directly into our path. The only "safe" plan of action is to create space. Drop back, open up the view, and distance yourself from the greatest risk, be it on the left or right side of the intersection. I urge my students to emulate nature's master of speed and position—the common housefly. And like said housefly, always, *always* know what's coming up behind you.

Think about what great lengths the human must go to in order to triumph over the fly. Because he can never match the fly's maneuverability, he must brandish a weapon a hundred times its size and nearly as fast. Still the tiny nemesis more often prevails.

Mental errors, not SUVs, are the real enemy. SUVs are big, but they're not a hundred times our size (those are 18-wheelers—the topic for another day).

They're fast, but nearly any bike will easily out-accelerate them. Maneuverability? Largely a state of mind. When we're prepared (and when traction is good), we can flick our bikes with catlike quickness. Surprised, our most common response is no action whatsoever.

Aggressive though they may be, SUV drivers wield nothing like the targeted malice of a fly swatter. All it really takes to stay out of their path is that we be smarter than they are. How tough can that be?

Urban Warfare

October 1998

Years back, I was fortunate to attend an education seminar and come away with some very valuable information. The concept discussed was the Quadrants of Knowledge and if you stop to think about them, the meaning is simple:
1. *You know you know*
2. *You know you don't know*
3. *You don't know you know*
4. *You don't know you don't know*

As a motorcycle instructor and rider, I am convinced this concept applies to motorcycling every bit, if not more, than it does in the education field. I am also convinced that it is the last category that contributes to most motorcycle crashes—especially those of new riders. As Larry implies in this article, it is a war zone out there. Too often we go "into battle" completely unprepared. Sometimes that means without our armor—more often it means without all of the mental strategy to win the battle.

I was fortunate enough to have taken one of Larry's instructional tours prior to taking a motorcycle tour in Europe. My husband and I had known Larry for several years and I happened to run into him a couple of weeks prior to our scheduled tour with him. I commented to Larry how I was looking forward to the tour. His reply, was that he was not sure what he could teach us . . . I knew at the time, that was a joke. But after the tour, I realized how many things Larry pointed out that I did not know that I did not know. Regardless of our training and experience, there is always more that we can learn!

JoAnna Murray, owner and lead instructor
Atlanta Motorcycle Schools

It was October of 1979, my first visit to San Francisco, and the Hells Angels trial was the big local news story. One of the more bizarre episodes involved President Sonny Barger's sister, described by the *Chronicle* as a "stylish Marin County housewife," who had to be forcibly evicted from the proceedings following a series of obscene outbursts.

My host, Pete Rudow, was hustling me, one Sunday afternoon, to a rendezvous with another of the Bay's notorious gangs—the Thundering Dummies MC. While jogging across a downtown intersection, helmets in hand, we were suddenly confronted by a mocking voice.

"Ooh—*helmets*. I wouldn't be caught dead wearing one of those!" snapped our antagonist—a stylish Marin County housewife by the looks of her. "Yeah, well I wouldn't be caught dead with you on the back of my motorcycle!" countered Rudow.

Although we weren't waiting for a fresh round of counterpoint, the air around us quickly blued with wildly speculative theories on our mothers' social lives. Each curse was appended with the warning: *Sonny's gettin' out!*

As a nation we prefer cheap gas and fiber-optic cable to crowded cities, but in San Fran, we have just about the best motorcycle city in the world. "Motorcycle city" might sound to you like an oxymoron, but in addition to its ever-mild riding climate and proximity to spectacular roads and scenery, Frisco has the hardware, the know-how, and the characters that only a pulsating, overpeopled metropolis can bring to this sport we love.

If you rode into mine (Pittsburgh), you'd find an abstruse gridwork of potholed surface streets and antiquated freeways, yet one block from my house there's a street called "Serpentine Drive," which, for one weekend each summer, becomes a 3.5 mile vintage grand prix racetrack. We also have steep, one-lane tracks which switchback through wooded hollows reminiscent of deepest Appalachia, then terminate at elegant cliffside restaurants from which to view cable cars and skyscrapers melting into a vitreous nighttime riverscape.

The first time I crashed a motorcycle was in the city—about six blocks from where I now live. The door to a parked car swung open; I swerved to the left, caught my front tire on a street car track, and down I went on the cobblestone street. Pure rookie mistake, but major cities are minefields just waiting for an innocent to take a wrong step. Ordinarily I do most of my on-road training in suburban and rural areas, but one Saturday morning last spring I made an exception when a student asked me to follow him on his daily commuting route.

The student had recently completed a MSF course, and it was clear from our parking lot warm-up that he'd been well trained, so we proceeded onto the street. We jogged through a park, over some quiet backstreets, and then he led me into the war zone.

Watching him turn right at a traffic light, I scanned around the corner and saw a van inching out of a parking space. Seconds later he was on the ground. No blood/no foul. I picked him up and wheeled the bike out of harm's way before any real damage could occur, but the student, in addition to being embarrassed by the episode, was completely mystified.

"What happened?" he wanted to know.

Well, the van driver wasn't really at fault; he'd seen the motorcyclist as soon as he'd rounded the corner and stopped in his tracks. An experienced city rider would have identified the hazard before entering the turn, but my student rounded the corner, spotted the van pulling out, and grabbed the front brake . . . just as the front wheel skimmed a manhole cover. *Boom.* Never had a chance.

By calling such incidents "spills" and not "accidents," the German moto-psychologist Dr. Ulrich Schutz has come up with scads of data which normally elude government number crunchers. His interviews with young German riders, who tend to rack up more commuter miles than Americans, revealed that five "spills" in the first year of riding wasn't at all uncommon.

"I figure that inner city traffic is about the safest place to practice," remarked one of my recent students, a London banker serving time at the World Bank in Washington, D.C. "I mean if you hit something you can't be going very fast." Curious logic, but then logical folks usually ride the bus.

Let's take a look at an average intersection in an average American city—Washington's DuPont Circle, a few blocks from our banker friend's flat. Here, where five principal streets converge, you have 30 crosswalks, 18 concrete medians, *80* or so traffic and pedestrian signals, two driveways, a metro station, and an underpass where drunk drivers with diplomatic immunity reach triple-digit speeds. Red light/green light coming *off* the circle; red light/flashing yellow arrow getting on . . . unless of course you're on Mass Avenue, and then you have to cross over the *outer* circle to the *inner* circle. Piece of cake.

Regarding speed: On suburban boulevards, a motorcycle's horsepower can be a boon, particularly if you've got the other skills to identify and capture juicy pockets of space. But most people are already moving along too rapidly on our city streets. The cars which lope along at 45 mph on my 25-mph street can't even stop for a pedestrian at the crosswalk (which no one seems to understand is the law), let alone a child who might suddenly bolt out from between parked cars.

If making time is your objective, your best opportunity is when the other traffic is stopped or nearly stopped. Unfortunately, "white lining" is probably frowned upon where you live, even though the Hurt Report found it to be a safer practice than sitting in stalled traffic. California may be the only state in which lane splitting is de facto legal, but motojournalist Bob Higdon told me that he split lanes daily during 16 years of lawyering in downtown Washington and received only one ticket for doing so.

If it's just a matter of wedging by one or two parked cars to get past a long line of traffic, I'll do it every time. When the signal changes I accelerate sufficiently to put some distance on the lead car, but only after a full signal/mirror/head check. If some jughead with an 8.0-liter Dodge Ram decides to make it a drag race, I'll let him win. Stupid and angry people belong in front of or way behind a motorcycle.

Like seeing-eye dogs who are trained to "intelligently disobey," city riders need to exercise creativity and common sense.

Hopping a curb to park your motorcycle may be a hundred times safer than stopping opposing lanes of rush-hour traffic to back it into the same space. If you ride in the same neighborhood every day, people will recognize you. Loud pipes will score big demerits. Talk to your neighbors. Get to know the police and meter maids. If you don't interfere with the mail carrier or the garbage collectors, you might land a convenient, secure parking spot on the sidewalk beneath your office window. *Communicate.*

Here are a few tips you might add to your personal survival list:

Dress conspicuously—Black is beautiful . . . and potentially deadly.

Cover the clutch and brakes.

Look for escape routes—Watch the mirrors and leave a car length between your bike and the preceding vehicle at traffic lights.

Ease off the front brake—It's easy to lock a front brake at the end of a stop . . . especially where there's oil or painted lines on the road.

Avoid drivers' blind spots—and don't hide behind vans and other obscuring vehicles.

Give taxi drivers wide birth—Expect them to change lanes without warning, run red lights, cut you off. It's what they're paid to do. On the other hand, taxis make ideal escorts across strange cities. Tell them to go slowly and pay them after you reach your destination.

Carry a good map (ever read *Bonfire of the Vanities?*).

Cover your horn button—But don't use it. Blasting the horn either startles or angers other drivers. A gentle "toot-toot-toot" may get the attention of someone up the road who's not looking in your direction.

Wear your lid every ride—One of motorcycling's greatest misconceptions is that helmets are only for high-speed use. In San Francisco—or any place where curbs and car hoods abound—your chances of being caught dead wearing one are about a fourth of being caught dead *without* one.

Wheelmen Ride in Traffic

September 2004

Most certainly drawing on his car-less earlier years as a Pittsburgh cyclist, Larry shares why he feels the urban crucible is an important proving ground for a two-wheeler pilot's abilities, with or without power.

Pete Tamblyn

A letter arrived the other day from my man, Lance. You know—that bicycle guy. "Dear Fellow Cyclist," it began.

"When I ride the Tour de France, I benefit from police escorts and roads closed to automobile traffic. But when I train hundreds of miles a week at home, I face the same difficulties riding on the road as you do."

Actually, though I greatly admire the urban cyclist's ability to carve through traffic, I've pretty much favored the troubles of the throttle twister, ever since the day when a Fort Lauderdale drawbridge operator failed to take notice of me pedaling across his causeway. Anyway, the solution to such difficulties, said Lance, is to join the League of American Bicyclists, an organization which strives to deliver to 57 million cyclists all that the American Motorcyclist Association and the Motorcycle Safety Foundation do for us.

For all of Armstrong's cachet as a five-time (maybe six by the time you read this) Tour de France champion, the League's dues-paying membership (40,000) is actually down 60 percent from its heyday. That would have been 1880, when they were known as the League of American Wheelmen. Compare those stats to our AMA, which draws six times the support from a pool one-tenth as deep.

But make no mistake: We owe a huge debt to those 19th-century wheelmen (the appellation bicyclists preferred in the day), and not merely for our basic two-wheeled platform. It was the League of American Wheelmen that mobilized 150,000 business leaders and 17 governors in the 1890s to build the nation's network of paved roads—horses and wagons having so decimated the dirt roads that it was nigh impossible to travel on two wheels. So when you hear impatient drivers (or,

sadly, some unenlightened motorcyclists) grouse that bicycles don't belong on "their" roads, ask them how they'd enjoy traveling in the rutted
tracks of horse-drawn buggies!

Maybe Lance and his League buddies should add the following statis-
tic to their marketing campaign. According to John Forester, a well-
known cycling advocate and author of *Bicycle Transportation*, members
of the League have far fewer accidents than other cyclists—113 per million miles, compared to 720 for child cyclists and 500 for "college-associ-
ated adults" (whoever they are). So I can't help but wonder: Are AMA
members safer than non-members? Who wouldn't pay $39 per year to
lower their chance of an accident by nearly 80 percent?

Now I've always assumed that riding a bicycle in traffic was riskier
than riding a motorcycle. There are those pesky car doors, don't you
know, and try accelerating out of harm's way with even Lance's Hercu-
lean 1,000-watt (1.5 horsepower) power spike. But a number of statisti-
cal accounts say that's not so. NHTSA's 1997 *Traffic Safety Facts* states
that 13.8 percent of all bicycling injuries are "incapacitating," a bit higher
than the rate for injured car occupants (11 percent) but far lower than
that of fallen motorcycle riders (27.7 percent). Expressed as fatalities per
million exposure hours, a table compiled by Failure Analysis Associates
Inc. (and I haven't a *clue* who those people are) presents bicycling as significantly safer than car travel (.26 per million hours vs. .47), way safer
than motorcycling (8.80 per) and about a bazillion times safer than
skydiving (128.71)! Parachuters, I suppose, might argue that no one ever
got killed jumping out of an airplane; it's the *ground* that gets you.

That's the argument we use, isn't it? That motorcycles aren't dangerous; it's the nuts driving around in cars who cause accidents. Unfortunately, that's never been quite true and may be even less so these days,
given the recent trends in motorcycle fatalities: older riders/large displacement machines/single vehicle accidents/rural roads. According to
NHTSA stats, half of all fatal motorcycle crashes occur on curves; two
thirds are associated with speeding; over half involve collisions with a
fixed object. And the 31 percent who were drunk when they bought it
(2002 FARS data)—did some "cagers" pour firewater down each of their
1,015 throats?

One of the more radical theories advanced by John Forester is that
construction of bike paths and bike lanes results in *higher* accident rates
for bicyclists. I won't bother to cite Forester's stats but will merely note

his assertion that government, in tandem with the bicycling establishment, has taken a passive approach to cycling safety: herding cyclists off busy streets and packing their heads in Styrofoam, rather than teaching—and *evaluating*—safe traffic strategies.

Mind you, Forester is a maverick, a man with a dedicated following but still floating outside the orbit of cycling's mainstream, including the League of American Bicyclists. However, his 1981 *Forester Cycling Proficiency Score Sheet* could be a model for a 2004 on-street motorcycle test, as it assesses critical lane positions and visual strategies in live traffic situations. And when I say *live* traffic, that includes real drivers turning left in front of the two-wheeler!

Now, I wouldn't favor the abolition of bike paths any more than I would favor the banning of older motorcyclists from rural roads, but I see some parallels worth noting. We build more bike paths, yet the Mom & Dad Limo Service outsells biking 51 percent to 3 percent among children who commute a mile or less to school—presumably because parents view the routes as too dangerous to bike on. On the motorcycling side, we have a generation of adult riders who want to ride on country roads, away from urban traffic and who think that a supervised weekend, riding a 250cc bike on a parking lot, qualifies them to operate the day's most sophisticated machinery. The people who sell the motorcycles and issue the licenses concur—provided that riders (duh) wear a helmet and (double duh) don't imbibe.

If the above statement sounds like an indictment of MSF training, so be it, but know this: MSF curricula are the envy of the drivers education *and* bicycle safety communities. Thanks to the Foundation, millions of riders have at least *heard* a consistent message on responsible riding in traffic. The League of American Bicyclists has been around for a century and a quarter, yet its training program is only in its infancy. Their challenge, they'll tell you, is to get bicyclists and motorists alike to recognize the bicycle as a vehicle.

Ironic. As I covet the bicyclist's ability to sluice through traffic unencumbered by the conventions which bind motorcycles to the same rate of progress as the most ponderous four-wheelers, bicycling's hierarchy strives to "domesticate" their own. I don't know how to advise a clock-racing bicycle messenger in D.C. or New York, but I'd tell any motorcyclist that riding a street bike is dealing with—not avoiding—traffic. You can have your track days and your $20,000 Harley haulers, but if you don't have the skills and confidence to attempt the daily grind across your city, then you're fooling yourself by thinking that you're safe on those blue highways.

Lance would tell you: *Wheel*men ride in traffic.

Danger Gets a Name

November 2004

Any motorcyclist who hasn't been living under a rock can identify the most frequent type of motorcycle/car collision—an approaching car left-turning in front of the bike. Far fewer can clearly state the next most frequent type—violation of the motorcyclist's right-of-way by a vehicle entering perpendicularly from the right side. Larry condenses that phrase into a single, ominous word. We don't see Mr. Safety angry often. . . .

Pete Tamblyn

Here's a not-so-gentle reminder that sometimes the quietest places are potentially the deadliest.

If you should visit Wisconsin some Easter weekend, you will find that not a blade of green sits upon her mud-colored hills. The snow may be gone, but it's guaranteed that the sand they've spread to provide some modicum of winter traction won't be.

Now flash forward three months. East Coast residents are complaining of the heat. The tops of the Appalachian hardwoods are looking a little blanched . . . and Wisconsin is a miracle of green. We have cornfields in Pennsylvania and West Virginia, but you know, they're just not the same. Wisconsin cornfields are flat-out *gorgeous*. What's more, the county roads which roll across its modest hills are cradled by true working farms. We're talking bright red barns and freshly whitewashed fences.

There are enough hills and curves in the upper Midwest to cavort butt up and chin down for a few hours at a clip, but cruising—feet forward with head held high—gives one a clearer appreciation for how this gently sculpted landscape shaped the classic American motorcycle. Randy Scott rode Milwaukee iron, though he hailed from Minnesota.

I came to Wisconsin for the express purpose of teaching an on-road safety course, like the ones I conduct throughout the Appalachian region. At Deal's Gap they boast of 318 turns in 11 miles on The Dragon—I like to boast of a training ride with 4,000 turns in two days, though honestly, I never counted them. Wisconsin, I knew, would be different. We'd have to adapt. There was, for example, a stretch of about 70 miles between the Kettle Moraine, just east of Milwaukee, and the hilly Wisconsin River Valley west of Madison, that contained few, if any, sharp curves. We adapted by creating a gear-shifting drill, and then—when the road *really* opened up—by practicing throttle/brake/throttle transitions. The weather was splendid, and before we knew it we were back on "good" (i.e. *crooked*) motorcycle roads.

That was more than a year ago. By now I've logged about 4,000 miles on three trips to America's Dairyland, and I understand a bit better how the riding there differs from Appalachia or California. Of course, riders everywhere want to avoid accidents, and when I pose the question, "What scenario is the single biggest cause of collisions between cars and motorcycles?" I get a correct answer more often than not *(car driver turning left across path of oncoming motorcyclist)*. I've no way of knowing the long-term effectiveness of my curricula, but after a few demonstrations of moving right and creating space—putting the motorcycle where car drivers *can't touch* it—I find that most riders adopt a more proactive defense policy toward potential left turners.

Question: What is the *number two* cause of collisions between cars and bikes? Have to scratch your head on that one? It's a simple scenario, really: *Car driver violates motorcyclist's right of way by pulling out of a perpendicular artery on the right.* "Officer, I never saw that motorcycle!"

And it's probably true. Stopped at a crossroads with a barn or a cornfield on the left, obstructing the view, it's understandable that a driver might fail to detect an approaching motorcycle. There are thousands of such crossroads in Wisconsin and the upper Midwest, just as we have thousands of dirt and gravel tertiary roads abutting the best asphalt in places like West Virginia and southeast Ohio. The big difference is that few of the county roads in Appalachia actually *cross* the two-lane blacktop.

Even though intersections account for the majority of collisions (regardless of vehicle type), the average motorist makes no concession to cross traffic when passing through a highway junction. If the posted speed limit is 55, most drivers will cruise through at six or seven mph over, never considering an adjustment in speed or position. Maybe motorcyclists are better in this regard, but I tend to think not. Too many riders fail to grasp how quickly quiet crossroads can turn chaotic . . . or what a dramatic difference a little space and a few mph make when the gauntlet is thrown into their path. Those rural junctions, so benign on the surface, had to be boosted to a higher place in rider consciousness. They needed a *name*. And then it hit me.

A *Janklow*.

Some legacies spring forth out of word association rather than the sum of an individual's accomplishments. Take the name Molotov, forever to be linked with the "Molotov cocktail." Vyacheslav Mikhailovich Molotov was one of the most powerful politicians of the Soviet era, yet to 99 percent of the world he's remembered for a crude and terrible weapon he may have sanctioned but did not invent. Fifty years from now few school children in the Midwest will be able to recite the legislative accomplishments of Bill Janklow, the ex-governor and congressman from South Dakota, but I hope that motorcyclists will still feel a shiver at the mention of his name. A *Janklow Intersection*. I think that he deserves no more and no less of a legacy.

You probably know the tragic tale that unfolded in Moody County, South Dakota, on August 16, 2003; how then Rep. Janklow sped his Cadillac at 70 mph through a familiar stop sign at the junction of Highway 13 and Trent Road, taking the life of 55-year-old farmer, Vietnam veteran, volunteer firefighter, and Harley rider, Randolph Scott of nearby Hardwick, Minnesota. No ink has been spared in bringing to light Janklow's history of reckless driving and flagrant disrespect for traffic laws. Maybe you've read that he previously pardoned his son-in-law for drunk driving. All of this puts me—a person who earns his living in an industry which often mocks traffic laws—in a fidgety position. Is it our actions we should be judged by . . . or their consequences?

Many argue that Janklow's sentence, 100 days in jail, was too light, but no amount of justice will bring Randy Scott back to life. His laughter won't be heard at the volunteer fire department, he won't attend his grandchildren's graduations, and he'll never again cruise his Harley along Highway 13. No court or citizens' action group can change that.

At a press conference Janklow told reporters, "You can't prepare in life to deal with the enormity of what I'm dealing with, and what I've put other people through." None of us can know his private thoughts or how long it takes him to find sleep at night. What I hope is that riders in all parts of the country will take an extra fraction of a second to put themselves where drivers who *aren't* flagrant scofflaws—who are maybe just a little distracted or impatient or temporarily blinded by the sun—won't permanently fracture the lives of whole families.

And what I really hope—what I fantasize—is that one summer day, years after he ceases to be recognized by those along the Minnesota/South Dakota border, the politician known as "Wild Bill" will be sitting in a café when two motorcyclists settle in, ruddy smiles upon their faces. They'll take off their helmets and the older of the two will nod to the younger.

"Son," he'll say, "you want to have fun and not ride overly cautious, but you've got to be real alert passing through those crossroads. You know—the *Janklows.*

"They can be deadly."

Pieces of a Circle

April 2002

Larry's stressing 360-degree awareness brings to mind my watching college basketball over the years. Players with superior passing skills quickly drew my attention, realizing that these individuals possessed excellent "court awareness." Those most skilled at passing exhibited unvarying consciousness of the other nine players' positions (current and next), strengths, and weaknesses. This court awareness allowed the passer to predict precisely where each of his teammates would be and pass the basketball to the most advantageously placed player. Never looking down, these players looked around and far ahead, allowing them to predict and place the ball with the best chance of scoring.

Today these players are called "point guards," and function much like a quarterback in football. I especially remember Bob Cousey, Larry Bird, Magic Johnson, and of course, Pete Maravich.

Motorcyclists, more than drivers of four wheel vehicles, need to develop a high level of "street awareness," using their peripheral vision and head checks to accurately predict traffic flow. This raised awareness separates those riders who rarely blunder from the majority, who comprise most of the crash statistics.

Ken Murray, owner and lead instructor
Atlanta Motorcycle Schools

When I started riding, you could count on the fingers of a peace sign the number of motorcycle models equipped with a disc brake. Stopping wasn't the motorcyclist's forte; it took light weight and maneuverability to gain any edge in traffic.

A lot has changed since then. Cars became smaller and slower . . . then bigger and faster. Motorcycle performance—including stopping—exceeded our wildest dreams. The cops who stopped us grew inexplicably younger, and for some, the heart rate wouldn't settle down without a pacemaker (. . . *potato, potato, potato*).

With so many different types of motorcycles and riders today, it's specious to stereotype, but I would venture a couple of general observations about the drivers we share the road with in this second century of motorcycling.

1) They're "multitaskers," i.e. they're preoccupied with more than simply negotiating the traffic matrix.

2) The "automotive lifestyle" has not only given us more drivers, but more authoritative ones. The notion, for example, of dominant male drivers and submissive females is utterly archaic.

3) They drive on boulevards and highways that have more lanes and driveways, so they're much more prone to sudden changes of direction.

Back in the bellbottom era, you might have felt unstoppable, weaseling through the traffic on a wispy two-stroke, but today's jam-buster might be racing from the boardroom to Lamaze class in a 6,000-pound, 450-horsepower turbo-diesel on off-road tires. A motorcyclist in today's traffic mix had better have eyes all around his or her head.

Statistically, the greatest risk of collision still lies in the foreground—between nine and three on your bike's "clock face," but to prepare for the future, you must have an appreciation of the past. You may easily swerve around the car at two o'clock on your visual screen, but are you certain there's nothing coming up behind you at seven or eight?

I've heard it said by many riders, "I feel safer moving a little faster than the traffic around me." Often it *is* safer—but space can close as quickly as you open it. You may swerve around car A, only to brake for car B . . . and get rear-ended by car C. To act without 360-degree awareness is to act without all the necessary facts.

When should you use your mirrors? I use them for passes, lane changes, and merges, of course—and I use them each time I plan to slow down. I use them when I sense danger on the right and when I sense danger on the left—I want to know where all available space is should I have to move laterally. When there's nothing blipping on my radar, I check them a minimum of every five to six seconds on the open road and every three to four seconds in traffic.

From what I've observed, most motorcyclists are better at swiveling their heads and covering their blind spots than the car drivers they share the road with. That doesn't mean, however, that their head checks are universally purposeful and well-timed. Peripheral vision, a rebel call for many who wage the helmet law battles, picks up changes in color, contrast, and motion . . . but it's too sketchy to record complex details.

Shifting the eyes in the sockets can bring objects into reasonably sharp focus perhaps 35 degrees from dead center; obviously the farther down the road the eyes are trained, the more driveways and parked cars that 70-degree arc can encompass. My "double blind" experiments with skeptical students have shown that full-face helmets sacrifice nothing—*not one degree*—of sharp vision.

Helmets *can,* however, inhibit one's head rotation, especially in adverse weather when collars are higher and thicker. Should I have to make a sharp right turn at an intersection with a limited view, I keep to the extreme right until I'm up to speed—just in case the radar has missed a phantom vehicle.

Similarly, keeping to the extreme right opens up a runway for merging onto the freeway. I often watch riders perform three—four—*five* head checks before actually merging with traffic. That's time that could be spent on the principal task of attaining freeway speed. And yes—I *do* like to accelerate to a speed greater than the ambient traffic flow. It gives me forward, backward, and sideways options for slotting into a safe gap. A single well-timed head check is all that's needed 99 percent of the time.

Acceleration is an invaluable tool, even on bikes having modest engine performance. Anyone with a bike with 40 horses and an opposable right thumb can dispatch a dawdling four-wheeler at triple-digit velocity, but low-risk passing is the product of acceleration and good timing. Naturally, the longer you spend overtaking, the longer your exposure to vehicles encroaching from the rear, the side, and the oncoming lane. Speed shrinks that window of risk . . . but it also can intensify the consequences, namely: 1) loss of lateral mobility relative to slower traffic, 2) increased stopping distance, and 3) higher impact speed, should a collision occur.

A better strategy than all-out speed is to "close down" the vehicle you wish to overtake, maintaining a modest speed advantage while retaining the facility for lateral movement. As you change lanes, the once-parallel projectiles assume divergent paths, and *that's* the time to light the wick. By learning the parameters of your "response bubble" (i.e. where you can pinpoint your bike at a given moment in time), you can learn to overtake swiftly, making it impossible for others to lay a glove on you.

Never is 360-degree awareness more important than in the moment preceding a quick lane change or pass. The British police instructor I trained under was the Garry Kasparov of overtaking maneuvers, mentally mapping the whereabouts of every vehicle, calculating the projected paths even as they slipped in and out of view.

If you're a conservative (not to be confused with "tentative" or "reluctant"—dangerous traits) passer, stick to a methodical "signal . . . mirror . . . head check" approach. More aggressive riders may eventually do themselves harm by looking over a shoulder while rapidly closing down their prey. Riders who overtake relentlessly, whether on the two lane or the expressway, need to live in their mirrors, but that still doesn't mean that they can forget about head checks.

These days, I'm training myself to watch the vehicle I'm overtaking with my right eye while checking the blind spot with my left one. But since peripheral vision runs out of bounds so quickly, I can't recommend the practice—not without a scientific study, using all the relevant controls.

Each of us processes data at our own rate. The safest riders aren't the super-computers with the fastest reflexes; they're the ones who know where they have been and where they're going . . . and where to escape to, just in case.

Chasing the Visual Point

April 2005

Stayin' Safe Motorcycle Training was always an evolving work in progress, it seemed. One of his assistants remembers it this way:

I first met Larry in the fall of 2000 in Washington, D.C., to discuss his training program over breakfast. Until this time, I knew of Larry only through his Stayin' Safe column and his picture therein. To my surprise, he walked in looking like he had hastily dressed after just rolling out of bed. I wondered to myself, "This is Larry Grodsky?"

Later, when I began training with Larry, I discovered what genius lay beneath the surface. Constantly looking for new methods of explaining ideas, he devised a creative way of illustrating his Vanishing Point concept. Arranging Velcro-edged dominoes on a small, Velcro-covered board to create the left and right boundaries of a curve, he'd pass this assembly among the students. Rotating it at eye level as if riding through the curve created the illusion of a moving vanishing point.

This worked surprisingly well, except when the dominoes fell . . . .

Randy Kuklis, senior instructor, Stayin' Safe
Motorcycle Training, MSF instructor

Why does the rider who cannot see call the turn blind? The first time I said it to myself, it seemed so palpably clear that I couldn't believe it had taken me 35 years of riding to figure it out. I had to share it with others.

"At every corner entry," I would tell my students "you'll find one of two things: a solid object . . . or a drop off." I couldn't wait for the next stop to share my epiphany, but in truth the concept still needed at least half an hour of final tooling on the word lathe. Waiting along the side of the road was the contradictory argument: four bikes haphazardly parked. A huddle by the ditch. *Rider down.* The impetus? A flat, feature-less 90-degree fence line turn.

OK, *most* corner entries . . . .

Be that as it may, roads seldom change direction without a reason. It could be property rights, but the vast majority of those reasons are features in the landscape. For the past seven years or so, I've spent a good deal of time teaching riders how to "read" a road. Paramount to this skill acquisition is the recognition of what we call the "visual point." Some people call it the "vanishing point," so named for the way in which a road appears to "vanish," even as you try to reel it in with the throttle. Others call it the "limit point," probably because smart riders make it their practice to be able to stop short of the farthest point they can see.

I suppose I avoid saying vanishing point because I like my students to look for features in the landscape and not just the road itself. For the same reason, I don't refer to the limit point, although I absolutely feel riders should be able to stop within their lines of sight. I just don't think that one should focus exclusively on the road surface when there are other features that can expand rider awareness of when the road bends and how sharply. There are a dozen or more of these features, but we can narrow them down to two categories: those which parallel the left side of the road and those which parallel the right. Where those two features intersect, you've got a curve, but before you can lean and swoosh through it, you must first point your motorcycle directly at those solid objects. Are you with me?

Let's paint a little more detail in this picture. The solid object on your right is a granite wall. The solid object on your left is a guardrail. The convergence point is getting closer. And closer. Hadn't you really ought to slow down? This we all know as setting entry speed. While you're doing this—miracle of miracles—that convergence point appears to move away. Watch the end of the guardrail, and it appears to be *growing longer.* This means that your curve is opening up.

The essence of reading the visual point is learning to detect motion where those paralleling features—what the British call "verges"—intersect. Hold your hands at eye level and imagine them to be two rock formations. Draw them toward each other. The *con*-verging features mean the road is changing directions. Draw your hands apart. *Di*-verging features mean the curve is opening up.

You know those successions of reflective arrows that highway departments sometimes post along the more severe bends on primary and secondary roads? They're more than mere warning signs; they're a useful tool, and clever riders will find similar ones embedded in the natural and manmade features of even poorly marked roads.

Say there are five arrows posted in a corner. These five arrows are set on the "far side verge." At the first sign of an arrow (skilled riders will recognize other clues before the arrows) one should start setting entry speed—at least mentally. The idea is to make the arrows approach—and then recede—at a manageable rate.

Maybe there are no arrows. Maybe there's just a guardrail with little round reflectors posted on its supports. That's even better. Now you've got dozens of fixed points of light syncopated into one moving target—the visual point. The rate at which it moves becomes a product of *your* actions—the smoothness with which you manipulate brakes and throttle.

Most riders don't have any difficulty stopping for a traffic signal or a red, octagonal sign—so why do so many become startled when they have to slow down for a landscape feature? Maybe it has something to do with the notion that we ride "in" turns, as if they were dark rooms or deprivation tanks. A blind turn—you can't know what it is until you're *in* it!

I prefer to think of turns as the paths we plan around and between obstacles, taking care to maintain a comfortable response bubble relative to those obstacles. Here, I like to use the analogy of social intercourse. In my work I interact about equally with Northerners and Southerners. Look a New Yorker in the eye from arm's length, and he'll probably lean in closer. Someone from a small town in Mississippi will more likely take a step back. Each knows his personal comfort zone and operates within it.

Getting back to those arrows or reflectors. The time between first sighting and arrival is the aforementioned response bubble. If your view time of each marker is successively less, then your bubble is compressing. It's probable that you're operating outside your personal comfort zone. It's certain that you're compromising your drive out of the turn. Had you maintained a more constant bubble, you would have been ready to accelerate as soon as the turn began to open up.

Some other examples of verges are trees, shrubs, cornfields, buildings, hillsides, fences—anything that can rise above the road surface and parallel its course. But what if there is no opposing verge? What if you have a solid object on the near side of the road and nothing on the far side? In such cases, you've almost certainly identified a drop-off. What's more, since you cannot reliably predict where the curve will open up, the prudent thing would be to predict the worst—a drop-off *and* a decreasing radius bend!

It's hard to say how many untrained riders read the terrain subconsciously. In Britain, where police Roadcraft training has elevated public awareness of these principles, many schools boast in magazine ads that they'll turn motorcyclists into more rapid pilots. After all, they're the same principles that enabled TT stalwarts like David Jeffries (RIP) to lap the Isle of Man at over 125 mph! In my training experience, the number of course grads who slow down—at least on the entry—is nearly as great as the number who find the confidence to corner harder.

Fast rider or slow, no sensible person would knowingly accelerate toward a solid object or a drop-off. Yet because of the way we look at turns, so many of us are blinded to what's right in front of us. As for fence line turns, that's a topic for another day.

The 10 Commandments of Making Progress (American Style)

October 2005

We all know how to pass because, well, we've all done it. But are we making progress or just shooting ourselves in the foot? There's probably room for a little improvement; maybe a lot of room!

Pete Tamblyn

Passing slower traffic is both a science and an art . . . but it's OK to get passed once in a while, too.

Sunday, July 10, 6:30 a.m. PDT: Comrades Tuttle, Freund, and Salvadori should be rolling out of bed in Monterey about now, taking their first sips of coffee and preparing to push through the peninsula's over-clogged arteries en route to the inaugural United States MotoGP race at Laguna Seca. I wish I could join them. I haven't attended a GP since the last "inaugural" USGP—the 500cc championship round, also run at Laguna, in 1988.

What a spectacular event that was. An American sweep, with 500cc world champion Eddie Lawson taking the checkered flag after Jimmy Filice—an unknown abroad, with no international résumé—ran away with the 250cc race. I still laugh at German champion Antong Mang's sour grapes remark that the Laguna event convinced him Americans had faked the lunar landing photos!

Between 1978 and 1993, the period in which Yanks claimed 12 world championships in racing's premier class, their astonishing success was credited to the tire-sliding style practiced on America's dirt ovals. Now that the rest of the world's learned to slide and spin, our best and brightest seem happy to finish on the podium at grand prix events. Where, I wonder, might today's American road racer recapture his competitive edge?

I'm thinking Interstate 495—Washington's frenzied Beltway, or L.A's nefarious Interstate 405 freeway. True, Italy, the land that currently claims the top three places in MotoGP, has faster, even more aggressive traffic, but it lacks our extremes, our split personality. We have urban freeways where drivers battle at frightening speeds, madly weaving between backmarkers, and quiet two-lane country roads with ribbons of double yellow unfurling into infinity. Extremes can be fun, but couldn't we, just maybe, find a way to reconcile the folks who want to get there quickly, with the ones who wish to smell the roses?

The Brits, in their droll way with the mother tongue, speak of motorcyclists "making progress." That usually means blowing the doors off everything with doors, but really, don't we all wish to make progress? I know that I do, and if I were in charge, the following would be my top 10 commandments. I hope you will pass the list on to your friends who share the roads, no matter the number of wheels beneath them. With luck a few of those friends will be open-minded law enforcement types.

1. Thou shalt signal thine intentions.

If you're planning to overtake (and we hope your passes are, in fact, planned) activate the turn signal two seconds before you change lanes.

2. Thou shalt not linger in thy neighbor's blind spot.

Each of us has a right to be on the road, and a need to know who else is.

3. Thou shalt not be a left-lane bandit.

Oh—if these people would just see the frustration and the havoc they wreak!

4. Thou shalt give way to faster traffic.

Use the mirrors! If you see that someone wants by, look for a safe place to pull over. Don't be offended when someone flashes the high beam (it's just a way of saying "pardon me . . ."). And guys and gals, when a fellow motorist gives way, always acknowledge this decent gesture with a friendly wave.

5. Thou shalt respect signs, signals and markings.

Your motorcycle may go from 40 to 80 mph in less than two seconds, but don't assume that the double yellow doesn't apply to you. Seeing Eye dogs are trained to intelligently disobey on occasion. Dogs that always disobey are liable to be put down. Planning and executing passes before the dashed line turns to solid is an exercise that will pay dividends when proper timing is critical.

6. *Thou shalt respect motorists of differing speeds.*

You wouldn't curse an airplane pilot for passing overhead at five times your speed, so if another road user doesn't make you swerve or brake, don't impose your standards of risk acceptance upon them. Anger clouds one's vision. Slow drivers, erratic drivers, and aggressive ones are all part of the landscape. A healthy mix of patience and opportunism is the best recipe for placing space between your vehicle and theirs. Take as many civilians as you can for rides on your bike, so that they'll better understand the anxiety of being boxed in and the exhilaration of rapid two-wheeled escape.

7. *Thou shalt not slam the door in thy neighbor's face.*

Always accelerate to a point well beyond the vehicle you've overtaken. Remember that images in mirrors are closer than they appear.

8. *Thou shalt not sully the image of motorcycling.*

Loud, close, overly aggressive passes (especially the blatantly illegal ones) make the landscape bumpier for the rest of us. When you accelerate past a car full of people, they should be saying, "Gee, that looks like fun!"

9. *Thou shalt learn passing skills.*

Time not only your passes, but how long approaching vehicles take to arrive from the distant curve or crest. It's not all about speed. Learn to use momentum to slip past sight-blocking vehicles when you exit curves. Observe how much easier (and safer) it is to pass on a left bend (clear sight line and shorter distance to travel) than on a right.

10. *Thou shalt not speed through hallowed areas.*

Nearly all of us tend to move too quickly through crowded urban areas. Studies show that REDUCE SPEED signs have no effect whatsoever at construction zones. Please be cool in school zones and in residential areas. Make progress if you will, but remember this: the number of collisions between parallel vehicles is a small percentage of those traveling perpendicularly on impact.

3:30 p.m. PDT: Never underestimate the power of 52,000 screaming Americans. Valentino Rossi, the fastest motorcycle racer in the world, perhaps the most gifted of all time, could manage no better than third place in California, as Nicky Hayden and Colin Edwards ignited Laguna's crowd with a one-two stars-and-stripes finish. American road racers, once again, are making progress on the international scene, but aside from a mid-race move that Edwards put on Rossi, the duo didn't display much in the way of passing skills. Nicky led from start to finish.

Riding Tips

Mr. Safety's Top 10

August 1990

In his Rider *magazine column, Larry Grodsky made the subject of motorcycle safety interesting every month for 18 years. He gave us invaluable tips on how to position ourselves out of harm's way and stressed the importance of practicing our techniques, and he always put it so eloquently. Over the years many readers wrote to tell us how Larry's advice had prevented them from getting injured or that he had even saved their lives. Larry would cringe if he heard that, as illustrated in his August 1990 column, "Mr. Safety's Top 10," but even as I re-read this column and many other ones years later, it's clear that his words are still saving lives. He had a perfect way of putting into words exactly what he meant, and in such a way that it made you really pay attention. Sometimes he'd come up with a word I'd never heard, which would send me flipping through the dictionary. There were more than a few phone calls that went something like this:*

"Larry, not all of us have an Ivy League vocabulary. How about let's substitute the word 'enroll' for 'matriculate'?"

There would be a pause on the other end while he was processing this. It always made me smile as I could picture him in intense thought. Then from him, "No, I mean 'matriculate.' The word 'enroll' just doesn't quite say it."

As precise as he was in his writing and safety expertise, in person he was lovably scatterbrained. When he came to visit, oftentimes he'd leave something behind—sometimes intentionally (he couldn't be bothered with packing it up; could I just mail it to his home?), sometimes not. I once found a duffel bag in my office after he'd left. Turns out it had clothes he needed for his trip but that was okay because he'd just bought some clean socks and shirts along the way. I could just return it to him one day—no worry, no hurry.

Don't hurry. There it is, number seven on the list of Mr. Safety's Top 10 commandments. Dang! If I'd just retained that *tip, I could have saved myself $1,000 in plastic and a broken mirror. "It's okay to ride fast, but never in a hurry," Larry quotes a fellow instructor. Great advice!*

I've read over this column a dozen times today and have memorized every commandment. I am now indoctrinated into his way of thinking. No, that doesn't quite say it: Larry would say inculcated in it.

Not only did Larry teach me much about stayin' safe on a motorcycle, he also taught me some new words.

Donya Carlson, senior managing editor, Rider *magazine*

There exists, in my business, a certain phenomenon which, for want of a better term, I shall call the "messianic complex." Rest assured, friends, that I suffer from no such malady, but certain of my colleagues and I occasionally find ourselves confronted with one or another of its permutations.

"Your course saved my life . . ." is a phrase that triggers a Pavlovian cringe in this motorcycle instructor, for it's bound to append a three- or four-minute monologue on how the former pupil snatched his/herself from the jaws of calamity, using some recondite technique known only to MSF graduates, and in so doing, robbed fate of all but a fraction of the certain disaster it had written for his/her epitaph.

My old instructor-friend, Celine, recounted just such a tale for me, one in which the protagonist was launched into the air by his sparkling new $5,000 sport-bike in concert with a left-turning automobile. The bike was history, as was his new $250 helmet and $300 leather jacket, but the broken leg was healing nicely and all would be well soon. "Your course saved my life," he said.

Celine is a rare individual. I haven't a doubt that she would plunge into an icy river or a blazing apartment building if some cherub's life were in the breach, but—help me out here—like, did crashing his motorcycle make this guy miss his plane to Bophal or what?

You know this stuff can get morbid after a while. Hey, I like this gig, but when the evening news signs off, I don't curl up with the Hurt Report. There was one dreary mid-winter night (and I confess there was some alcohol involved here) when my evil friend Neil and I reached into our dark souls to compile the "dirty dozen"—street riding's 12 forbidden acts. What a column that would make! *(Remember kids, don't try these at home!)*

Ahh, but all things worthy sprout from a mere germ of an idea—even a disease germ like the dirty dozen. So maybe, I thought, some good might come of this. Why not compile a list of 10 *positive* actions? Actually, this had a compelling synergy to it, because, for some time, I had been bemoaning the fiscally mandated shortening of motorcycle riding courses and the consequent lost opportunities for effective behavior modification.

I posed a question to a number of experts in the field. What if, I suggested, you had a single goal—*lower the motorcycle accident rate*—and you could bring to bear all of your resources, but only in an effort to change one aspect of rider behavior. Which behavior would that be?

The experts were reluctant to play ball. Educators, understandably, strive for broad-based conceptual programs, ones which heighten students' understanding and awareness. However, people who voluntarily enroll in safety classes are already sensitive to safety issues; that sensitivity is validated by a well-rounded curriculum (which could explain the sport-bike pilot's need to believe the course saved his life). If Mr. Safety wanted a simple behavior modification scheme he would have to devise it (mostly) by himself. So here it is, a sort of "top 10 commandments" for cycle survival:

1. Maintain a space cushion.

"There is no single magic bullet," insisted one leading safety expert, and indeed no miracle cure is going to suddenly erase all motorcycle accidents. But "space cushioning"—putting yourself where a car can't touch you—can prevent most accidents, especially the 40,000 or so annual collisions between motorcycles and left-turning autos. Moving to the right third of the lane keeps you one step ahead of that car and virtually eliminates any chance of contact.

2. Don't speed through town.

Where do accidents occur? *Intersections,* of course. This elegantly simple advice arrives courtesy of Raynald Marchand, national coordinator of motorcycle training for the Canada Safety Council.

3. Check tire pressure weekly.

More than half of us are running daily on underinflated rubber.

4. Practice braking.

Ten minutes a week could ensure that you have this most essential skill when you need it.

5. Practice swerving.

Same as above.

6. Take a riding course.

Any riding course. Every repetition, good or bad, reinforces the way you do things. By recognizing a higher authority, even for one day, you open up pathways of rational thought that habituation may have clogged.

7. Don't hurry.

My fellow instructor, Don Myers, says, "It's okay to ride fast, but never in a hurry." *Fast,* to my way of thinking, is any speed that provides feelings of exhilaration that a lower speed will not. Those sensations can be enjoyed within a framework of discipline and sound strategies, but *hurrying*—racing the clock, ignoring fundamentals—opens you to all sorts of hazards your defense system would normally deflect.

8. Follow nothing you can't see over.

Vans, buses, trucks; even if you can see beyond them, chances are others don't see you. Pass when it's safe, let a few cars fill the gap, or just pull over momentarily. It's no big deal, really.

9. Use turn signals.

Use them early and often, and cancel them when you're done. I have no idea how many accidents this could prevent; it's just plain right.

10. Don't tailgate.

If Jim follows one second behind Bill for 100 miles, he'll arrive one second sooner than if he followed at two seconds . . . that is, *if* he arrives.

Animal trainers use yummies and whips to shape behavior. Humans are more perverse. Ply them with drugs, electric shock, and heart-stopping bills, and Freud himself still couldn't predict what, if any, changes you'll effect. No list is going to change the way Americans ride. The items on this one were selected because they place the responsibility for safe riding squarely where it should rest: on the shoulders of you, the rider.

. . . And because they're hard to argue. I could say, "Don't wear black—it makes you invisible," but to hundreds of thousands, black leather is the quintessence of motorcycling. I could say, "Don't drink and ride," but some will insist they're fine with one beer (or five). I dare say there are no such equivocations on this list . . . and no miracles either. Yet, if I've persuaded you to faithfully adopt one item as your own, it will have been my most successful column.

Now if you'll excuse me, it's been a long time since I've adjusted my tire pressure.

Practically Everyone

August 1997

The previous selection gave suggestions for curing motorcy-clists' most common bad habits. Seven years later, the riding community still needs a few reminders to call their common sense back from sabbatical. Here's Mr. Safety's list of our most egregious offenses.

Pete Tamblyn

Remember when you were a kid, and you wanted to stay up to watch television or hang out at the pool hall or comb your hair in a DA and ride a motorcycle . . . but your parents wouldn't let you? Without logic and reason on your side, nor bargaining power or moral conviction, you entreated your parents with that pathetic, time-worn strategy: "*. . . everyone else* does/has/is allowed to!"

To which your parents predictably (they didn't need imagination; they were your parents) replied, "*You're* not everyone else!"

And indeed, now that you've fully evolved, you're glad they were right. Much better to be your own man/ woman; an individual unique among all others. You ride a motorcycle, for goodness sakes—maybe even to the office!

Years ago, when I first started teaching motorcycle courses, I recognized what an enormous challenge it would be to apply a single curriculum to a large and diverse group of learners. Some learned through listening, others by watching, some by reading, and others only by doing. Each time I thought I'd seen it all, some new student would come along and throw me a teaching challenge I never could have imagined.

When I left the confines of the parking lot four years ago and began offering on-street training, I discovered that every mile with every student poses a unique learning challenge. One of my early lessons, for instance, was with a short student who'd purchased a very tall motorcycle. We were approaching a stop sign on a steep off-camber slope, when it struck me that the student might not be able to reach the ground with his left foot. What was I to do? I was a safety instructor. I *had* to stop for a stop sign. The student flopped right on top of me and my bike!

For many of my students, even those who have ridden for decades, learning new skills takes them back to their school days—which in turn can lead to feelings of insecurity which they believed they'd forever left behind. When that happens, a little childhood voice cries from within: "Does everybody else have this much trouble?"

Well, no—the 6-foot 10-inch guy doesn't fall over at stoplights. And the guy who used to race motocross doesn't dump the clutch and stall, but believe me, there are common threads. Certain skills are just plain difficult to master, while other difficulties might be common sense on sabbatical. Many more are mental or physical techniques that no one's ever called to the rider's attention. Perhaps some day I'll do a column on the most aberrant student disorders. The following are the most common. In fact, *practically everyone's.*

. . . *follows other vehicles too closely (less than two seconds).*

. . . *starts left turns too soon,* hugging the inside so that oncoming cars can take a crack at their left kneecap.

. . . *fails to make proper lane adjustments* (move as far to the right as practical) *when they see an oncoming car preparing to turn left.*

. . . *watches mirrors too infrequently.*

. . . *pulls up too closely behind stopped vehicles at intersections,* thus forfeiting one of the few safety advantages that motorcyclists hold over automobile drivers: the ability to flee if another car, approaching from the rear, can't stop. Mr. Safety's lady friend hounds him repeatedly on this one.

. . . *signals too late for lane changes* . . . or doesn't signal at all.

. . . *admits to riding a little faster than he or she should, some or most of the time.*

. . . *wishes* (secretly perhaps) *that he or she could ride a little faster.*

. . . *has difficulty braking and downshifting at the same time.*

. . . *makes sharp left turns more easily than right ones.*

. . . *locks the rear brake when unexpectedly having to stop in a hurry.*

. . . *grips the handlebars too tightly.*

. . . *doesn't turn his or her head enough while cornering and making low-speed turns.*

. . . *runs the tires down too far.* Fortunately, modern tires are so good that even the criminally negligent usually get by without tire failure

However, performance—especially on wet roads—is bound to be compromised. A wise man once said "better to ride a bad bike on good tires, than a good bike on bad tires."

. . . *has failed to check the bike's tire pressure this week.*

. . . *would ride more smoothly and effectively if riding a smaller motorcycle.*

. . . *could improve transitions from throttle to brakes and from brakes to throttle.*

. . . *believes to have improved motorcycle's performance with an aftermarket exhaust system, but has actually worsened it* (usually with weakened midrange and poorer throttle response).

. . . *could get better ride and handling by accurately adjusting the motorcycle's stock suspension settings.*

. . . *could get better ride and handling by improving throttle control.*

. . . *pays extra for premium gasoline, when the bike would run just fine on regular.*

. . . *assumes that leather garments provide the best protection in a motorcycle tumble.*

. . . *fails to recognize the huge difference in abrasion protection between competition-grade leathers and most off-the-rack leather garments.* In fact, certain synthetic fabrics outperform some leathers in this area.

. . . *underestimates the importance of protective armor in knees, shoulders, elbows, hips, and back.* It's your first bony impact with the pavement which probably determines whether you'll report for work on Monday or spend months in painful rehab.

. . . *when surveyed, underestimates the likelihood that he or she will be involved in any sort of accident.*

. . . *tenses up when confronted with riding through gravel.*

. . . *finds it easier to spend $$ on performance/appearance than on comfort/protection.*

. . . *underestimates the distances and times needed to execute various maneuvers.* Few realize, for example, that it takes a skilled rider a full second to achieve a decent lean angle at 30 mph.

. . . *fails to recognize and hence fails to exploit the benefits of throttle steering.* When asked to predict the path that a motorcycle will assume when gassed mid-corner, fewer than half of all riders correctly predict that the bike will straighten and run wide.

. . . *will find several things in this column he or she disagrees with.*

. . . will find something in this column which he or she vehemently disagrees with.

Nothing in this column, however, is really worth getting hot and bothered about. After all, none of these things applies to you. You're not everyone else!

Speed Kings

June 2004

Sometimes you are guilty of riding too fast. Sometimes you are even aware of this fact—but not always. Larry gives some thought-provoking mistakes to be alert for in your own riding which say only one thing: back off.

Pete Tamblyn

How do you know when you're riding too fast? Well, by watching how you ride, of course!

Chances are, you know the feeling when a motorcycle you're grooving on suddenly escapes your control. But a friend of mine once experienced something that you and I will never live to tell about. While traveling in one of the world's unsettled regions, he was invited to ride the king's own motorcycle, and—well—you guessed it!

Actually, the Harley-riding potentate was very understanding (didn't even cut off a hand!) and accepted my friend's truthful explanation that he lost control of the bike when an inattentive driver pulled out in front of him. My friend, who spent a few years as a club-level road racer, admitted that he should have been able to stop short of the errant driver but instead, overreacted and locked the front brake. He estimated his speed at not much more than 25 mph—about the average for the 4,000 accidents Harry Hurt and his team of investigators studied in their landmark Hurt Report.

According to our good friends at NHTSA, a fatally injured motorcyclist is 37 percent more likely to have been speeding than a car driver meeting his demise. Speeding, according to the agency, can mean "too fast for conditions," which I learned, as a teenager, needn't be any faster than you can run. After wheelieing myself off the back of my 305 Laredo, I subsequently chased it for half a block—still clinging to the throttle—before it crash-landed between two parked cars. Experiences such as these have made me uniquely qualified to tell others when they are going too fast.

Quite often it surprises people. The main reason, I think, why people are surprised to hear this is that almost everybody knows someone faster. The fastest street rider I ever knew is no longer with us. He blew through an intersection at the posted speed limit, never noticing that beyond the big pickup truck was a driver waiting to turn left across his path.

Some people belong on the track. Period. They just can't ever bring themselves to ride at speeds with which polite society can coexist. They're rare. For most of us, it's situational. A little too fast on a well-known bend or a neighborhood intersection. I see it every week when I train others . . . and every day, practically, when I monitor my own behavior. Here is a list of clues that you could be traveling too fast for conditions:

Hitting a pothole. Or perhaps a big rock, or even a muffler. You didn't see it because you were tailgating—following a second or less behind another vehicle. Did you really want to arrive *one second* earlier? Of course not; you just let your restlessness get the better of you instead of laying back and waiting for an appropriate moment to accelerate around the other driver.

The car that could have nailed you. You know the feeling: when you clear a busy intersection or a hidden driveway and suddenly see a car that you'd have been powerless to avoid had the driver floored it a second earlier.

Locking the rear brake. One of the classic panic reactions. I've seen some of the smoothest riders lock up the rear wheels when the scenery coughed up a surprise. In a study I once conducted, the unexpected flashing of a red light caused the best riders to lay down a dark stripe— even some who claimed they never *use* the rear brakes!

Upsetting the bike while shifting. Jason Pridmore (when he was a callow 19 years old) once chastised me for bucking like a bull rider every time I upshifted. I'm sure that my gyrations didn't lower my lap times any, but they surely proved that I was working too hard at *trying* to be fast.

Passenger gongs your helmet. I've said it before: the passenger is the ultimate "smoothometer." Take a fraction of a second to ensure a smooth shift or braking transition and you'll have a happier companion. Someday, who knows? Your calmness could be a life-saver.

Missing a turnoff. A favorite instructor trick of mine is to tell a student to turn when they arrive at a particular sign. When they blow past it, I know that their scanning rate isn't up to their velocity. Anytime you make two wrong turns you should seriously consider the possibility that you're riding over your head.

Dabbing brakes at the turn entry. Racebikes don't have brake lights, of course, but if they did, you'd never see a competent racer flash one going into the turn. Brakes take time to modulate smoothly (three seconds minimum is my observation), and every new corner calls for a strategy— whether it requires brakes or not. Reaching for the brakes as you enter is a sure sign that you're carrying more speed than you can comfortably control.

Flirting with the centerline on left turns. I personally don't have a problem with hanging parts of the motorcycle or your anatomy over the centerline, provided you're absolutely assured that there's no oncoming traffic. Tires are another matter. That centerline can get slippery, and besides, it's the perfect reminder that the roadway is a cooperative, not a competitive, venue. When riders can't (or won't) keep a safe space cushion in left-handers, it's usually because they have too much entry speed and must choose a bigger arc.

Unwillingness to use the right wheel track to set up for left turns. This might seem like a strange item, since "edge fear" is a common weakness among timid riders. Nevertheless, riders who won't use the right half of their lane should reduce their speed until they're comfortable operating near the shoulder (on the straightaway). With time and practice, the speed will gradually come back, but the important thing is that the bike will be in the safest part of the lane.

Failing to use turn signals when passing. Some riders believe that because they can maneuver laterally and accelerate more quickly than other traffic there's no point in communicating their intentions. Let's just say I disagree. If nothing else, turn signals give a cadence to the ride and keep one grounded to the reality that making progress through traffic is not the same as racing through it. Two seconds before each lane change is about right.

Total disregard for the double yellow. If a student makes a risky pass, it's my obligation to say so, but I've never dinged a pupil simply for passing on the double yellow. Sure, the DOT wasn't taking into account the superior acceleration of a modern sport-bike, but they had to be thinking of *something.* What? Once, after a few dozen passes on one of Vancouver Island's sinuous but well-traveled roads, I overtook in a curve, having ascertained that there was no risk of oncoming traffic. Only halfway through the pass did I realize that there was a turnout with a car aimed at my path! I parked and took five after that one.

Riding more aggressively with friends. This one is the classic, probably responsible for more accidents than all the others combined. Sure, you may be able to keep a faster pace by following that helmet over the hill, but you're not riding better when you leave your most critical judgment tool—speed selection—in someone else's hands. I know I've turned faster laps when following instructors around a repetitive course, but they were professionals who knew how to assess my abilities and were circulating at a mere fraction of their personal race pace. The person you're following down racer road is more likely to be seeking his own gratification. Seriously, if following is your thing, pay the money to follow a real professional like CLASS's Reg Pridmore or one of Keith Code's highly qualified instructors.

"King" Kenny Roberts, unfortunately, closed his famous minibike school in Spain a few years ago. But then again, it's never wise to mess with the King. My friend was lucky this time.

The Big Ugly

June 1990

Admit it; you've never wished it would rain when you had a ride planned. It's a fair bet that you've occasionally cancelled when the weather seriously threatened. Some of the, er, more seasoned among us (recalling soaked skivvies and bone-chilling cold) may simply pass on the opportunity, legitimately declaring they have nothing to prove. The "Riding in the Wet" section of many riders' résumés includes no more than a dash to the nearest shelter. Unfortunate, if that's the case, because there is much to be learned from riding in the rain. First, it makes you smoother. Read on for some plain-spoken advice on how to handle this element.

Pete Tamblyn

As near as I've been able to ascertain, rain has three known causes. The first of these is when warm air rises, gathering moisture (clouds) until the air bubbles turn into droplets of water that grow heavier, finally falling through the floor of the clouds. The other two are washing your bike and forgetting to carry your rain suit.

According to the Hurt Report, rain isn't that big a deal; only 0.2 percent of the investigated accidents occurred on wet roads. Of course, Dr. Hurt would probably be the first to admit that on the Los Angeles freeways he studied, a motorcyclist is as likely to be struck by a .38 caliber bullet as a steady downpour.

A University of North Carolina study, *Analyses of Fatal and Non-Fatal Motorcycle Crashes and Comparisons With Passenger Cars* by Carroll and Waller, found that 11.2 percent of motorcycle accidents occurred on wet roads, compared to 29.1 percent for passenger cars.

"This seemingly lower rate of motorcycle accidents," concluded the researchers, "is likely due to reduced travel by motorcyclists during inclement weather conditions."

Now for some truly astonishing findings. A team of Swedish epidemiologists (remember Dr. Jess Krauss and his infamous superbike paper?) discovered that wet roads were present in 24 of the 180 accidents they studied. Their conclusion: "People do not like to ride motorcycles in the rain." Unbelievable.

I'm not any kind of an "ologist," but I'm gonna go out on a limb and say that motorcycling in the rain is riskier than in the dry. I won't be totally alone out there; a New Zealand study, one of the few to weigh exposure data, pegged rain riding as 60 percent more perilous. All things being equal, I believe it would've been higher, but if any good comes out of rain, it's that it makes us more careful.

My hat goes off to America's driver education teachers for the extraordinary job they've done at disseminating one crucial bit of information, that being that the most dangerous time to drive wet roads is during the first 15 minutes of a storm. *Every*body knows that's when the streets get really greasy.

Water gets painted the villain, but its crime is just commiserating with the wrong elements: dirt, grease, fog, cold, and darkness. A couple of years ago, when I was practicing on Keith Code's outrigger bike for our *Roamin' Wyoming Rally,* I discovered that even with the asphalt hosed down, I could generate enough front-wheel braking traction to loft the back wheel off the ground. This, of course, was on a pit road, with no sand, no spilled engine oil or gasoline, no mud, and no leaves. You don't even need a motorcycle to replicate this experiment. Simply rub your rubber-soled shoes across wet, clean pavement—and then repeat with any of the aforementioned contaminants.

Ducks love the rain, but nobody gets around in it like an Englishman. Reg Pridmore, the former racing great who now operates the CLASS safety schools, was considered something of a rain specialist during his competition days. So if a monsoon strikes one of his CLASS events, he sees it not as a deterrent, but as a valuable teaching tool.

"Slow down!" is Pridmore's initial advice. "I take the first drops on my face shield to be an immediate warning sign. But after the rain washes away the grease and dirt that've risen to the surface, you can get good lean angles."

Pridmore reckons that riders exacerbate the rain by running on subpar tires and expending too much of their energy through tensed-up muscles.

"It should be a matter of common sense. Just tell yourself, 'I'm not gonna let it upset me.' Relax, slow down, and enjoy it."

Perhaps one reason that average street riders become overly tensed by rain is that they're accustomed to feeling totally "planted." But when traction is less than ideal, wrestling with the handlebars won't make your tires stick any harder.

"Let the front end do more of what it wants to do," advises Pridmore.

It does'nt take a genius to recover from a routine skid—just two big gyros and the composure to let them do their job. Low-speed (5 mph) skids are less retrievable, so, stops and starts on slippery surfaces demand deft manipulation of brakes and throttle.

You simply have to allow yourself more time—time to settle the weight onto the front wheel for braking—time to bank it over for turns—time to spot painted lines and manhole covers—and time for the other guy to see you. MSF curricula suggest tripling the normal 2–3 seconds following distance on rain-soaked roads. True, rain increases everyone's stopping distance, but it also raises the stakes, and with oncoming motorists scanning less effectively, you're more likely to disappear behind cars and trucks.

When roads are slippery, the dominant survival instinct is keeping the bike upright, but keeping it *visible* is probably more crucial. According to Bragg, Dawson, and Jonah *(Profile of the Accident Involved Motorcyclist in Canada),* "Light condition was significantly related to accident likelihood with significantly more accidents occurring at dusk than the amount of dusk riding would predict." The ambient light during a heavy shower is roughly equivalent to dusk, and other studies have shown headlights and bright clothing to increase a bike's conspicuousness by up to 400 percent in those conditions.

And finally: How well can *you* see in the rain? My most terror-filled riding memories are the miles traveled at night, on poorly marked roads, my view expunged by the glare of headlights against my fogged faceshield. When you made your most recent helmet purchase, I wonder—did you consider whether the manufacturer produces an effective anti-fog shield? I've tried everything from scuba mask defoggers to potato juice but found only one product effective, the gooey liquid in the mini-helmet once peddled by Nava—which no longer sells helmets in the American market.

Rain doesn't have to be ugly. Before you drew your first breath, you spent a blissful nine months submerged in water. One of my favorite things is to watch old swimmers as they take leave of their weary, arthritic joints and stroke calmly, smoothly, dreamily back to their first memories. Motorcycles should move like that—the roadway gliding effortlessly beneath them en route to magic memories. But realistically, we're not always after memories; sometime we just want to get there. *That's* the Big Ugly.

Drills and Skills

Perfectly Basic

October 2001

Larry had an ability to make a lesson out of the simplest things. I looked forward to reading his monthly article—most of the time thinking "You know, if the same thing happened to me, it would probably not even register in my conscience!" And I would never have been able to write such an entertaining and informative article about it. This article is a perfect example of a great lesson in the most basic area of motorcycling.

We so often overlook the importance of basics. Many learned to ride by having someone simply say, "Here's the clutch, throttle, brakes, and shifter. Now go—it's easy!" As an "experienced" rider, do you ever stop to think there is more to operating the controls than simply knowing where they are located and how they operate? Do you ever stop to think why they are called controls?

We try to stress to new riders the importance of operating the controls smoothly and gripping them lightly. When doing so, the motorcycle's suspension can work the way it is intended to work—rather than us controlling the motorcycle's actions. Let the motorcycle have the control and you simply guide it. It's basic—and it works!

JoAnna Murray, owner and lead instructor
Atlanta Motorcycle Schools

In motorcycling, like live rock 'n' roll, one man's techno wizardry is another's wretched excess. In either venue it's still the basics, thankfully, which separate virtuosity from showmanship. According to the Motorcycle Safety Foundation, a modern motorcycle has five "primary" or basic controls—ones that dictate where it's headed and when it'll get there. *Clutch, front brake, rear brake, shift lever, throttle.*

And we should be thankful that the five basic controls change about as often as the strings on a guitar (but don't be surprised to see revised brake controls within the next decade). I don't think it's far-fetched to say that most experienced riders would significantly improve their smoothness if they worked to perfect just one of the five primary control applications. What do you say we scrutinize these so-called basics?

Handlebars: Yo, man—a proper git-box has *six* strings, not five! "Give me a lever, and I'll move the world," a wise man once said, but a lot of riders limp along with steering so flaccid they can't change lanes without a windblast from a passing truck. What's their problem?

Well, maybe if we called them hand *rests* instead of "grips" . . . then riders might convert some lost energy into useful steering torque. I'm talking about the energy spent pushing on one bar to overcome the grip on the other. By the way, countersteering (i.e. push left/go left; push right/go right) works at even walking speeds. You may think you're turning the bars or "car steering" at low speeds, but it's really the handlebar swinging back on its own . . . something it can do only if you employ a light touch.

Clutch: The clutch is the beginning rider's "lifeline," and a friendly exhortation to "cover the lever" has no doubt made the difference between happy riding careers and some lifelong aversions to motorbikes. Unfortunately, once over the stall or wheelie hump, most riders assume that they've "mastered" this simple-looking device. It's like looking at the surface of a vast sea, teeming with life, and assuming that it's no more than a conveyance to the other side.

Many riders fail to grasp that the clutch is "pressure sensitive" rather than "motion sensitive," For a glimpse at how good your clutch control really is, try this reversed-world experiment:

With the engine off and the motorcycle in first gear, slowly back the bike down a moderately steep slope. If the surface is at all slippery or loose, you'll find that the front wheel locks easily—you don't necessarily have to grab the brake. The better technique is to stay off the front brake and control the rate of descent with the clutch lever . . . effectively using the engine to brake the rear (weighted) wheel while keeping both feet solidly on the ground. If you have good clutch control, you'll lower the bike down the slope as if you have a rope and pulley; if not, it'll lurch down in fits and spurts.

If it takes more than a few seconds to adapt to the idea of the clutch action working "in reverse," then you're probably a victim of "squeeze it in/ let it out" mentality. You'd be well served to practice until your left hand is fully pressure sensitive . . . just like the device it's operating.

Front Brake: Put simply, the front brake is *the* brake—or at least the *stopping* brake (commentary on the other device to follow). If I said that you'll enjoy superior feel and control by using two fingers on the brake lever, that would ensure that I receive a dozen argumentative letters. I really don't care whether you use one, two, three or four fingers. Top racers all prefer one or two, but it's *rider*-specific and *bike*-specific. Bottom line is that riders should use the fingers necessary to control their machines, and the truest measure of control is the ability to consistently reach impending skid.

When I teach, I typically see two obstacles to smooth, effective stopping—type of lever action and timing. As with the aforementioned hand*grip* the term brake "lever" may suggest certain inputs that aren't the most bike friendly. Gloved fingers gliding smoothly across the blade will usually produce finer control than will a true "in/out" lever action . . . an observation which led one of my students to christen such form, "cam braking."

The brake's release is nearly as critical as its application. After all, a sudden weight shift isn't the subtlest message you can communicate to your bike's chassis as it starts to settle into a turn.

To gain proficiency on the front brake I'd recommend two things: 1) Practice settling weight on the front wheel by applying sufficient pressure to bottom the fork. Do so in first gear, skimming both feet along the pavement at about 15–20 mph. Make sure you have a good clean surface—and don't forget to squeeze the clutch lever in. 2) To further hone your "touch," find a deserted stretch of road. Modulation is easier when you can brake from 60 or 70 mph than it is in a parking lot where you might reach 30 mph max—especially when it comes time to practice easing *off* the brake.

Rear Brake: If you ride a dirt bike, you need no reminder of what a marvelous control the rear brake is. That's why we call it the "control" brake. As a stopping device, however, it's pretty impotent. It *may* provide 30 percent of the stopping force in *some* applications, but certainly not in any sort of authoritative stop, when most of the bike's weight has shifted to the front tire. I've tried on some of the longest, heaviest bikes (we're talking conventional, not linked brakes here), and I've never shaved more than a couple of feet off of my front-only stops when I added rear brake pressure.

The control comes in when the weight has started to return to the rear wheel, or in lesser applications when there's not much weight transfer to begin with. Don't take it on my authority, but do yourself a favor and experiment with the British technique of first applying the front brake and then gently adding some rear after the weight has shifted forward. In an emergency you may forget to apply the rear brake, which is just as well, as locking it is one of the foremost errors found in accident investigations.

If you don't use the rear brake to assist on U-turns and other low-speed maneuvers (we're still talking conventional systems here) then you'll need to be more expert with the other controls. Because its simpler to "un-apply" than a front brake, the rear also helps to smooth out the difficult transition back onto the throttle before entering a turn. In the tighter stuff, there's no harm in holding down the rear pedal a bit to soften the hit as you throttle forward. Just a tool . . . not a rule.

Gear Change Lever: Grinding, clanging gears—the *savagery!* More calamitous shifts are probably fomented by clutch, throttle, and plain bad timing than by sins of the shifter itself. You can start, however, by examining the position of the lever. Can you easily rotate your toe over and under it? When it comes time to effect the change, instead of giving it a solid thwack through the free play and into the subsequent gear, try "preloading" it for just a moment, i.e. pressure it just long and forcefully enough to take the freeplay out. If you're correctly matching rpm to wheel speed it should slip easily into gear. Typically your lower speed changes must be slower, more deliberate, perhaps with more clutch work. By the time you're reaching for the higher gears, you scarcely need more than a "fanning" of the clutch lever. Just remember—don't force the lever. It'll engage when it's ready.

Throttle: If your eyes were built into the motorcycle, they'd be the most important control. But since they're not, the throttle is like a seeing-eye dog—taking incoming visual data and converting it into useable physical space. Treat it as you would man's best friend. On the road, strive for long, fluid, purposeful throttle applications. More than all the others combined, it's the control you use to create motorcycling's most vital commodity—space.

Though it seems we're losing a bit each day, there's still space enough on our roads to accommodate riders of manifold tastes and skill levels. Loud or soft, fast or slow, each might consider the simple goal that guitar great Eric Clapton once expressed: to some day play "one perfect note."

Parking Lot Pragmatism

November 1998

Your own personal tune-up training range is as close as the nearest box store. The advantages of the parking lot over the street for honing particular skills are many. Just go early, before the shoppers arrive and don't ask (maybe best not to tell, either).

Pete Tamblyn

It's the end of July, as I write this, and it seems my bald spot gets a little redder and my feet a little flatter with each passing day. People think I ride motorcycles for a living, but the truth is that I *chase* motorcycles for a living . . . across a parking lot.

Dozens of parking lots actually. Trainers like Reg Pridmore and Keith Code disseminate their ample knowledge on some legendary race circuits, but none as famous as some of the places where I train. How many of your neighbors have heard of Laguna Seca . . . compared to K-Mart? Or Road Atlanta . . . to the Pentagon? I don't mean to brag, but I'll bet I have one of the largest bodies of parking-lot motorcycling experience in the world.

For my money the single best thing you can do to boost your skill level or clear out the cobwebs is a "staggered" or "offset" weave. It reinforces smooth throttle control, visual directional control (by forcing you to turn your head), balance, and steering. The dimensions you choose are arbitrary and should reflect the size and type of bike, your present skill level, and whatever aspect of your riding you wish to hone. For example, if it's counterbalancing you want to master, practice a wide offset. To tighten your handlebar grip and develop knee and foot control, place the cones close together, dictating a rapid fire left/right/left technique.

If you ride a large-displacement machine and are reasonably confident in your basic control, you might start with two setups: the first using cones spaced at 10 paces (30 feet), with alternating cones offset by 2 1/2 paces; your second run might be five or six paces between cones, with an offset of two to three feet. Perhaps the most valuable lesson of the offset weave is how dramatically it illustrates the effects of muscular tension, particularly in the arms. Oh, one more thing . . . make sure you ride around the *outside* of the cones, Einstein!

Before you begin, a casual walkabout will alert you to errant nails, broken glass, and so forth. Run your boot sole over the various surfaces (though I'd long been wary of them, I recently heard my first documented report of a bike crashing out on tar strips), paying special attention to dropped oil and anti-freeze. If you think of it, bring along a water bottle; you might be surprised at how a little H$_2$0 affects painted lines and other surfaces.

If you can't stop your motorcycle within 45 feet at 30 mph, either you or the bike needs work. Most of today's bikes can stop in significantly shorter distances. But before you get hung up on numbers, train yourself to smoothly settle weight onto the front wheel, using firm front brake pressure, and all of the bike's fork travel. You can start by trundling along in first gear with your feet dragging on the pavement. Don't forget to squeeze the clutch in and to release a little pressure at the end, when weight returns to the rear wheel.

A big parking lot is also the safest place to scuff in slippery, new tires; circle repetitively, adding lean angle increments. And if you *must* master the wheelie/brakie, a deserted lot is second only to a soft field. A cell phone and a riding partner wouldn't hurt, and if you mess up, you didn't get the idea from me.

Can you get in trouble using a parking lot? I live by the maxim, "It's easier to beg forgiveness than to ask permission." Phone the manager of Warehouse World for permission to practice motorcycle drills there, and I'll bet I know what his or her response will be. But unless the property is posted or you're doing burn-outs on your pro-stock drag racer, your presence doesn't violate any laws (I've been chatted up by hundreds of curious police and store managers and never evicted yet). Some of today's suburban high schools have huge parking lots—suitable for speeds up to 40 mph when no one's around. Best bet on commercial lots is to arrive at sunrise and depart before the first employee clocks in.

Unlike public roads, racetracks and parking lots don't require so much effort just to stay on them. Motorcycles prefer sweeping, uninterrupted arcs of the "pie are squared" variety. On the track if you don't like your lean angle, you add a little or subtract to suit your tastes. On the street, too often, each action begets an opposite and equal reaction just to keep the tires from eclipsing the center line or shoulder.

But while the racetrack meets the scientist's demands for repeatability, each lap requires 10 or 12 more combinations of braking, gear changing, looking, leaning, and accelerating, before you get to make even a single correction. Contrast that with a serious musician, who might practice one riff or even the same note dozens of times before he's sufficiently satisfied to move on.

If you want to experience steeper lean angles, you need only ride a circle. You can go around and around, adding lean angle until you start to scrape, slide, or soil yourself. If it's a quicker "flick" you desire, make an oval of two semi-circles and two straights.

In the days before Sunday sales, legions of rumbly little red-and-green cars used to swarm shopping centers each Sabbath for some spirited, short-circuit time trials called "autocross." The Sports Car Club of America (SCCA) still sanctions events around the country, and about two years ago, a certain V-twin fraternity enlisted their aid in establishing an "autocross for motorcycles." Buell Motorcycle Company debuted the resulting event, dubbed "BattleTrax," at the '97 Daytona Bike Week.

"For those of us who always wanted to be a performance rider of sorts, it gives us the opportunity to sport ride in the safety and confines of that parking lot," explains Buell's general sales manager, Scott Miller.

" . . . in many cases you never leave first gear. You're riding between zero and 40 mph, and you've got sweeping corners, closing radius corners, switchbacks, chicanes, and straightaways."

According to Miller, less than .5 percent of all street riders ever experience a real racetrack. He and course designer Reg Kittrelle (editor of *Battle 2win*, a Buell and high-performance Sportster publication), believe that the course provides riders with a special opportunity to hone routine street riding and evasive skills in addition to performance riding. A typical event features four hours of "fun runs" (with Buell test bikes available), an hour-and-a-half of competition, and then some more fun runs.

Riders who compete do so against the clock, not elbow to elbow, and healthy competition is ensured by the creation of different classes for different types of bikes. What's the fastest way around a BattleTrax course? KTM's lithe Duke has set some of the hottest lap times.

"In more cases than not we've been able to beat 'em with a Buell,"

Miller boasts, barely containing his laughter, "... since we made up the event, we kinda like to win it."

A 300- by 300-foot layout (the size of two MSF ranges) is the ideal, according to Miller, but one of his favorite was a "double figure 8" run on a teeny 150- by 100-foot lot. At parent company Harley-Davidson's 95th Anniversary celebration, they invited spectators to come ride the factory prepared race-bikes of Scott Parker, Jay Springstein, et al., while the engines were still warm from the Milwaukee Mile!

"Probably the most exciting piece of BattleTrax," says Miller, "is that the event comes to the rider. We look around now at just about any K-Mart parking lot and we could effectively have an event.

"BattleTrax," he concludes with typical Milwaukee restraint, "could be the event of the new millennium."

The 20-Minute Tune-Up

December 1992

When I first met Larry nearly 20 years ago he was teaching the MSF course at the Community College. Fresh out of the US Park Service Police M/C School myself, I was curious about these safety classes, and spent my breaks observing when I could. That's where our friendship began. We often debated opposing theories over lunch at a local restaurant, understanding each other's point in the end. Larry was uncanny in his ability to listen to the opposite viewpoint, and then be willing to actually give it a try to see for himself—the sign of a true trainer.

Occasionally we would practice our skills together. We differed on braking technique and I would demonstrate my point that general rules just don't apply in all situations. "Always use the front brake when stopping" doesn't work in slow, controlled turns (unless you want to pick up your bike). He agreed with me there. The first time I took him up and down steps, he asked "Why?" I answered, "point of escape." Definitely not an MSF consideration!

I have often reflected on the way he helped others, and what he has done for motorcycle riders all over the world. He could teach without preaching, and add a little Grodsky humor. I learned a lot from our talks. Some of my fondest memories are of two people, two points of view, but always with the common element of safety.

It was truly an honor to have known Larry, and to have been featured in one of his articles.

Larry D. Shaw, M/C police officer (retired)
Monroeville, Penn., Police Department

I'll admit it was the lights and sirens that drew me to ride the big FLH police bike—my chance to brazenly flaunt the paraphernalia of authority. "Shamu" is accustomed to crowds. First-time acquaintances observe this simple name stenciled on the right side of officer Larry Shaw's bike and summarily ask, "Is that you or your bike?"

"Take your pick," is the usual response of Officer Shaw, a bear-like man whose handshake is always remembered even if his appellation isn't. "Community relations" is another phrase he freely dispenses . . . and his rationale for letting me herd the copsickle around his U.S. Park Service pursuit course at a recent holiday picnic. The lessons that followed were a necessary show of force; our rounds of the mall this bright summer morning are, well . . . *street theater?* The cleaning lady inside the department store scarcely bats an eyelash, even as our front tires turn and dart away, inches from the plate glass window she's washing. To the 30,000 residents of Monroeville, Pennsylvania, the sight of Shamu's urban trials maneuvers is endemic—like a spotted dog in a Norman Rockwell painting. In fact, it gives the sprawling suburban community a beat policeman's familiar presence—but with even greater range than a patrol car.

Clutch in the friction zone, little bit of rear brake, slowly weaving in and out of the 10 stone pillars; about two feet is all the clearance between the barrier and the curb. Watch the mailbox—never make it with those saddlebags and mirrors poking out. Turn around—now back the other way, 15 mph this time—just cleared that Coke machine. U-turns—left then right— then a 75-foot slow ride with the tight side mirror close enough to warm the bricks in the wall. What's the point?

"You don't feel the same every day," explains Shaw. "Some days you're a little tight, a little stiff. Some days you can't do right-hand turns as well as left. But when you ride for a living, you have to be able to execute all your skills when you're called upon. So I come down here to warm up, and I don't go out on the road until I feel right."

The kids at the school playground swarm around us like pigeons at feeding time. They must have seen Shaw's Harley climb those schoolyard steps a hundred times, but the shower of sparks still signals a happening.

Up and over the dirt mound. In and out, in and out of the little round pyramids, on tracks barely wide enough for our tires. How did I get on top of this four-foot wall? Oops! Curbside pull-outs: lean 'er way over, turn the wheel and don't look back—good practice. But what's this? How was I led to the top of this toboggan run? And why am I sliding down the hill . . . back-wards!?

STOP! Thank you, Officer Shaw. I think I'm warmed up now.

"These are things that anyone can do," says Shaw. "You don't need any special equipment or a special area. I mean this is a playground, a public place. We're not breaking any laws. The toboggan run? You know, it helps sometimes if you have a badge."

Short of a get-out-of-jail-free card the following is the best usage of free space that I can recommend to tune up your riding on a weekly basis. A dozen four-inch traffic cones will fit easily in your saddlebags (all MS instructors have a list of suppliers) or saw some old tennis balls in half.

THE DRIVEWAY:

U-turns—No matter how narrow your driveway, you can use it for valuable turning practice; just adjust your pre-turn angle accordingly. Shaw, who practices 140-degree curbside pull-outs (about halfway between a 90-degree and a full U-turn), says you should determine the turning radius of your bike, then give yourself a foot or two of leeway. Start with the front wheel already turned, the bike leaned and one or both feet on the ground. Turn your head sharply and strive to hold your lean angle and full steering lock through smooth clutch and throttle.

Slow Ride—Take some jumbo chalk or find a painted line 30 feet long. Eyes up, knees in. Best control is achieved with steady throttle and clutch, adjusting speed via rear brake modulation. Should be able to ride the line for 15 seconds.

Stop 'n' Plant—From 10 to 15 mph, squeeze front brake progressively but firmly enough that forks bottom. Keep eyes up and knees on tank until forks are fully rebounded, then plant left foot.

Stop 'n' Go—Before you leave home, try stopping momentarily at the end of the driveway without putting either foot down.

THE PARKING LOT:

Stabilizing highway speeds make convenient camouflage for aberrant throttle and turning behaviors. But the dynamics of a five-mph parking lot turn are nearly identical to the 70-mph sweeper.

Figure Eights—Mark a box 20 feet by 60 feet (bigger or smaller, according to your skills and equipment). Only the clutch work and counterbalancing (optional) make this different from highway-speed turns. Running wide? Most riders run out of space because they don't turn quickly enough. So practice until you can "flick 'er in there."

Offset Weave—String four cones at 60-foot intervals and, on a parallel line 60 feet away, three more in the gaps. Start outside the first cone and commence weaving. Loosen up those butt cheeks, turn your head, and hold that throttle nice and steady. Also, try accelerating, then braking the machine before each turn, but finish all braking before leaning the bike.

Stop in a Box—One of motoring's great myths is the "panic stop." Besides the fact that there is no place for panic on the highways, it assumes that you've exhausted your reserve and a collision is almost inevitable. A better plan is to practice smooth stops with a goal of narrowing the reserve you need to operate at the same or lower risk levels. Chalk a four-foot box, choose a speed, and then see how long you can delay your braking and still plant the front tire smoothly in the box. Eventually you will learn to detect impending skid. Just make certain that you keep both feet on the pegs until you're virtually stopped. That way if you do lock the front brake, you can easily release it without losing your balance.

Swerving—You *do* understand, countersteering, right? If not, enroll in a rider education course at once. Find one at www.msf-usa.org. Play around with your own dimensions, but strive for a loose and easy style that enables the motorcycle to move independently of your body. Principles of swerving: 1) the harder you push, the quicker the bike leans; 2) the longer you hold the push, the farther out it goes.

THE ROAD:

Swooping—On a familiar piece of road, select a gear, and settle into a rhythm that lets you set up for corners without braking or shifting.

Late Apexing—Works great in concert with swooping. Approach on the outside of the turn. By increments, delay the moment when you turn the bike (never at the expense of smoothness). From your parking-lot practice you know the importance of turning the head, and late apexing has the real-world advantages of increased ground clearance, greater visibility, elimination of wasteful directional changes, and—most important—a space cushion against oncoming cars.

Smoothness is the logical aim of every rider, from enduro champion to freeway flier. But smooth riding takes planning; you don't get there by simply hopping on the bike and riding off. And one more bit of advice from the man in blue.

"Practice on the bike the way you ride the bike," advises Larry Shaw. "So if you ride two-up, do your drills with your passenger on the back."

But hey—not on the toboggan run!

Rust Bucket

May 2000

One of the things that I admired about L.G. was his ability to learn from a myriad of situations and apply the lesson to his teachings. I remember the day in question and the green plastic all over the trail. It really didn't phase L.G., he just learned a lesson, and then applied the lesson to his teachings. I realized this about L.G. early on, whether we were mountain bike riding, dirt bike riding, riding on the street, or just hanging out. He was constantly analyzing, learning, and refining his teachings and himself.

I met L.G. officially when I scheduled a riding lesson. I had actually known him for some time as a customer, but had no idea what he did. When I picked up my first street bike, got to the end of the alley, and didn't know how to make a turn, I realized that a 550 pound K100RS was a completely different animal. In preparation for this day I had been reading Rider *regularly. One day I realized that Grodsky was a name on a list at my shop and thought, what a coincidence. After that first lesson, I surprised L.G., who was on his trusty Transalp, when I followed him off road on the K100RS. Our friendship grew from that day forward. I think of him often and miss his friendship. God speed, L.G.*

Alan R. Patterson III, Esquire
dirt bike teacher, street bike student

"What is he, nuts?" I asked when I heard that Mike was on his way over to pick up the helmet I'd promised him. Utter rigor mortis gripped the evening rush hour, and that was the *good* news, since forward progress could only be made skating across a fresh, inch-thick coating of ice.

A half hour later, he stood in the foyer, shivering uncontrollably. It took another half hour before he could find his own fingers. Why hadn't he waited until morning or simply walked the two miles? I doubt, in the three days since he bought my Suzuki DR350, that he'd purchased insurance, and I know he had no license—maybe a permit. He'd had to hail a car to jump-start the frozen motor and the borrowed helmet he arrived in was so tight as to cause brain hemorrhaging.

"You're a complete knucklehead," I said, but secretly I admired him.

My personal jellification has been a steady, gradual transformation, so the passing of the DR isn't of any real historical significance. Had someone paid me two grand to compete in a 50-yard dash, I'd have taken the money and run (sort of), but it wouldn't have proven that I'd suddenly turned slow afoot.

About Mike I'll make a couple of predictions. I don't know if he'll seek formal training or not, but either way, he'll probably take a spill or two. A German study of new, year-round urban riders showed that *five* minor tumbles was the first-year average. But I also predict he'll become a heckuva rider. He's a professional bicycle messenger, so his reflexes and balance are sharp. I expect he'll master the physical skills quickly, and as a messenger, that traffic which doesn't kill him can only make him stronger.

When I was a little younger than Mike, I rode my Triumph daily until the pushrods fell out the bottom—a streak I kept alive by braving single digit temperatures. But a couple of years ago, after performing a complete service on my Honda TransAlp in preparation for a Mexico tour, I off-loaded it from the pickup in Austin, Texas, only to discover that the carburetors were full of varnish. The same fuel had languished in the tank for more than three months!

As my belly sags, so (nearly) sags the gut of the American motorcyclist. If, collectively, we continue to age at our fourth-quarter 20th century rate, the average rider in 2100 will be 83.6! Now, you might holler at Junior for not practicing the piano, but who's gonna rag on Gramps for failing to put miles on his Yamaha R1?

Back to the DR350. DRs are the soul of motorcycling. Like Yamaha's funky two-stroke DTs—bikes that set the hook for so many boomers— they simply don't know the meaning of the word "can't." My justification for ditching it is that I purchased a "proper" dirt bike . . . the formula for which is: one hour of riding = one hour of trucking + one hour of cleaning + three hours of maintenance. My new Kawasaki KLX300 is a sweet-handling machine, but I really don't ride it any better than the thoroughly neglected DR; I only pick it up more easily. Did I mention one hour of kickstarting?

I won't let this descend into another "dirt bikes make you such a better street rider" tirade. So far I've ridden mine twice in my first frigid month of ownership. But I had to have it. You know the old saw about rationalization and sex . . . the one that ends: "When did you ever make it through a day without a rationalization?" My excuse for dirt riding is that it makes me a better teacher.

The majority of my off-roading I do with my friend Alan, another street rider who returned to his dirt bike roots several years back when law school was turning him ooby-shooby. Now Alan gets out maybe four times as often as I, but his friend Jeff, who started riding five years ago, is a fanatic. He never misses a weekend and often loads up the trailer after work on summer evenings. Both are stalwart companions who never grouse when I'm stuck on a hill, but Jeff's Toyota Land Cruiser has heated seats. You can't put a price tag on friendship like that when your gutchies are oozing 35-degree mud.

Jeff may be faster than Alan, which means that Alan rides a bit more conservatively on his own, but can hang with him just about all the time. About two or three times per ride I'll slam myself hard . . . and it's always when I'm behind Jeff, not Alan. Since the groups I train on the street usually have three riders, analogies to my students are easy to draw.

Once, on a five-mile, uphill section I convinced the "weak" rider to lay back and meet us at the top of the ridge. The group's alpha dog cut loose, and I pursued him to the top. Upon arrival we waited all of 15 seconds for the last man to show.

Now this percentage stuff is pretty arbitrary, but the actual time difference on that section of road worked out to 3 percent . . . far less than either party would have reported had you asked them to assign a speed differential. So often, I go on rides where one rider apologizes for "being slow" or "holding the others up," but those two or three hard falls per dirt ride prove to me where the catch-up mentality leads.

When we pull the bikes off the trailer, Jeff takes off like a shot, whereas I like to warm up slowly, practicing the various body positions and weight shifts. I should forget about the others, they're so quickly out of sight, but I don't, and so I usually take my first hard fall less than five minutes into the woods. Later, about two hours into the ride, I feel the rust washing away, and the lesson is clear: *Occasional riders need longer warm-ups than regular riders.*

Then there's a point—about halfway through the ride, if the woods are really tight—where I start to feel like I can run with these guys. They're both entirely self-taught, but I was fortunate a few years ago, to receive some expert training from Dale Van De Ven, one of the key curriculum developers for both the MSF and the U.S. Marine Corps dirt bike courses.

By the way, this is precisely the point on the ride where I take my *second* hard fall. If I reviewed my Dick Burleson tape, I might be able to explain how to cross a slippery log at an acute angle, but Jeff and Alan just *do* it; they've surmounted thousands more than I have. So it was, as I chased after Jeff, that the icy log spit me head-on into the oak tree, showering poor Alan with shards of "unbreakable" green plastic.

The lesson: *Technique will conquer a known obstacle, but experience triumphs in inexplicable ways.* I see this phenomenon often on street rides. A grizzled veteran insults proper form, yet he repeatedly recovers from ham-fistedness and even faulty judgment. On the other hand, a newer rider with no repertoire of wrong moves systematically molds the basics into a smooth, even speedy package ... right up until the first surprise.

They say rust never sleeps, but I think it naps—in fits—with one eye closed, rolling over, then waking you with a sudden elbow to the face, about the time you're starting to feel comfortable. One day I'm going to make the time to really learn how to handle a dirt bike. I swear. But I wonder if the brilliance of today's specialized equipment could be turning on us, raising our expectations to where a toot to the mall is no longer worthy. Next month's the big tour or track day. I'll just take the car.

I should saunter down to the Suzuki store and see if the new DR-Z400Ss are in yet.

Brown Highways

March 1995

Lawrence Grodsky's gift of communication, simultaneously efficient and artistic, served him well as writer and teacher. In few words, he imparted information, stimulated thought, triggered conclusions, and evoked emotion. This piece on riding motorcycles on low-traction surfaces, whether poor roads or unimproved terrain, is a perfect example; it informs, instructs, and entertains.

As Larry says, "Sooner or later, no matter where you tour, you'll run out of pavement." Implicit is also, no matter what you are riding. *It is certainly true that a motorcycle designed for the purpose will make continuing, when the pavement ends, easier. It is equally true that some basic skills and a spirit of adventure will make continuing, when the pavement ends, possible. The same techniques employed by skilled riders on purpose-built machines to traverse seemingly insane terrain, will stand you in good stead when you need to coax your street bike through a bit of the loose stuff. This brief column packs a lot of information and food for thought into a few minutes' reading. So, whether you just want to keep moving on your street-oriented machine when the pavement ends or you aspire to serious off-road riding on a pure dirt bike, read, enjoy, then go ride!*

Ernie Middleton, student, Stayin' Safe Motorcycle Training

The readers of a trucking publication recently voted my state's roads the worst in the country—for the sixth straight year. If you visit Pennsylvania, I hope you have good suspension and tires, and that you can handle broken pavement. Come to think of it, maybe you should just ride in the dirt.

Sooner or later, no matter where you tour, you'll run out of pavement. Whether you keep moving or turn around is probably less a product of your motorcycle than of your personality and riding skills. Authors Ed

Culberson and Per Johansson are good examples. Culberson, *conquistador* of the brutal Darien Gap, inspired legions of BMW adventurers with his jungle journal, *Obsessions Die Hard*—but his early R80G/S, "Gringo," was little more than a road bike on knobby tires. Johansson? All he did was cross the rocky steppes and mountains of central Asia (*Rider*, October 1987) . . . on a Suzuki GSX-R 1100!

There probably are no more taboos that a touring rider can break by merely plonking a wheel off the paved road—only more shocks, frames, tibias and fibulas. If you're deadly serious, companies like ATK and KTM can put you on a competition-ready machine that is (nominally) street legal. However, a 37-inch seat height and a hair-trigger throttle may be more than you really need to find a decent campsite.

Oh, you want some suspension, but many of today's street bikes have more usable travel than dirt bikes of 20 years ago. Even cruisers can give a good account on smooth dirt roads, where long wheelbases and 21-inch front wheels provide reassuring stability.

And you want tires that bite. People who think that dual-sport tires get all slithery on the street haven't kept abreast of the latest rubber technology. You can buy DOT-approved tires in 10-percent increments that range from 90 percent pavement to 90 percent dirt. Some of the 80/20 and 90/10 tires, designed for bikes like the BMW GSs and Triumph Tigers, stick as well as pure street tires on wet pavement, and many are available in sizes which fit standard and cruiser models.

How light do you want it to be? Well, you don't carry the bike on your back, but until you're confident of your skills, it's best to stick with gentle terrain or else ride something you can easily support.

That brings up the delicate question of falling. Forget the rich, loamy soil you see spewing off the tires in those magazine shots. Unpaved roads are typically full of rocks and gravel—stuff that hurts when you land on it. But while falling is an inescapable aspect of racing and woods riding, discreet fire-road specialists often ride for years without a spill.

Nevertheless, the better protected you are, the more relaxed you'll be; and the more relaxed you ride, the less chance that you'll take a spill. So,

Rule No. 1—Dress Right.

Most of today's enduro jackets feature closed-cell foam, or hard plastic and foam armor. Many include back protectors. Separate elbow and knee pads, sold in most bike shops, fit under almost any riding gear, but don't forget that your hips are also a vulnerable area.

I personally do *not* recommend rigid motocross boots, which are designed for maximum support and impact protection. In minor spills they can transmit twisting forces farther up the leg, where more serious injury may occur. The more flexible dual sport style (e.g. Aerostich Combat Touring Boots) or a sturdy pair of work boots make an excellent compromise.

Also, dirt roads make you sweat even on cool days. Be sure to pack dry clothes for the ride home.

Rule No. 2—Know the Roads

Exploring can be half the fun, but inquire about local conditions (particularly after storms). Use high quality maps, such as the DeLorme State Atlases and the AMA Trail Riding Atlas (www.amadirectlink.com). Unless you're with riding companions, stick to graded roads which see regular (hourly) traffic. Attempt deep sand or mud only if you have solid off-road skills, and never on tires that are biased toward pavement.

Rule No. 3—Steer with the Rear.

You don't have to be able to hang the back end out at 90 mph like Scott Parker at the Parkersburg Mile. You needn't slide the motorcycle at all to enjoy unpaved roads, although the ability to handle a little drift or wheel spin is certainly a useful skill. The truth is that *all* motorcycles, on all surfaces, should be guided by the throttle and rear wheel after a brief initial handlebar input.

You want the motorcycle to be stable, and that necessitates a minimum speed. If the bike wanders in ruts or gravel, try a bit more speed instead of tightening up on the handlebar—but only the *minimum* speed for stability. Look for the exit of the turn (just as you would on pavement), turn with one concise motion, then feed it gas smoothly.

What if the back end breaks loose? *Don't* roll off the throttle. Unlike a car in snow, it will not "spin out." Hold the throttle steady and the back end will gradually self-stabilize.

Rule No. 4—Easy on the Brakes.

Few things will put you on the ground faster than locking the front wheel on a loose surface. Use one or two fingers, max. Off-road riders all know how to use a locked back brake to change directions, but ask your-self if this is something you're anxious to practice. Unlike the power slide, you *can* spin out from a rear brake slide, so never stomp on the foot brake, and if it locks, ease off gradually.

Rule No. 5—Mo-MEN-Tum . . .

Put rules No. 3 and No. 4 together and it's plain to see that "quality time" is that which you spend on the throttle. Plan each section of road to allow for long, fluid roll-ons. Motorcycles aren't monorails; they can bounce and flex—hop, skip and wiggle—and *still* remain on a positive course.

Stand on the pegs over rougher sections (lowers your "polar moment of inertia," says my physicist friend) and use your legs as shock absorb-ers. Shift weight forward to go up hills, back to descend. When corner-ing, slide forward to weight the front wheel. Try to keep your feet on the pegs as much as possible, but stay loose and avoid looking at hazards.

Unless it's overloaded or badly maintained, even a full-size touring bike can comfortably handle smooth, graded roads. The biggest obsta-cles to enjoyment are fear and weak skills. A small dirt bike, even an older one, can help you to overcome both. I'd suggest a single-cylinder four-stroke with a relatively low seat height.

If you want to be a motocross star, there are plenty of schools to choose from, but if you're old enough to have discovered pain, you'll probably opt for something less strenuous, The Specialty Vehicle Insti-tute of America (SVIA)—the ATV people—recently began training off-road "coaches" who conduct a one-day, hands-on program. Call (800) 887-2887 or visit www.atvsafety.org.

Northern Illinois University's Motorcycle Safety Project offers several riding courses. Register at www.outreach.niu.edu/mcycle/. Or, if you'd like a truly memorable education, the "Yamaha Off-Road Experience" combines expert training by British champion Geraint Jones, with a sce-nic Welsh bed-and-breakfast holiday. The cost is about $175 per day, in-cluding bike rental. Call 011-44-686-413324.

The MSF's new book, *Motorcycling Excellence,* contains an informa-tive chapter on off-roading, but a more extensive primer is SVIA's *Tips and Practice Guide for the Off-Highway Motorcyclist.*

Between the lunatic fringe of motocross and the perfect ribbon of as-phalt, there's a hidden universe of lumpy, bumpy brown highways. The Pennsylvania Turnpike is just the start.

Secrets of Smoothness

April 1994

When you look over the past 20 years, it is easy to see that there are only a few real seekers of information on how to ride. Schools of thought on the subject range from opinions to committee decisions to pet techniques backed up by nothing more than the air they are printed on.

Larry Grodsky really was a seeker and in many ways, at least to me, the most visible one of the past several decades as far as motojournalists go.

I didn't always agree with Larry's points but the fact that he was doing something, thinking about riding, and experimenting, always made me cut him slack on those points of disagreement. I felt he was a real player in the rider improvement game, not just a spectator.

Keith Code, California Superbike School

I don't like the guy who lives across the street from me. I'm not jealous of his youthful mop of hair, his Barbie Doll girlfriend, or even his new motorcycle. Last winter, after a blizzard dumped a foot and a half of snow on the sidewalks, he refused to let an 80-year-old neighbor ride in his car—but that's not it, either. What galls me about this young cretin is the way he shifts gears!

That, and the onanistic throttle blipping with which he announces each outing to the entire neighborhood. Lack of talent, experience, or practice can't explain his penchant for racket, nor the terror he wreaks on innocent, drive-chain links, gears, and shifter forks every time he bangs a shift. I know I'm getting old and crotchety, but I want someone to please tell me—when did it become "cool" to ride badly?

You and I are, of course, paragons of smoothness, but there's always the odd clunk, lurch, or wobble to intrude on our reverie. One problem is that street riding is a difficult activity to simulate within a tight, repeatable context. Consider this: over the course of a summer, a golf or tennis pro would observe your swing *thousands* of times. Take a yearly

Motorcycle Safety Foundation (MSF) Experienced RiderCourse, and your instructor may get a half-dozen looks at your braking. *Shifting*—a skill which I'd argue is far more complex than any golf or tennis swing—won't even get a mention, because it's considered so basic.

One of the smoothest riders I've had the good fortune to watch is the MSF's Bob Reichenberg. He'd better be; as education manager, one of his primary duties is to train chief instructors—the riders who train the riders who train the nation's riders.

"The first step to smoothness," says Reichenberg, "is good visual habits. You're not gonna be smooth if you're always surprised."

Motoki and Yamazaki, researchers from the Japan Automobile Research Institute and Honda Safety Driving Center, used an eye camera to record the visual patterns of motorcyclists watching a traffic video. Print-outs show that experienced riders (safety instructors in the study) scanned much more aggressively and had fewer fixations than student riders.

"Another thing," adds Reichenberg, "is to really consciously practice control transitions. If you do it properly, you don't get unexpected chassis movements."

One of the most common sources of transitional wobbles is going from the brakes to the throttle, as you do at the entrance of a turn. AMA Legislative Affairs Specialist Jim Bensberg is another seriously smooth rider, but he took four trips to Reg Pridmore's CLASS (see *Rider*, March 1994) before figuring it out.

"It's really pretty simple," relates Bensberg, a trace of incredulity in his voice, " . . . you just keep the front brake on a little bit with two fingers as you start to roll the throttle, and the front end doesn't suddenly pop up on you." He credits CLASS's David Murray with toggling the right light bulb for him.

Keith Code, the legendary road race coach and author of the world's best-selling books on riding technique, the *Twist of the Wrist* series, has given considerable thought to the brake/throttle transition. When he ran the California Superbike School, he developed the "smoothometer," which is simply a hydraulic pressure gauge spliced into the brake line of a stationary control layout. During simulated transitions, the gauge was able to predict wild chassis gyrations before a rider ever turned a wheel on the track.

"You don't want to squeeze the brake lever directly with your fingers," warns Code. "What you want is a rotating surface—either your glove slides over the lever, or your fingers slide inside the glove, depending upon how tight your glove is." He recommends installing a piece of shrink tubing over the brake lever—just loose enough to rotate freely. There's another, more tangible reason for the addition. "... so your glove doesn't get pooched out. Gloves are expensive!"

Transitional difficulties can be exacerbated by the machinery, particularly on motorcycles with a fair amount of driveline lash. Both chain- and shaft-drive bikes can suffer this affliction, characterized by the "thunks" and chassis pitching as the throttle is opened or closed. Those whose riding includes lots of bumps, sharp corners, or steep grades are most likely to notice it.

One remedy for driveline lash is the old dirt-biker's trick of feathering the clutch with one or two fingers as you go through sharp turns—you know, the kind that are too fast for a downshift to first gear but too slow for second. Another useful strategy on certain bikes is to lightly drag the rear brake, even as you throttle through the turn. This also helps to keep the rear suspension under steady compression.

The idea of both techniques is to maximize your good throttle manners. For a lesson in throttle smoothness I suggest you order a copy of *On Any Sunday* and check out the Japanese speedway sequences. In one of the world's more bizarre racing venues, competitors duel on a paved oval—with rigid-framed British twins! To the hardcore gamblers who patronize the events, these racers are of no more interest than the mechanical rabbit at a greyhound track, but they are the Nijinskys and Nureyevs of throttle control, turning lap after lap with nary a bobble. The aftermarket shock builders do *not* want you to see how smoothly these guys go around the track!

Shifting is a skill which the average rider gives little thought to, but not the expert. "One of the biggest problems," claims Reichenberg, "is riders disengaging the clutch too far. Once you've found your engagement point, don't squeeze the lever in any further than you have to.'

"Another thing that helps, I think, is to preload the shift lever a little before you shift gears." (This is a *momentary* action, not the drag racing maneuver of holding the lever up and waiting for the engine to hit the rev limiter!)

"I'm for things that make riding simpler," adds Code, who rarely uses the clutch to upshift. His personal advice is to back off the throttle quickly—"just long enough for the motor to go into neutral load." That would be the point at which the engine is turning at exactly the right rate to match road speed to the new gear, thereby making the clutch redundant.

Personally, I like to believe that there is no motorcycle on which I can't execute clunkless shifts, although I admit it sometimes requires a lot of practice and experimentation. A friend of mine, a master mechanic, takes that one step further. He claims that by riding any bike for 20 minutes, he can make it *run* smoother! It makes some sense. After all, high-performance engines prefer to be worked throughout their rev bands, receiving a smooth, steady fuel delivery. Which kind of brings us full circle, in that the rider without good visual habits—who's constantly surprised—is going to make unsure erratic throttle applications.

"When I think I'm getting real good," concludes Reichenberg, "I put a passenger on the back. You can't hide from those little turtle kisses on the helmet."

A good passenger just might be the ultimate secret of smoothness. Code says he applies the same test to his clutchless shifts and Pete Woodruff, the education director of the Gold Wing Road Riders Association, has been promoting two-up Experienced RiderCourses across the country. He's enthused with the results.

"It helps shifting, turning, and especially mountain riding," say Woodruff. "We find that the two-up rider is better trained, because he's got Momma sittin' behind him talkin' to him on the intercom!"

Perhaps my feckless neighbor should trade the Barbie Doll for something more stable and reliable. A Ford Taurus wagon, perhaps?

The Meaning of Whoosh

September 2001

I'll never forget discovering "whoosh."

There I was, very happy to be one of six students, listening intently during a roadside chat on a 3-day Ohio training tour. I had known Larry for some time, and had finally coordinated my work schedule with his tours. Feeling myself to be the least experienced rider in the group, and the only woman, I was excited and nervous. I put 100 percent of my energy into learning, wanting very much to improve and not look like a fool in the process.

The previous year, when I had first started riding, as I approached curves my mantra of comfort was Larry's advice, "You can never go into a turn too slowly," (adding the qualifier, "... unless you're wobbling"). I might not ride as fast as the other "guys", but at least Larry had promised this was no disadvantage when it came to cornering. Now he seemed to contradict his advice.

"I want you to give the bike a little throttle entering these upcoming turns." He continued, "You can never enter a turn too slowly, but you can proceed through a turn too slowly." What? No way! I thought it was "Slow, Look, Lean, and Roll;" not "Slow, Look, Speed Up, Lean ..." This was new. Had I misunderstood all along?

I asked him to repeat this very strange concept—add throttle as you go into a turn? With delight and patience, Larry explained about speed lost as one leans the bike, the difference in the circumference of the tire in the middle vs. the outer edges, gear ratios, etc. That sounded a bit like Greek to me, but the thought that I might be stabilized by a slight increase in throttle was very enticing.

I gave it a try. All that afternoon I practiced on a zillion curves in those crazy Ohio roads. What a revelation! What a thrill. Whoosh! Every turn—whoosh on through!

My riding confidence and fun ratio went sky high. Larry

gave me the gift of whoosh that day and I've not forgotten it. The new feeling of stability and control that came with that "simple" lesson elevated me to the category of riders who experience wind in the face as a thrill rather than fear. I began to embrace riding in a new way—one closer to Larry's clear passion for this thrilling sport.

Donn Joann Brous, gallery manager, writer, artist,
Stayin' Safe Motorcycle Training student

Motorcycling is sensational. Though MSFniks (Motorcycle Safety Foundation-niks) are fond of saying that it's "90 percent mental and 10 percent physical," we don't ride because it makes us feel like Einstein; the pay-off for engaging our cerebra is that we get to tickle our fun buttons.

I'll leave it to our ineffable touring editor to extol the planet's natural and cultural wonders as experienced from two wheels. As I see it, motorcycling's seminal sensations—any one of which is reason enough to ride a bike—are 1) wind in the face, 2) euphoric feelings produced by escalating G-forces in positive and negative acceleration, 3) the mood-enhancing pulses of machinery transmitted through the muscular-skeletal system, 4) sound waves emitted within an inexplicably pleasing frequency range, 5) the perception of beauty in a man-made object, and 6) . . . *whoosh.*

What is *whoosh?* Well, it has something to do with leaning, but if leaning was such a pleasure in and of itself, California would be filled with New Age leaning parlors, and cable television would abound with miraculous new home-leaning products that nick your Visa card for $99.99 plus shipping and handling. There's got to be more to it.

Whoosh, quite simply, is cornering, but cornering isn't quite that simple. Why do you think Keith Code has devoted an entire school to it? I consulted my Webster's, and the closest I came to a satisfying explanation was definition #23 "(of an automobile) to turn, esp. at a speed, relatively high for the angle of the turn involved."

By "relatively high" I suppose they mean higher than the average driver would negotiate it—which makes cornering sound rather naughty. But even though the average automobile can corner harder than the average motorcycle, it needs no speed whatsoever to remain, stable in a turn. Alas, without speed, the motorcycle requires an inordinate amount of balance and/or steering. That said, the motorcycle really doesn't need a higher than average speed in order to "corner"—to go *whoosh.*

What it needs is a rider with correct timing, one who is willing and able to combine leaning and power in the correct amounts for the entry speed and radius of the turn. It's almost impossible to approach a turn too slowly to corner. Watch a top motor cop swing his Harley around from a dead stop and what you're watching is cornering. "Swerving" and "counterbalancing" are equally valuable turning skills, but the police-style 140-degree curb-side pullout is leaning 'er in and driving 'er out from the lowest possible entry speed—*zero.*

The reason some riders wobble into turns probably isn't because they approach too slowly. More likely, it's because they slow down and stay there for too long. Anyone who's ever taken an MSF course probably remembers the "slow/look/lean and roll" mantra, but I coach my students to apply a smidgen of throttle before they initiate the lean. One of my students, fresh from two days at Freddie Spencer's High Performance Riding School, recently brought to my attention that Spencer and his chief instructor, Nick Ienatsch, instruct students to do practically the opposite of what I teach—to brake all the way to the apex of the turn. What do those guys know? *Faaast* Freddie—hah! One of his three world championships wasn't even in the 500cc class. And Ienatsch? A mere *U.S. 250 GP champion*—not even an international competitor!

Resumes aside, safely lapping the Las Vegas Motor Speedway, where Spencer and Ienatsch teach, has got to be simpler than negotiating Ohio's "Triple Nickel" (SR555—58 rail-thin miles with over a thousand changes of direction and elevation, scatologically improvised with gravel and equine emissions). The lines between the fastest experts at LVMS might differ by only inches, but recreational riders can rely on the track's generous dimensions to carry plenty of momentum into each corner, confident that they have the time and space to smoothly transfer weight from the front (steering) wheel to the rear (driving).

Already 50–80 percent narrower than a racetrack, a twisty road throws in ditches, guardrails, and oncoming traffic—much of which you can't see upon entering the turn—to further shrink the tolerable line. If one is to safely carry momentum into the bend, he'd better know where the turn goes or set an entry speed low enough to feed in some chassis-stabilizing throttle. To see what I mean, grab a pen and some notebook-size sheets of paper (or better yet a dry marker board) and try the following experiment:

First, start in the upper right corner and draw a rapid, counterclockwise arc toward the lower right corner, tightening the arc into a U before you reach the bottom of the page. Maybe you'll need a couple of tries, but it's not that difficult (remember—you might do 50 laps on a typical track day).

Second step: Draw the same big rapid arc, but then curl your U in the opposite direction (clockwise) at about the halfway mark. Within a few attempts, you'll no doubt smooth the transition on that one, too.

Third step: Starting with a clean sheet of paper, ask a friend to verbally instruct you to hook "left" or "right" as you sweep through the major arc. I seriously doubt that you can carry your former speed across the page and still make the turn without running off the page. You're going to have to slow down enough to process the information, and when you do, you'll discover that you achieve the smoothest arc by re-accelerating slightly, then adding more speed once you're assured of being on the correct path. *Whoosh!*

It really matters not whether you ride a sport-bike, a cruiser, or a touring machine, the formula for *whoosh* is the same: A touch of throttle to stabilize the bike; steer in proportion to your entry speed; power through the bend. If you cannot set your lean angle quickly (lazy steering), what you'll experience instead of whoosh, is LYSOB syndrome *(c'mon, lean you . . . !)*. Better to either slow down the entry speed or steer harder. Option A would be the wiser as a first measure.

Although most riders would benefit from more forceful steering, sometimes riders steer too hard in proportion to their speed. I see this primarily in left bends after they've shut off the power, making the bike eager to dive across the centerline. The remedy is to slow down to a speed where you can confidently go in deeper and still give it a "power boost"—i.e. enough throttle to push the bike away from the oncoming lane but not so much that you can't countersteer effectively.

One last thing: a lot of riders lack the confidence to "flick" the bike and to throttle through the bend because they don't realize the effect that leaning has on speed. Take a look at your tires and you'll see that the circumference at the outer tread limit is significantly smaller than the center tread. Therefore, in addition to the energy losses created by turning, you effectively lower your gear ratio every time you lean the bike over. It takes additional throttle just to maintain the entry speed.

Anyhow, all of this presumes that you get a buzz out of #6, going *whoosh*. If it's loud pipes that excite you, I know a bar on the other side of town...

Counting Mississippis

October 2004

You remember the Sesame Street character—an OCD muppet with the Transylvanian accent—who unabashedly loved to count? Substitute "Pennsylvanian" accent-wise and that would be Larry. Whether keeping tally of his own mistakes during a ride, or enumerating drivers failing to signal their intentions to make a lane-change, Mr. Safety could tell you how many times the event in question happened. Quite naturally, it followed when a student asked a question, Larry preferred to quantify the answer, often measured in that simplest element of time—the lowly second.

Pete Tamblyn

Good judgment isn't something you're born with, but improving yours is only a matter of seconds.

About 10 years ago, while riding in the Adirondack Mountains in preparation for a tour article, I came upon what I believed was an excellent photo opportunity. The setting was a river gorge not far from Lake George, and it was such a glorious May morning that I was certain I could capture a trophy shot with the help of my willing travel companion.

We climbed well up the side of the gorge to where we found a window in the trees, I set the camera and tripod for a practically overhead vantage, and scrambled back down to the bike. I don't recall how many takes we shot, but I felt confident that it was enough to get that special shot. I'm no Rich Cox (Slide Action Photography), but sometimes, as the saying goes, even the blind squirrel finds a nut.

This wasn't one of those times. The photo was probably lacking in several key elements, but what I remember most was that it looked like I was riding the motorcycle along the ditch—where you'd expect to find a bicyclist or an old man on a moped. Definitely not cover material.

Had the photo been taken from a different angle—say, road level and behind the bike with a long telephoto lens—it would have been clear that the rider (me) was setting up for a left bend. Well, I've blown lots of photos over the years, but I recall that particular one because a student approached me last month with a question I'd never heard before.

"How soon do you go into position for the left bend?"

I asked for a clarification. "Do you mean when coming down a long straightaway?"

"Yes," replied the student. So, it being a unique question, I asked for the evening to ponder it. In the morning I had my answer.

"Six or seven seconds," I proclaimed, then issued the caveat that my figure precluded the presence of any offending driveways on the right side of the road.

I didn't resort to any higher math to come up with the number. I simply watched a little videotape, then observed my habits over the first half hour of the subsequent morning ride. The more I thought about it, however, the more convinced I grew of the answer's correctness. For starters, we teach that the left wheel track is the "home base" on two-lane roads. On a straightaway, it gives the best road view and places the rider equidistant between driveways on the left and right sides. Jousting with oncoming vehicles is foolhardy to be sure, but it's far easier to migrate over a few feet for an approaching car than it is to swerve or brake when a driver darts out of a blind driveway on your right.

Back to the "six or seven seconds." MSF courses refer to the four-second "immediate path of travel." In other words, scenarios four seconds out front are more than just data gathered during the scanning process; they are cause for action. So, four seconds would be the absolute latest that you'd set your lane position, but why not get over there another two seconds early and improve your view in the bargain?

That little exercise in bonehead math got me thinking about all of the other riding situations that can be better managed by quantifying—in seconds—how much time should be allotted to the task. Some of you readers probably have a few of your own to add to the following list.

One second

Because lane positioning is such a dynamic process, I ask my students not to pull away from a traffic signal or stop sign at the same instant I do. I figure one second should allow a riding partner to establish where they wish to position their bike for passing through the intersection.

Two seconds

The minimum following distance. Everyone knows this, right? Maybe not. I doubt there's one motorist in 10 who can accurately estimate "car lengths" at 60 mph, yet that remains the standard of reference for so many. I reckon two seconds is also a good interval between signaling for and executing a lane change.

Three seconds

The minimum time needed to apply brakes smoothly before a bend. The idea is to efficiently transfer weight onto the front wheel (for deceleration) and then return it to the back wheel (for acceleration). That all takes time, and when it's done effectively the brake light typically remains lit for at least three seconds.

Three-four seconds

That's how often I like to check mirrors in dense traffic situations.

Four seconds

MSFs "immediate path of travel" is possibly the most significant number in street riding. For me it's the minimum sight line in a corner. I think it's also the maximum amount of time one should spend in the act of overtaking on a two-lane road. Think about this: if you can see four seconds into a curve (or to a blind summit), an approaching car could be *two* seconds or less away from intercepting your path. I submit that by *definition,* anything which requires a full response (search/predict/act) in less than two seconds is an "emergency" response.

Five-six seconds

Normal mirror check intervals on open stretches of road. Also, a good interval between signaling for and initiating a turn or freeway exit.

Six-seven seconds

As noted above, the transition time from straightaway (left wheel track) to left corner entry position (right wheel track).

Ten seconds

Beginner gap selection. I know that a lot of new riders read this column, and when I take rookies on the road for the first time, I have them wait at a few stop signs and count the seconds between a vehicle's appearance on the horizon and its arrival at the intersection. At first we don't pull out if there are *any* cars in sight, but we strive to quickly recognize a 10-second gap when we see one. From there we incrementally reduce the gap selection until it is similar to what the new rider would find acceptable behind the wheel of his or her automobile.

12 seconds

Normal scanning distance. How far up the road we'd *like* to be able to see. Think of it as information to be processed but not necessarily acted upon.

What is 12 seconds? Or six? Or three? I think that a clear appreciation of "one Mississippi, two Mississippi . . ." should be a prerequisite to using the road, whether on two, four or 18 wheels. When I've been off the bike for a while or when I'm on a strange bike or a busy two-lane road, I like to practice my "Mississippis" by estimating the arrival time of each vehicle as it first appears on the horizon. For example: "eight Mississippi, seven Mississippi, six. . . ." Normally I'm accurate to within a second, but if I'm not, I don't pull out to pass until my estimates are consistently accurate.

Speed and distance judgment is a well-known casualty of the aging process, but like strength and endurance losses it can be greatly mitigated with training. And you don't have to sweat for hours in a gym. It's just a matter of seconds.

Gimmee Five

May 2004

"Is it really safe to ride that many miles like they do in the Iron Butt?" a student once asked. Always one to enjoy answering a question with a question, Larry responded, "Which do you think is safer; riding 11,000 miles in eleven days or 1,000 miles each year over eleven years?" He assured the student the stats were in favor of the long distance riding community.

A mid-life career change for me once forced this question: shall I still occasionally fly private aircraft whenever I can afford the extra bucks? During the last visit to the airport following over a month's absence from the cockpit, I was stale and out of touch. Knowing the absences would likely lengthen, I flew no more. The essence of Larry's message in this column is identical: if you're not riding at least 5,000 miles per year, find another hobby.

Pete Tamblyn

NHTSA stats indicate that motorcycle fatalities have been climbing since 1998. Could it be that we've forgotten how to ride?

This week I won a major battle in the war against winter. It snowed 25 days in the last month, but on Sunday I did something I hadn't done in 10 years—race around a frozen pond on a big thumper with 200 spikes in each tire. I figure each of the four hours I spent churning ice bought a week of mental health.

Now I know that doesn't seem an appropriate opening for a May column, but fret not—this isn't a primer on winter riding. Hack writers just like to use winter as a metaphor for loneliness, despair, and even death—which, coincidentally, are the three stages of motorcycle deprivation.

As I write this, I've not ridden a motorcycle beyond my little neighborhood in two and a half months.

Never before, not in the coldest winter, have I gone so long without a real ride, and that makes me wonder—maybe it's not just winter. Maybe it's me.

I know it's my friends. Within my inner circle, few still commute to work regularly on their bikes, and only one does so faithfully all winter long. They all have electric vests and cold-weather riding suits. Most have fairings. They're not sissies. Were they on tour when the arctic clipper swooped in, I'm sure most would layer up and keep riding until the roads became dangerously slick. But they've all got cars, too, and warm homes full of projects that not riding might make a dent in.

Maybe you noticed—no, of course you noticed—that motorcycle accidents and fatalities are on the rise again. Now NHTSA can give you figures for fatalities per million miles ridden, but no one at the agency would dare claim that their mileage figures are anything more than educated guesses. So far they've hitched their theories to the empirical fact that more older riders are dying on rural roads . . . but could it be that more rusty riders are accidents waiting for nice, sunny, country weekends to happen?

Like many riders, I'm addicted to the motorcycle classifieds. In the old days, you wouldn't find diddly this time of year, but thanks to the Internet, you can now find a 1962 Tohatsu Runpet Sport and kick its tires over your dining room table at 3 a.m. on the coldest day in January. So I conducted a little online research project, admittedly not scientific, but valid enough for our informal venue. I picked Zip Codes from three major cities—Miami, San Francisco and Chicago—and then I randomly searched for three-year-old (2001) motorcycles within a 25-mile radius, jotting down odometer mileage until I had 20 samples from each region.

I didn't bother with any details of style or hardware; they could be cruisers, sport-bikes, or tourers, so long as they displaced 250cc or more. There were flaws in my research, no doubt. I don't know how many motorcycles each advertiser owned or what year these '01 bikes were first registered, but like most real (i.e. funded) scientists I got the result I'd hypothesized.

Chicago, with its insufferably long winters, yielded the bikes with the lowest mileage—an average of 3,375 or 1,125 per year. In Miami, where some riders scale back their riding to escape the intense summer heat, average mileage was about 50 percent greater than Chi-town's—4,790, or 1,597 per year. San Francisco, with year-round riding, a vibrant moto culture and good access to brilliant roads, averaged 6,970, or 2,323 per year.

Flushed with success (and not all that anxious to go for a ride in single-digit temperatures), I turned my prognosticative powers on the larger world. I've reported before on this page that many western European nations, despite their statistically deadlier highways, show lower fatality rates among their two-wheeled populations. A partial explanation might be the more rigorous training and licensing standards of most EC nations, but I hypothesized that Europeans stay sharper by racking up more miles on a daily basis. Not wanting to do any more math than I had to, I pointed my mouse where the odometers already count in miles. Good old eBay Motors UK proved me right once again, though not to the extent I'd expected.

In the '70s and '80s, I learned about English motorcycling in the company of London dispatch riders—merry misfits who averaged over a thousand miles a week in traffic that was even more oppressive than their rainy weather. The British bike industry was dead, the economy was wobbly, and biking as a hobby had lost just about all its appeal. Today, Britain once again has a thriving motorcycle scene, fueled by the rise of "Born Again Bikers"—middle-agers who can afford a car for necessary travel and a cycle for fun. So I shouldn't have been surprised to see lots of low-mileage bikes across the pond as well—average: 10,441 or 3,180 per year. Hardly dispatch-rider mileage, but still triple the Chicago average and double that of Miami, a place with 20 times as many warm, sunny days.

During my online interlude in Miami, I stumbled upon a more startling discovery: the mother lode of wrecked motorcycles. Ad after ad reverberated with the words "rebuildable title" and "certificate of destruction." I quit counting after the first 30 ads, 19 of which made reference to bikes which had been crashed hard enough in their brief three-year lives to have been written off by an insurance company.

I probably shouldn't have been surprised. Today's motorcycles have so many more pieces to break, and who has the time to master all their explosive complexities? Many of us who once bungeed duffel bags to our seats, then rode day and night to explore new destinations, have acquired a taste for instant gratification. In the '90s, we enjoyed an ever-increasing variety of rental and package tour options, but it appears that trend is reversing. A number of U.S. rental agencies have folded since 9/11, unable to afford their escalating insurance premiums.

It always comes down to greedy insurance companies, right? Well, not always. One large rental company, having enjoyed good success with touring bikes, recently purchased a fleet of 10 Honda VFRs as an experiment. If things went well, they were going to go nationwide with soft-core sport-bikes—but things didn't. Not one of the 10 survived its rookie season without crashing and going on the injured reserve list.

Meanwhile, down in Mexico, where it's easier to buy bullfighting insurance than to rent a moto, a group of bodacious investors has been eyeing a snowcapped volcano and envisioning one of the world's highest ski resorts, within two hours of 45 million people! In a country already beset with environmental nightmares, they'll have to level mountains of opposition, but what if they succeed? Try to imagine the epidemic of heart attacks and other health calamities that would ensue if the doors of Mexico City's offices and factories suddenly swung open, releasing millions with no previous ski experience and already corroded lungs to engage in eight-hour exercise binges at 14,000 feet above sea level!

That's what I see in my mind's eye, when I watch so many motorcyclists parade their cherished escape vehicles on so few perfect Sundays.

Do me a favor. Gimme five—5,000 miles. While the year is young, make a pledge to ride to work at least twice a week when the temperature's more than 50 degrees. Twice a month, April through October, turn your cell phone off and don't touch it until you've added at least 200 miles to your odometer. Once per week, while the evenings are long, spend a half hour practicing quick stops and low-speed maneuvers in a parking lot. . . then take off on a two-hour mental health ride.

You'll need to draw on those reserves in January when it's five below.

Gear

Wear a Real Riding Suit

The Face People

May 1994

Larry Grodsky was never afraid to take on a tough topic and this discussion of facial protection in helmets is a prime example. Larry looked at the complex issues surrounding facial and related head protection and did his darndest to throw the doo-doo out there hoping that it would get cleaned up. He was shameless in calling up those of us who knew something, to pick our brains and didn't always call back to double-check his facts or conclusions. But that was part of Larry's writings' appeal—intelligent ideas floated out into the world of motorcycling to shake things up and help us all at Stayin' Safe. The irony of his death on a motorcycle is painful to all of us who try to beat the odds by training ourselves and wearing the right gear. Larry's legacy lives on in his writings which are still topical and worth reading again and again.

David Thom, Collision and Injury Dynamics, Inc.
El Segundo, California

Touring riders will never wear full-face helmets. So said the motorcycle industry pundits, years after the integral design had become the standard in racing. But then sometime, probably around the mid-'80s, things began to change. Touring riders did start to trade in their open-face lids. Having counted heads at several recent Rider rallies, I'd peg full-face use at about two-thirds.

Why the change? Could it be that air of poised aggression so coveted by knee-draggers and bank robbers? Maybe, but I'd contend it's a manifestation of the self-indulgent "Me Generation;" when the lid comes off, people want a face that looks beautiful . . . or at least "normal."

Remember "face" is the operative word here. When guys in lab coats use the term "full coverage" helmets, they're speaking of the ones that shroud the cranium. Jawbones, cheekbones, noses, and the like mean big bucks to skilled surgeons—but they're generally not considered life threatening.

They are also useful—in the now-famous lexicon of Australian hellbender Dr. Rodney Cooter—"energy absorbing" material. Apparently two out of three touring riders would prefer to relegate that task to a fiberglass or polycarbonate chinbar, but the truth is, we're not exactly sure how the thing is supposed to work.

Cooter, whose study "Motorcyclist Craniofacial Injury Patterns" rocked MSF's 1990 International Conference, has called for a collapsible chinbar. But the Snell Memorial Foundation, the only U.S. testing organization with a chinbar standard, tests for *rigidity*—by pressing the bar backward into the immobilized helmet. Even the University of Southern California's Dave Thom, a vocal critic of Cooter's work, concedes that Snell's chinbar test makes little sense. "In a motorcycle accident, you normally slam your helmet against something," says Thom.

Here's where the two part company: Cooter has devoted two papers to his hypothesis that blows delivered to the chinbar can cause a forward rotation of the helmet, resulting in extreme chinstrap forces loaded into the mandibular rami (jawbone pivots). The jawbone, says the Australian, can then fracture the skull base in a region called the *spheno-occipital synchondrosis*—a mortal wound.

A 1991 paper by Germany's Dietmar Otte states that Cooter's findings "absolutely correspond" with his own. However, Otte at no point singles out the chinstrap as an injury mechanism—just the jaw itself.

"Accident data is filled with cases of the jawbone fracturing the skull base," asserts Thom. In fact, as early as 1981, the Hurt report (of which Thom is the No. 2 author) stated, "In those instances of severe impact to the mandible, the transmitted force can generate fractures at the base of the skull with deadly consequences."

So what gives—are chinbars smoking guns, or not? Stay with me; maybe you can decide for yourself.

Otte gathered impact data from periodic tests of Europe's popular helmets (1984, '87, '91). In the '84 test each helmet was dropped onto its chinbar from a height of one meter (at a rate of about 7 mph). Inside each lid, an ECE "test head" with an integrated triaxial accelerometer recorded the Gs upon impact. Thirteen of 20 helmets exceeded the instrument's measurable ceiling of 400 Gs, although there were several strong performers. The Shoei, one of the few of that era to feature EPS in the chinbar, registered a mere 88 Gs.

Three years later another group of helmets was tested, using a Hybrid

II headform, which, unlike the ECE and DOT models, features an anatomically correct human face. Deceleration values dropped by an average of two-thirds on the Hybrid II, which suggests something about the importance of a good fit. In addition to deceleration, the '87 test also measured forces (in Newtons) at the chin and chinstrap.

Not surprisingly, chin force closely correlated to deceleration, but strap force proved *inversely* proportional to the performance of the chinbar! The model with the worst face protection had the lowest strap force (140 N—2.5 percent of its chin force), while one of the "better" chinbars transmitted an astonishing 1,200 N (270 pounds-feet) to the strap—more, even, than went into the chin!

Otte attributes the poor chinbar performance to tight clearance and insufficient padding. The high strap force on the other helmet he blames on too much clearance. Neither model, by the way, was ever sold in America.

Round 3: In 1991—*after* Cooter's charges had enraged motorcycling's intelligentsia, 13 fresh models were assembled for the same test battery. Both measures of chinbar performance continued to show improvement, and seven models registered chinstrap forces of 250 N or less—compared to only one in '87. Shoei's RF200 showed a 75-percent reduction in strap force over the earlier RF105. Had it been available four years earlier, the 200 would have claimed the laurels for lowest deceleration *and* chinstrap load. Do *you* think the Shoei people regard Cooter as a quack?

Shoei wasn't the only star of the 1991 test. BMWs System III (manufactured by Schuberth) was equally impressive. What—did I hear a beemerphile groan that you can't buy a System III here? *Quelle Surprise!* Actually, there are lots of excellent helmets you won't find on your dealer's shelf. The Japanese brand DIC won the '92 helmet shootout in Germany's *Motorrad* magazine, beating out the best from Japan and Europe. Won't it be interesting if, in a few years' time, we have 50 helmet-law states and *no* manufacturers offering lids for sale in them. In case you haven't already noticed, virtually all helmets are now manufactured overseas.

By the way, while I don't know how they'd withstand a high-speed blow, or one from an oblique angle, neither the System II nor System III models exhibited evidence of flaws in their hinged chinbar designs.

Now, if you want to take this article and ring up that lawyer who advertises at 2 a.m. on your local UHF channel, there's one more thing you ought to know. Otte, like our Harry Hurt, has collected a whole lot of data on a whole lot of motorcycle accidents. And not even the owner of the oldest, cheesiest, full-face helmet was found to have suffered a skull base fracture from a chin impact of less than 25 mph.

Snell tests helmets at about 17 mph, DOT calls for 13 . . . and neither one certifies that you'll *live* after one of those blows. Can a human survive a 25-mph frontal impact—with or without a full-face helmet? I'll let your shiny-suited lawyer see what kind of expert testimony he can recruit.

Maybe we still don't know exactly how a chinbar should work, but there's no doubt they save face. To maintain the optimum balance between chin forces and strap forces, choose a helmet whose chinbar has adequate but not excessive clearance (try using your index finger as a feeler gauge). Look for a bar that's rounded—not squared or pointy—to better deflect forces. And be sure it's lined with EPS (expanded polystyrene foam).

We, at *Rider*, would like to see DOT rid us of its antiquated chinstrap requirement (Snell '95 will have a superior retention test that necessitates no strap). As we've repeatedly emphasized in these pages, the state of the art is continually improving, and we think standards should reflect that. When did you last replace your helmet?

A Slippery Slope for Head Protection

March 2003

I first met Larry back in the 1980s when he introduced himself at a motorcycle safety gathering and started discussing helmets. Larry had lots of ideas and opinions and wasn't afraid to air them.

I remember Larry's phone call clearly because it became part of my life for more than two years. Larry's idea was that riders would be better off wearing a light-weight, well-ventilated helmet (sort of like a bicycle or ski helmet) rather than a fake helmet or nothing at all. Larry and I took the idea to the only active, multidisciplinary helmet committee in the country. Larry attended meetings and presented a survey he had done about helmet choices. The project led us to the halls of DOT where it ultimately was mired down by governmental red tape and liability concerns.

Plus, who but Larry would quote a "leading authority" as saying, "Oh s—t, I forgot my helmet!" (I'm sure I said "shoot" . . . or maybe shout . . .) If you are, or know, a rider who likes the feel of a bare head parting the wind, follow Larry's logic and get yourself a nice bike or ski helmet that you can forget you even have on.

David Thom, Collision and Injury Dynamics, Inc.
El Segundo, California

My first full-face helmet, a polycarbonate Nava, was absolutely the rage in 1980, thanks to its jaunty Italian design and affordable price point. It was also one noisy SOB, and a hard gaze would scratch its delicate shield, but I never once considered going back to an open-face model. Three years later I bought a Shoei RF105, a fiberglass unit which cost more but fit securely, offered a durable shield, and even featured adjustable vents.

I've owned dozens of helmets since that old Shoei, but none struck me as having broken new ground. To my knowledge, neither the

Department of Transportation nor the Snell Memorial Foundation have revised their standards over the last 20 years in response to technical advances in helmet design.

Ah, but I'm *in love* with the new Giro Fuse, a unit which, like all ski and snowboard helmets, carries a clear warning that it is *not* intended for motorsports use. My adoration springs first and foremost from its lightness—14.5 ounces, or about one quarter the weight of a top-line Arai or Suomy. The Fuse is an open-face unit, which partially explains its lightness, but the greatest weight savings is in the shell. Its gossamer-thin latticework looks much like a bicycling helmet, which should come as no surprise; Giro is one of the two largest manufacturers of cycling headgear.

Even before the Fuse I marveled over the lightness of ski helmets and pondered how they might offer an alternative to so-called "fake" helmets, the strap-on skull caps designed to appease law enforcement even though they have no energy absorbing expanded polystyrene foam (EPS). Forty-seven states require helmet use, if only for minors, yet voluntary use is no better than 50 percent. Put another way, there are probably 3 or 4 million U.S. motorcyclists and passengers who ride bareheaded or with fake helmets. Wouldn't they be better served by a government which encouraged—or at least permitted—the use of lightweight ski helmets such as the Fuse?

I put my idea before the Head Protection Research Laboratory's Senior Program Manager David Thom, perhaps the nation's leading authority on crash helmets. Thom is a scientist, suffers fools politely at best, and has known me for 15 years. He has never hesitated to tell me when I'm suffering from a hare-brained delusion, so imagine my delight at his response.

"Oh yeah, that would be a *great* alternative!" he said. "They'd be wearing a *real* helmet!" An avid runner and bicyclist, Thom went on to recount a recent experience while downhill mountain biking in California.

"I got a couple minutes down the mountain, when suddenly I thought, 'Oh s—t, I forgot my helmet!'" But Thom had *not* forgotten his helmet. He'd borrowed Qiro's top-line bicycle hat, the Switchblade (so named for its detachable chinbar). Now, have you ever owned a motorcycle helmet so light and unobtrusive that you forgot that you were wearing it? Not likely.

Brightened by my positive response from Dave Thom, I turned to Ed

Becker, executive director of the Snell Memorial Foundation, whose voluntary M2000 standard is widely considered to be more stringent than the mandatory DOT certification. Would Snell ever consider a "B standard" for riders who don't really like helmets?

"We think that an M2000 helmet is the minimum you should wear every time you ride," replied Becker, obviously not so enamored of the idea. "You need to wear all of the helmet you can get."

When he says "We think," Mr. Becker, an MIT trained engineer, is obviously editorializing. Although dedicated to scientific research, the Snell Foundation's roots are emotional. It was founded as a tribute to amateur car racer William "Pete" Snell, who died of massive head injuries suffered in a 1956 crash. Nearly three decades passed before the foundation established a standard unique to motorcycling (M1985). Are the protective needs of cruising and touring riders significantly different than an SCCA or AMA racer's? Snell says "no," but half of America's riders say "yes."

For those riders who demand maximum protection, the cost of test fees, acquisition, shipping, and random testing comes to 80 cents per Snell-approved helmet, and Becker doesn't hesitate to remind us that manufacturer participation is purely voluntary.

"If DOT comes out with a Snell standard, we're out of business. We'll dry up and blow away."

Don't worry about Becker's job security. Even though DOT is at work on an updated and presumably "better" standard, the Snell Foundation is far from dust. Not only has the organization developed separate standards for car racing and motorcycling, it's also branched into karting, bicycling, rollerblading, skateboarding, equestrian sports (separate standards for horseback and harness racing), snowboarding, and—of course—skiing. To my eye it appears that they not only have a "B standard" but "C" through "J" as well.

So how does a Snell-approved ski helmet stack up against an approved motorcycle lid? In the principal tests—the flat and hemi anvil impacts— the Snell moto helmet must survive a more than three-meter drop onto each, while the Snell ski lid must survive drops of two-plus meters and 1.6-plus meters. Put another way, that's 150 joules for *la moto* and 100/80 for *le ski*. But that's just part of the story.

DOT's hemi and flat anvil setup is actually *less* severe than the Snell ski tests—90 joules and 67.6 respectively! Plus, all Snell tests specify a pass/fail threshold of 300g peak acceleration, while DOT permits up to 400g. So the Snell ski standard is actually tougher than the DOT motorcycle standard, no? Well . . . there's more to it.

Approved motorcycle helmets must survive *two* impacts. It's doubtful that a thin-shelled ski or bicycle helmet would fare well in such a competition, or against the sharp "edge anvil" used by Snell (but not by DOT). DOT imposes a strict (though controversial) chinstrap test which the lovely Giro with its plastic buckle would probably fail. The Feds do not, however, have a roll-off test (such as the one which Thom and his HPRL associates have devised), which is a better measure of helmet retention. Many DOT-approved "shorty" helmets fail the roll-off test miserably, while the Fuse ski helmet, thanks to its generous basal skull coverage, would probably breeze through the test.

Besides its weight advantage, there's another area where the Giro Fuse opens a big can of whupass on all motorcycle helmets—climate control. It features probably 100 times the venting area, and yet all of those vents close with the flick of one easily accessible lever. Combine that with a snuggly, washable, and detachable ear flap/liner and you have a hat that warms you in cold weather and cools you in hot.

David Thom's former boss, the noted Professor Harry Hurt, once quipped, "Tell me what kind of accident you're going to have, and I'll design the perfect helmet for it." If today is the day you're going to run afoul of a pointy wrought iron fence, I hope you're not wearing a Swiss-cheese ski or bicycle hat . . . but I'd say blunt force traumas far outnumber the head injuries inflicted by sharp and pointy objects.

Whatever your preferences, *please* don't mistake this column for a scientific treatise on helmet effectiveness. Much as I love the Giro ski helmet, I'll continue to ride with a full-face Snell- or DOT-approved motorcycle model. I just wonder how many tragedies might be averted if we gave riders a reasonable alternative to novelty helmets.

To learn more about helmet design and standards, visit the Snell Memorial website at www.smf.org.

Putting a Lid on the Bull

March 2004

Larry was a vocal critic of the unyielding, single set of DOT standards governing the sale of any item labeled "motorcycle helmet" which doggedly refused to recognize the possibility of a middle ground. Unfortunately, no bureaucratic break-throughs came of a dialog he joined regarding the merits of a compromise helmet—one perhaps more acceptable to those who otherwise chose a bare head .

Richard Black, one of Larry's favorite riding buddies, comes to mind. The comments of his wife, Patti Troth Black, are sum-marized:

"My husband Richard rides daily, prefers motorcycles to any car, and simply and without fanfare does not wear a hel-met. Instead, he wears an ancient leather aviator's cap, or sim-ply good eye protection. I envisage his first encounter with Larry was filled with contention. Although often colorfully and indefatigably opinionated, Grodsky could switch posi-tions on a given issue with enviable agility. Richard—who nei-ther defends nor explains—quietly perceived this to show Grodsky's thoroughness at not only seeing, but assuming, all aspects of a controversy—even one as fraught with dissension as the helmet question. Larry's openness allowed them to prog-ress to becoming fast and genuine friends, quickly discarding their opening banter.

"In 1995, the three of us spent several weeks in Central Mex-ico together. Each time they set out, Larry donned the latest safety "lid." Richard pulled on an old pair of beveled aviator goggles, or occasionally the leather cap that went with them. Off they would go. Like the air in the Central Mexico moun-tains, tension over the helmet issue thinned to almost non-ex-istent. These riders were too busy admiring and respecting one another's riding ability and safety awareness. With time I, too, ceased noticing the difference in their headgear. They

appeared exactly the same—each a single streamlined, lyrical motion — aware, skilled, and clearly enamored of riding."

Pete Tamblyn

The age-old argument rages on: Which is the better helmet safety standard, Snell or DOT . . . or should it be something else altogether?

Question: Why don't they have helmet standards for bull riding?

Answer: Because the testing laboratories don't have head forms for bulls.

Ba-BING!

OK, I'm not joking. The American Society for Testing and Materials (ASTM) publishes helmet standards for bicycling, snow sports, equestrian competitions, and dozens of other pursuits in which someone inevitably gongs his or her head. At a November meeting in Tampa, Florida, the organization's 50-member headgear committee entertained standards proposals for soccer, Segways (the standup gyro-driven urban scooters), pole vaulting . . . *and* bull riding. You might peg them for safetycrats who want to wrap us all in plastic bubbles and insulate us from anything that might remotely look like fun—but you'd be wrong. They just pay closer attention to the mechanics of head injury than we do.

When track and field officials approached ASTM a few years back, requesting a standard for a pole-vaulting helmet, the committee examined the evidence presented and then plainly told them that they must first fix their sport. Pole vaulters, as you may be aware, can sail up to 20 feet in the air—a height from which no helmet can negate a direct hit. But pole vaulters don't dive bomb onto their heads from 20 feet any more often than motorcyclists ram their helmets at 100 mph into the pavement. Skid lids protect against common injury events such as striking a curb or a car hood. Pole vaulting's nemesis is the "bounce out."

Vaulters, you see, land in a pit of deep foam, usually upon their well-muscled torsos. When a head injury occurs, it's typically after the athlete has bounced off the foam and smacked his head on the surrounding floor. So ASTM told the track-and-field guys to increase the pit size, and *then* they would talk about head protection.

Nowadays when a rodeo cowboy tosses his Stetson into the ring, he may reach for a "Bull Tough" in its place—a 2½-pound helmet with a titanium face guard. Rodeo experts say that a cowboy's greatest risk of head trauma arises when the bull angrily snaps his head back and gores (or at least conks) him in the noggin. In fact—I kid you not—rodeo rules stipulate that an animal be destroyed once it has ascertained that it can eject the rider in this fashion!

"The solution," one Canadian engineer remarked in a sidebar, "is to pad the *bull's* head!" He went on to describe how this could be done in a fashion that lusty rodeo fans would scarcely notice.

You may wonder why, upon scrutinizing your hard-earned purchases, you've never seen an ASTM sticker grace a motorcycle helmet. Well, motorsports are about the only head-banging activities that the organization *doesn't* publish helmet standards for, reasoning that the mandatory DOT and voluntary Snell standards should pretty well cover the field. I'd traveled to Tampa because I didn't feel that was the case, and amazingly the ASTM folks required minimal persuasion. The group voted unanimously to initiate a task force aimed at designing a new motorcycle helmet standard to replace DOT's FM 218—little changed over the past 30 years. These are the reasons why:

1) The number of states which permit adult motorcyclists to ride without a helmet is now 31 and rising.

2) Where helmets are not required by law, voluntary usage is typically 40 percent or less.

3) In helmet-law states the use of "novelty" or "fake" helmets (hard shells with no energy absorbing layer intended only to skirt law enforcement) is rampant.

4) The penetration tests stipulated by DOT and Snell have necessarily resulted in helmets which are hot and heavy—two of the most strenuous objections to helmet usage.

5) The overwhelming majority of head impacts during motorcycle accidents are with flat objects. Penetration injuries are almost unheard of.

I never imagined the level of enthusiasm that the subject would spark. A show of hands revealed that half of the members were active or retired motorcyclists—and what a combined résumé they presented! Dean Fisher, a tack-sharp 80-year-old and the "godfather" of Bell helmets, almost single-handedly authored the original Snell and DOT standards. David Thom of Collision and Injury Dynamics Inc. (and one of the three Hurt Report authors) introduced Dr. Jim Newman as ". . . the man who taught Harry Hurt how to investigate motorcycle accidents. " Regardless of their personal involvement with motorbikes, all of the assembled engineers, physicians, and—yes—*lawyers* seemed to regard the polystyrene-based helmet as motorcycling's magic-bullet gift to head trauma prevention.

Enthusiasm is one thing, but no headdress, regardless of state law, may be legally sold as a "motorcycle helmet" in the United States unless it carries DOT approval. So that could have (and *would* have) been the end of it, had not Dr. Newman turned the tide.

"By building a helmet that is lighter, we can actually make it *more* protective," he emphatically stated. Many helmet experts feel that modern motorcycle helmets, particularly Snell-approved ones, are too hard, a paradox for which Newman provided a curious insight. Polystyrene-lined helmets are designed to absorb "one hit" as opposed to the closed-cell foam used in "multihit" applications such as football helmets. Multihit headgear guards against concussions, but the purpose of a single-hit helmet (and this goes for featherweight bicycle helmets as well as motorcycle lids weighing four times as much) is to prevent skull fractures and severe brain injuries. Snell and DOT differ from most international motorcycle standards by requiring two direct hits in the exact same place—even though the odds against that happening in a real world accident are incalculably high.

"That test," said Newman, "dates back to the days when nobody had a laboratory ceiling high enough to administer a drop test from the optimum height, so instead they dropped the helmet *two* times!"

Another shortcoming of the DOT test (which was reported six years ago in a study that the department funded) is its omission of a roll-off standard. Snell and the European Community (EC) require that motorcycle helmets meet tough standards for retention in an accident. So does our Consumer Product Safety Council (CPSC), the agency which presides over the sale of bicycle helmets in the United States.

Good intentions aside, my recent visit to a dealer open house revealed that our task will be tougher than merely convincing DOT to modernize. When confronted with eight different helmet designs, including snow sports, BMX, and a perforated EC-approved motorcycle helmet, the great majority of riders—lid lovers and lid haters alike—found the lightweight helmets generally off-putting. Many believed that our very hard-shelled novelty helmet would provide more protection than the full-face—*so light you don't know you have it on*—Giro Switchblade, built for downhill bicycle racing! The majority of the riders we surveyed simply could not grasp that the one thing standing between a motorcyclist and a life-threatening brain injury is a six-ounce hemisphere of crushable Styrofoam—even one shot full of holes and covered with a wafer-thin laminate.

Don't get me wrong—there are very good reasons for putting a tough shell on a motorcycle helmet (e.g. a long, fast slide down the asphalt), and maybe somewhere across this vast land there's a rider who's going to impale his or her head on a pointy wrought-iron fence before he or she gets home from the 7-Eleven. But the chances are much greater of slamming it on a curb or car hood and dying from an injury that could have been prevented by a $15 BMX helmet sold at Pep Boys.

Many say motorcycle riders are either for or against helmets, that there's no middle ground. I disagree. Look around and you'll see riders making choices based on weather, speed, and distance traveled. Unfortunately, my survey suggests that they're also basing them on misinformation. Solutions aren't always where or what you expect them to be; sometimes you've gotta put a lid on the bull.

Sartorially Safe

May 1992

Larry was selective about what he wore. He admits to having passed through a "shorts and sneakers" stage in his early riding days, but as an adult, he wore the best gear he could find. Protection came first, followed closely by versatility and comfort considerations. Style was always a distant third; he couldn't care less if the graphics of helmet, boots, and gloves matched so long as they functioned well. Over the years I watched with interest as he searched for the perfect combination of a crash-resistant outer garment that had adequate ventilation, yet was lightweight and easy to slip into. Often he field-tested products for journalistic review, and wasn't shy in telling the manufacturer when an item didn't cut the mustard.

Pete Tamblyn

Inside my closet, there's a riding outfit for every occasion: something to stay warm in; something to stay dry. Something for staying warm *and* dry . . . plus, of course, my lovely goat-skin falling-down, sliding-along-the-road ensemble.

I have heard of lifelong riders who've never fallen off a street bike, and I don't doubt that it's mathematically possible, but among my personal friends—those dozens of riders whose lengthy careers are open to my scrutiny—none can make such a boast. As for myself, the longest I've gone between tumbles is seven years. The shortest, maybe two weeks. Is it any wonder I can never decide what to wear?

Let's ponder all of the things that we ask of a riding suit. In no particular order they are:
1. keep out the wind
2. keep in body heat
3. circulate fresh air
4. protect against abrasions
5. pad bony protuberances such as elbows and knees
6. seal out moisture

7. provide storage for convenience items

8. alert other motorists to our presence

Does that sound like your daily riding outfit?

If you answered "yes," you must be the lucky owner of an Aerostich suit, or something similar. Suppose that, as a working hypothesis, we assume the Aerostich to be the finest example of street-riding attire ever constructed. Logically, our first question would then be, why isn't every motorcycle rider wearing one?

At approximately $550 [$700 in 2007] the Aerostich's initial cost is a deterrent to many riders, though with a life expectancy of perhaps 10 years it's an outstanding investment. I think weight (14 pounds average) and storage have a lot to do with it. Where will you put it on an 85-degree afternoon when you park your already loaded dresser? Will you wear it to ride your cruiser down to the mall?

So, the Aerostich is costly and labors against its own bulk, but let's not stop there. Top Dog must be able to fend off angrier attacks than those. Fit? No problem because the manufacturer, Rider Wearhouse, will happily custom-tailor each one- and two-piece suit. You merely supply your measurements and decide if you want a trim, roadrace type fit, or if you'd rather slip it on over your civvies. Most riders opt for the latter, preferring the freedom of movement and the option of layering to meet prevailing weather conditions.

Unless you've roadraced, you may not appreciate the benefits of a trim riding suit. In a long slide, snug fit cuts down on friction inside the suit, and, if the outfit has protective padding (of which the A-suit is amply endowed), assures that those pads remain centered on the likely impact points. Now, with the advent of electrically heated garments and ultra-high insulative materials, bulky layering is practically a thing of the past. So, why don't more manufacturers feature zippered expansion panels that enable a trim fit in warm *and* cold weather? Or even better, why not let the material itself expand?

In front of me at this moment is a copy of the British publication, *Motorcycle International,* in which the editors have comparison tested five riding suits, all tailored with Kevlar, the lightweight synthetic found throughout exotic racebikes and in many of our helmets. It's also the active ingredient in bulletproof vests. Most roadracing organizations have sanctioned Kevlar as a substitute for leather, and various manufacturers claim that it is five—even *10*—times as strong. Plus, it can—like the heavy nylon Cordura of an Aerostich—be interwoven with that other miracle fiber . . . waterproof, breathable Gore-Tex. Some manufacturers even mate it to a fabric resembling Lycra, the silky, stinky stuff they make some lingerie out of (if you've ever seen a glossy European motorcycle apparel catalogue, you'll appreciate the parallel).

Against an opponent half the weight of leather—one which boasts superior flexibility and one-third the storage requirement of bulky touring suits—our friend Mr. Aerostich (and our working hypothesis) would appear to be toast.

Not so fast. Each of the Kevlar suits, in the view of the English authors, is seriously flawed in some way—too hot in summer, too cold in winter. Too leaky, too few pockets, padding too skimpy or ill-fitting. Unlike Aerostich designer Andy Goldfine, who's achieved a near total symbiosis with the American rider, the Kevlar boys appear to lack clear marketing vision. Some suits are clearly targeted for racing, others as waterproof oversuits, some plain look like Halloween costumes.

I'm not suggesting that the demands of touring and commuting are identical to racing, but at any speed higher than a school zone, there are more similarities than differences. And therein lies the myth of one of our great American institutions: Kiss the pavement at 60 mph with Uncle Levi Strauss as your chaperon, and you might as well get caught fondling the mullah's daughter behind the mosque; your butt is *schwarma*.

Even among touring riders who wear full leather, too few give enough thought to its construction. What's the grade of the leather? How about the seams—are they lap stitched or merely butted together? Are the hips, knees, elbows, and shoulders genuinely padded, or do they just have cosmetic patches?

After an incident-free weekend of roadracing, I once dropped my beloved Ducati at less than five mph, a few blocks from my home. It was dark and rainy, and the manhole cover I braked on put me down so fast I didn't know what'd hit me. The fact that my elbow throbbed for about six months afterward shouldn't sound so surprising. After all, the drop height in a DOT helmet test is only six feet—with an 11-pound weight inside. The weight behind my elbow surely must have been higher. Lightweight body armor could have saved me a lot of pain, and—who knows—maybe some arthritis down the road.

Will the body armor be in place when the pavement comes calling? The extra hundred dollars you spend for a custom-made suit could ensure that it will. A two-piece suit needs a sturdy zippered attachment, or, in the case of a bib suit, an ample overlapping area.

Don't look now, but we're fast approaching the era of motorcycle airbags, possibly before they're technologically feasible and probably by unpopular mandate. We can wait for a flood of all kinds of hackneyed passive safety measures, or we can fight the current by pumping out fresh ideas from within—and by looking like we know what we're doing.

After all, the refinement in the modern motorcycle can be traced to the conviction of one man—Soichiro Honda—that motorcyclists deserve the same quality as automobile drivers. In performance we've surpassed them, but even after quantum leaps in motorcycle comfort, the total integration of rider, machine, and environment—that "oneness" we wax philosophical over—still eludes us.

Andy Goldfine, when you produce your three-pound Aerostich KGL (Kevlar/Gore-Tex/Lycra) suit, please put me down for your first delivery. Stowing it in my little compartment where primitive man put his gasoline, I'll wear it on every ride, long and short. Only when I arrive—fresh, clean, and whole—will I don my black leather jacket.

Safety's one thing. When I park my bike, man, I wanna look *cool*.

Adding the Safety Component

Keep Groups Small.

Yee-Hah! The 25 Best All-Time Safety Tips

May 2000

If you know someone who, um, doesn't read a lot (or maybe doesn't get out much) but you think might absorb some good advice if you made it really easy for him, direct him to these six compact pages. This is the good stuff. Have him read slowly (it's OK if his lips move) and read often.

. . . and after all that stuffy safety advice, make sure he doesn't miss the final suggestion about the fast sweeper. Yee-hah, indeed!

Pete Tamblyn

Say you just turned 40, and realizing that half of your expected life was behind you and the other half carried no warranties, written, oral, or otherwise implied, you pay a visit to your physician.

"Doc, what are 25 things I can do to stay alive and healthy?" you implore (hypothetically—in real life no HMO would cover you for 25 answers!).

He might prescribe a magnetic mattress pad or a daily poultice of sheep's blood and *cojones,* but chances are most if not all of his recommendations would be things you already knew you should do. Only people with serious psychological disorders deliberately make themselves ill, but we all put ourselves at varying degrees of risk because life has taught us we can get away with it much of the time.

But let's say that after depressing your tongue, bonking your knee and—well, yee-hah—it is your *40th* birthday exam, he icily looks you in the eye and declares, "You have a rare genetic disorder which is escalating daily. You'll be dead within a fortnight unless you at once and forever refrain from eating blueberry pie."

Well, it just so happens that you *love* blueberry pie, and as luck would have it, fresh blueberries are in season—a bumper crop. What to do? Well, unless you just lost job and pension, your wife emptied your bank account and took off on your bike with your best friend, and your kids ratted you out to the IRS, you'll do what you have to do. You'll alter your lifestyle immediately and permanently, because whatever the frailties of your particular flesh, your single, most powerful instinct is to remain alive.

Perhaps nothing in this article will affect you so profoundly, but you owe it to yourself to read these 25 tips today.

1. It's as plain as the big, swollen red orb on your face.

You can be killed riding a motorcycle, and the surest way to prove it is to have four or more drinks and go riding at night. Unfortunately, the news items that taint the non-riding public's view of our sport begin with "motorcyclist" and not "drunk," which is what 50 percent of all fatal crash victims were.

2. Mind your throttle.

Enjoying your bike's acceleration is one of motorcycling's consummate sensations, but the extra time needed to close the throttle can as much as *double* your stopping distance. Example: An expert rider, cruising through an intersection at a constant 30 mph, might need 50 feet to react and stop quickly. The same rider, accelerating through the intersection, could need 100 feet to stop, even if he were going the same 30 mph when the need to stop became clear.

Acceleration is one of the primary evasive tactics, but research shows that the vast majority of hazards emerge in front of us. Whatever your evasive action, you'll need a properly timed arrival, and to do that you need to keep your throttle poised and ready.

3. Check mirrors before changing lanes or slowing.

Times are changing. More vehicles, more lanes, more of everything that has nothing to do with driving going on inside cars. Your awareness needs to be 360 degrees.

4. Have escape routes when stopped at controlled intersections.

Leave a car length between your motorcycle and the preceding vehicle. Hold the clutch in, keep the bike in first gear, check the mirrors, and listen for squealing tires. Scan the area to both sides and know where you'll flee to if you must.

5. Take two and call me in the morning.

If long rides frequently leave you with a sore back, neck, etc., you might try taking Ibuprofen before you ride. Not a pain killer but an anti-inflammatory, 600mg can make the difference between arriving refreshed or doubled over in pain. Consult your doctor.

6. Avoid fatty foods before riding, especially on hot days.

Fat molecules are just waiting to attach themselves to your red blood cells, where they'll cut off your oxygen and turn you into an afternoon zombie.

7. Take a dirt-bike course.

It's a traction thaang. If there are none in your state, try the Ganaraska Offroad Motorcycle Adventures (GOMA) outside of Toronto, Ontario. Their one-day programs are inexpensive, and they provide the bike and all necessary protective gear. Phone (toll free) 877-939-5267 or www.trailtour.com. Information on other courses in Canada can be found at http://ridertraining.ca

8. Observe features above the road surface.

Fences, trees, rooflines, utility wires, etc., will often indicate direction changes well before you can actually see the pavement.

9. Watch out for "vanishing points."

When you're rounding bends (or even taking straightaways), the horizon should either remain constant or appear to recede. If it looks as if it's rolling toward you, your ability to change direction or respond to a hazard is steadily deteriorating

10. Practice quick stops.

Once you've settled weight onto the front wheel, the danger of locking it is greatly diminished. Squ-*eee*-ze is the correct action, releasing a little pressure so as not to lock up at the end, as weight returns to the rear wheel. With practice, you'll settle weight more quickly, which is the key to short stops. Always use light pressure on the rear brake pedal.

11. Practice U-turns.

Not being able to turn your bike around sucks. Borrow a lightweight bike if you have to, but practice. Key points are to really turn your head (don't look where you're going, look where you *want* to go), drag the rear brake a little and feather the clutch as necessary. Add a little counterbalance, and you'll be an ace in no time.

12. Watch for "shadow vehicles."

Those are the vehicles that disappear behind other oncoming vehicles on straight stretches of two-lane road. You may first spot them on distant curves, but check under the chassis and to the sides to avoid surprises should one suddenly pull out to pass. If you even think you see a shadow vehicle, move toward the shoulder (your right) to present yourself to bunched-up traffic.

13. Practice timing things.

Some people have a natural gift for estimating arrival points, but most need to work a little at it. Inexperienced and aging motorists are the most likely to make judgment errors, but you can avoid them by practicing. Count "one thousand one, one thousand two," then try working backward from your estimated arrival point "six, one thousand, five, one thousand," etc.

14. Practice countersteering aggressively.

I regularly encounter safety course graduates who believe that you countersteer by pushing *down* on the handlebar. That has no effect; you must rotate the steering axis by pushing forward or pulling back on the bar. Parking lots are great, but find an empty stretch of highway, CHECK YOUR MIRRORS, and rapidly weave across two lanes.

15. Position the bike for every potential hazard.

The Golden Rule of riding in traffic is to simply put the bike where others cannot do unto you. If you adjust your speed accordingly, there's almost no scenario where a collision is unavoidable.

16. Keep groups small.

If you want to ride with 30 friends, get a parade permit or else split up into smaller groups of four or less. A long, tight formation diminishes your ability to change speed and direction and can be unsettling or irritating to other motorists.

17. Wear a full-face helmet.

If today just happens to be the day you gong your head, chances are one in four you'll do a face plant.

18. Remember to scrub in new tires.

Like the gift of life itself, they bring hope and joy, arriving all smooth and in need of immediate attention. Ride for several minutes to bring them up to operating temperature, then weave from side to side, gradually at first, then more aggressively. If you haven't access to a twisty loop, locate a big parking lot and ride in circles, leaning gradually at first, then progressively harder and deeper. You might want to dismount once or twice to check your progress. Try not to leave the job half done.

19. Wear a real riding suit.

Dense, closed cell foam, particularly in the elbows, knees and shoulders, can prevent a high percentage of the foreseeable injuries in a spill. Make sure they don't flop around.

20. Oxygenate, don't caffeinate!

If you're like me, you can't function in the morning before you imbibe a tall, dark mug of Columbian Supremo. Caffeine is an effective stimulant, but if you're having trouble keeping your eyes open in the afternoon or evening, you need to get off the bike and start pumping oxygen up to your brain. Walk, jog, skip rope, push your bike (a great way to get rid of a chill)—whatever it takes to recoup the alertness you need to keep accumulating miles. Not even fresh air and exercise are substitutes for rest, however. Know when to nap or pull over for the night.

21. Perform a head check for each lane change.

Mirrors aren't enough, although you may wish to skip the return head check during really fast passes on two-lane roads.

22. Beware of SUVs.

Even before O.J. turned national attention to his infamous white

Bronco, SUVs had become an inescapable public menace. Sure, they're practical, but they cast a dual curse on us as motorcyclists, simultaneously cutting off our road view and rendering us invisible to others. Remember that the accepted practice of following at two seconds may not be sufficient when trailing these and other obstructive vehicles. You may have to drop back to four or more. Also, hordes of kids, cell phones, and now televisions cast doubt upon the alertness of whomever is at the helm.

23. Make your butt stick out.

This year's hot bike color is yellow, but from the rear even a brightly colored machine blends into the asphalt if it has black saddlebags and a rider with a dark suit and helmet. A bright helmet and/or torso are best. Prominent reflective material not only makes you safer at night, it shows consideration for those who must follow you.

24. Learn rear brake control.

It's practically useless in emergency stops, so resist the urge to mash that pedal (just your big toe is sufficient on most rear disc brakes), but it's a great tool for controlling jerkiness and chassis pitch. Add a bit more at the end of your stops, just as weight begins to return to the rear end. Below 5 mph you can avoid embarrassing spills by using it in place of the front brake—especially where traction is suspect.

25. Have fun.

You can't spend your life dwelling on the NASDAQ or the crisis in Rwanda. If you don't want to get hurt or killed riding motorcycles, take a long, hard look at your preparedness, and if, when you're done, you still ride off giggling inside your helmet, your doctor would probably tell you that you've found a healthy outlet for stress. Ask him, if you don't believe me. And just one last thing: If you really are turning 40, some doctors now say you can safely stall part three of that exam I mentioned earlier for another 10 years. So bend over and shout, *Yee-hah!* in a 70-mph sweeper. If you're 50, well, you know the drill.

The Zone

January 2000

What's the Magic Bullet to eliminate the majority of motorcycle crashes? The respected Professor Harry Hurt claims there is none. Undaunted, Larry thinks he's hot on the trail, suggesting it might be associated with the right wrist . . . and when the rider chooses to adjust it.

Pete Tamblyn

One of my earliest memories is of trying to illicitly cross the busy street outside our family apartment at the age of five. Frightened as I was, I managed to convince my four-year-old sidekick that it would be okay . . . we just had to get the speeding drivers to yield the right-of-way, which we could accomplish by hurling rocks in their direction.

Now at age five I was no Sandy Koufax, and the four-year-old was an utter candy arm. What seemed like hours passed before I finally made contact, and I remember it as clearly as if it were yesterday: The solid *crack* when the rock struck the car's windshield, the squeal of the brakes, and the speed with which our little feet took flight to our respective apartments, where news of our escapades had already arrived and corporal punishment awaited.

That incident resonates with me still, as each morning, 10 blocks from the spot of my first traffic violation, I risk life and limb for a cup of coffee. Believe me, when the drivers whiz by at double the posted 25-mph limit, oblivious to the freshly painted crosswalk, I'm tempted to pick up a big one and hurl it with all my full-grown might. Instead I play a more mental, more strategic, but equally confrontational game, feinting and faking and strolling coolly toward the paths of these speeding miscreants.

Broken down (and this is based upon years of scientific documentation), the number of courteous drivers—those who stop at the crosswalk and allow me to cross—is one in eight. The majority, five in eight, carry on at a steady speed, without regard for the pedestrian's rights, but will pull back when they recognize that a collision is imminent. The remainder—fully 25 percent—will not back off. Period. For these I reserve my fanciest footwork and the occasional rude gesture.

"What would you say is the one key to staying alive on a motorcycle?" asked a student of mine last week as we were winding down an intensive two-day session. When I started doing these columns more than a decade ago, I authored a piece called "The Magic Bullet," which dealt with strategies for evading the dreaded car driver who turns left across the motorcyclist's path. The title was derived from my personal belief that proper lane positioning would virtually eliminate what the Hurt Report identified as 43.8 percent of all car/motorcycle collisions.

"There is no magic bullet," said none other than Professor Harry Hurt himself, as we chatted three years later in a hotel lounge during the MSF's 1991 international safety conference. For sure my humble column wasn't one, because all these years later I don't see many riders exercising their freedom of mobility to put the motorcycle in the safest lane position.

Anyway, even if we could purge all of those nasty left turn accidents, that would still leave more than half of the collisions unaccounted for, plus all of the "crashes, spills, tumbles, dumps" and other dirty little single-vehicle mishaps, many of which never get reported to the agencies that churn out the data. What common thread, if any, could these incidents and accidents share which could help a trainer send his charge down the road, knowing he'd offered bona fide value for money?

Even before my "magic bullet" ramblings I went through a period when I thought we could save the world from motorcycle accidents with a three-part prescription: "countersteering reflexively, braking authoritatively (i.e. possessing the ability to quickly bring the front wheel to impending skid), and developing strategies for positioning the bike in traffic." Courses in motorcycle safety were relatively new at the time, and I could count on several reporters per year who would devote space and airtime to my "expert" views.

Which brings me to the Next Big Thing, a buzzword for the new millennium: *the zone*. You see, experience has taught me that there are some riders out there who either can't or won't brake very hard, and yet they don't have accidents. There are still, despite our best efforts to publish instructive articles and increase enrollment in rider courses, millions who haven't even *heard* of countersteering . . . and many of them don't have accidents either. Street strategies? I've heard the cockamamie and the self-righteous from riders who profess to never having had an accident—something I could never claim.

I'll tell you what I can claim: Virtually every manifestation of "Oh S—t!" that you can experience on two wheels. Those include, but are not limited to, rear-wheel skid, front-wheel skid, tank-slapper, high-side, and wheelie gone bad. I want to say this as unemotionally as possible because, unlike those fabulously entertaining British bike rags, I try to preserve in this space the realization that the line between photo op and disaster is often a fine one.

And that's where the zone comes in—the *roll-off* zone. A self-important commuter who hasn't the time to stop for a crosswalk knows that 999 out of 1,000 pedestrians will back off before he does. Furthermore, with anti-lock brakes he needn't fear any of the above-mentioned tentacles waiting to snare the single-track traveler.

When I've participated in laboratory-style studies of rider performance—ones in which subjects knew that an event was coming and that their person was in no real physical peril—response times typically ranged in the .5- to .8-second range. However, accident researchers report far longer intervals before motorists are able to take physical action on the highway. For several years I've invoked what I call the "three-second rule of braking," which, broken down, comes to one second for easing the brakes on (settling weight onto the front wheel), one second for easing them off (transferring weight back to the rear), and at least a second for some meaningful brake friction in between—therefore a minimum of three seconds in which the brake light is visible.

In coaching over the radio, I typically prep riders with an "okay . . . ready," the length of which is close to two seconds. In that time I expect them to calmly roll off the throttle, because the most career-shortening activity for a motorcycle instructor is watching brake lights fire off at corner entries.

Several states use an exam called the Motorcycle License Skill Test (MLST), but which I call the "anti-SIPDE" test. I call it that because, while it focuses on skill deficiencies common to accident-involved riders (hard braking, cornering, and swerving), it requires licensed candidates who only know they're about to receive some sort of signal to react, using the hardest swerve (left or right) or stop they can muster. To me it's anathema to the critical process of "scan, identify, predict, decide, and execute," which we "safety experts" claim is the key to street survival.

It's not surprising that MLST users have a nasty accident rate, but despite my obvious prejudices, the test has taught me just how critical throttle position becomes when a rider must respond quickly. I've watched some novices squeak through on trailing throttle with pathetically weak swerves and stops, and I've watched others with strong physical skills fail the test because they were still accelerating slightly at the moment they received their signal. My own experiments on the MLST grid have shown that throttle position can *double* the stopping distance, even when the actual speed at the time of the signal is identical.

To twist the throttle and feel the bike's forward thrust—be it on a Suzuki Hayabusa or a dual-sport 250, is one of motorcycling's indescribable rushes. But if you can't figure out when to close it, you're more defenseless against a Ford Explorer than a five-year-old with a rock in his hand.

Mistakes, Near and Far

April 1995

Without beating himself up, Larry observes his own riding, noting where he could improve, differentiating between sporadic and chronic errors.

Pete Tamblyn

This month's safety tip: If you're passing through the town of Tamazunchale on the great Pan American Highway, don't try to tempt fate by eating in a restaurant called "Montezuma's."

The Pan Am Highway from Tamazunchale to Zimapan is perhaps the most breathtaking road I've ever ridden. "The Route of a Thousand Curves," as it's called, winds from jungle to prairie in a hundred deceptively long miles; in between it scales cloud forest and Alpine massifs with sheer drops of thousands of feet. It is mind-numbingly gorgeous, but it smells of diesel fuel and death. I soon lost count of the bloody carcasses I saw strewn along the road—horses, cattle, and burros—but I won't easily erase the images of human carnage: a driver and a pedestrian.

It's the last week of December as I write this, and I've observed—wishfully perhaps—that several events made me a better rider this year. Taking student riders on road trips forced me to ride with exemplary care and precision, while writing this column gave me opportunities to pick the brains of people whose advice I consider unassailable—guys like Keith Code and Motorcycle Safety Foundation Education Manager Bob Reichenberg.

But Mexico gives me pause. I see here that I'm not as good as I believed. My gringo riding companion, who headed back north several days ago, called me "obsessive" when I told him that I keep track of my mistakes. Perhaps so.

What do I grade myself on? I have a regular loop at home, and skillwise, it's fairly simple. I try to stop precisely at painted lines, with one smooth lever application. I practice shifting in all the various modes—

uphill, downhill, hard and modest acceleration—and deduct for any clunks or unnecessary chassis pitch.

I'm mindful of my brake/throttle transitions, which I feel are pretty smooth . . . but I wonder if I'll ever master simultaneous braking and downshifting. I have many good places to practice stopping on a curve, mostly stop signs at the bottoms of steep hills. And I do lots and lots of U-turns, though not enough to make right-handers second nature.

Before I even leave the city I plunge down a steep wooded road with— let me think—nine turns. The trickiest is number seven, a blind, off-camber right-hander with a driveway just past the apex . . . used only for Irish weddings. There's a tiny clearing in the trees which affords me a sneak preview before I have to commit myself. Usually I brake before the turn, but sometimes for practice, I "swoop" (i.e. engine braking only) all nine turns. On my little dual sport, the feeling is just like free fall.

Besides sharpening my scanning technique, turn seven reinforces an important mountain road skill—one which, for want of another term, I'll call "gravitizing." Motorcycles, you see, don't like to turn with their brakes on. On steep grades there comes a time when you must decide to trust physics (i.e. gravity and centrifugal force), or ride the brakes off a cliff.

The mental stuff is a greater challenge—adhering to rules that no one else seems aware of. *Two second following distance . . . keep to the right except when passing . . . stay out of other drivers' blind spots.* Perhaps I'll never know where the line is drawn between an opportune "squeeze" and that which is rude, dangerous, or illegal. Still, I try to find consistency—to be ruled by intellect, not emotion or impatience.

More than anything, I work on my space cushion, striving for early, proactive adjustments, as opposed to late, reactive ones. When I round a blind curve, then spot a driveway I didn't position for, that's a definite point deduction.

I take pride in my belief that no left-turning car will ever nail me, but you know—things change. Six-lane boulevards with designated left-turn lanes scarcely existed 15 years ago. To be visually cut off from a car turning into McDonald's—or by a van turning into Burger King—is now a routine but potentially lethal occurrence. But risk always appears smaller through the lens of familiarity.

I'm certain that state and national bureaucracies keep tabs on the comparative accident rates of residents vs. non-residents, but what they can't do is monitor the subtle transitions and irregularities that contribute to accidents.

Once, when I was giving one of my first on-street lessons, I became separated from my novice student at a traffic signal. Though I'd been through the intersection hundreds of times, something felt different and more confusing riding at novice speed. So I went back later to investigate and was amazed at my findings. Within 300 yards there were arrows indicating *five* different directional changes . . . all within the same lane!

I'm not sure how I safely made it through the intersection all those other times. Probably a combination of acceleration and agility enabled me to simply be where I wanted to be at the right instant. Lots of motorcyclists who have ridden many thousands of safe miles are strictly intuitive—guys who could never explain what they do or why they do it.

But intuition can also work against you. One of my most predictable errors occurs when I want to turn right from a driveway, stop sign, or red light. Naturally, my first priority is a safe gap, so I concentrate on looking over my left shoulder, while an invisible magnet pulls me into a rolling start, oblivious to possible pedestrian and bicycle traffic. It's the classic "I never saw him" scenario on which we thought car drivers had a patent.

Still, transitions hold the key to smooth motorcycling. Reg Pridmore made this crystal clear when he took me for a ride around Grattan Raceway on the back of his BMW. Two-up, we circulated the track more quickly than I could solo—yet with less speed and lean angle. On the street, we use all sorts of "contractions" to get from point A to point B, but do they make us more or less safe? Coming to a full stop and putting your foot down may enable you to gather valuable information . . . or it may increase your risk exposure.

Every rider has his own information-gathering speed, and even that is far from constant. Riding in unfamiliar locations is like learning a foreign language. At first you must translate everything back into our native tongue; you can't make transitions as smoothly because you're unsure of what comes next. Then, in time (I'm told), the words become second nature and you learn to "think" in the new tongue . . . which, of course, presents a new danger.

An Englishman, on meeting an American lass, would be ill-advised to tell her he'd like to "knock her up" (come calling), though his reception couldn't be more horrified than that of an American man I knew, who once told a swimming class of seven- and eight-year-old New Zealand girls to slide into the pool " . . . on your fannies." (Use your imagination.) Even when you think you're speaking the same language, misinterpretations may arise.

In California, for example, drivers in the right-hand lane are legally responsible for giving way to vehicles merging from freeway on-ramps *(Bravo!)*. It's a foolish motorist, however, who assumes that even his fellow Californian is a scholar of motor vehicle law. Because of my work I periodically review my state's operator's manual and vehicle code, but once, in Prague, I narrowly escaped a head-on collision because I hadn't taken time to memorize simple traffic signs.

If you had to take a test today on signs and traffic laws, would you pass it? Better still, could you map out your Sunday ride or daily commute, accurately documenting your braking and shifting points, and all of the special "hidden" hazards?

One of my recent students—a doctor—told me that what drew him to motorcycling was "the danger." He hardly seemed like a risk-taker: wore full leathers, a good helmet, and rode at sensible speeds—but he *knew*. He'd totaled a BMW—not on the Pan Am Highway, but in Virginia. He didn't hit a bull, but rather what the bull spends its days manufacturing.

I guess the reason he wanted more training was that he'd had his fill of . . . mistakes.

Groundhog Day

February 1995

Corpulent does not adequately describe that groundhog. It remains, to this day, the largest groundhog that I have ever seen. The groundhog had to cross one traffic lane to escape its onrushing doom. Watching its slow progress and hearing the car wind through the gears, I never doubted the outcome.

Managing space and time is one of the critical tasks that every motorcyclist must master. Larry discussed the techniques used for space/time management early and often during his training rides. Master them to avoid the groundhog's fate.

Chris Freed, MSF instructor

We were sitting outside a frozen custard stand, my instructor buddy, Chris Freed, and I, when my eyes fell on a particularly corpulent groundhog, about to embark on his long journey across the road.

"Chris . . ." I asked, "what do you suppose that hog's chances of making it are?" From the valley floor, we could hear the low drone of a V-eight, roughly 30 seconds off.

"Oh, I'd say about zero," he replied. *Four, three, two . . .*

Has a groundhog *ever* made it across the road? I don't think so. Like the salmon swimming to his fated spawning ground, *Marmota monax* is guided by his very own genetic imprint—typically three to 5/32 of an inch.

I've heard more than one motorcyclist opine that, since most accidents take place in intersections, the safest strategy is to run through them as fast as one can! There is an element of truth in that . . . if one presupposes an existing window of opportunity. In the real world, however, such windows are too often shuttered by groundhogs, masquerading as motor vehicles.

These pages have sung both the glories and dangers of speed, but there can be no speed without space. A Ferrari has 10 times the top speed of a moped, but the moped will whip its butt in a downtown traffic jam.

What the moped has and the Ferrari lacks is "quickness"—the ability to rapidly effect change.

My aging 286 IBM-compatible computer is about as fast as a moped, but its processor speed is immaterial, since it spends most of its time idling, while I stare at the screen, contemplating my next move.

Where mental quickness comes from is an enduring mystery, but I would say preparation: knowing your environment, being able to prioritize hazards, and having a plan which minimizes them. My only accident in two years of on-street training occurred last summer, when I took a student on an unplanned lunch ride.

The student had come to me with perhaps 400 miles on his permit—all in a rural area. I selected a route devoid of complicated in-traffic maneuvers—just a left turn protected by a traffic light, and then, 100 yards later, a right into the restaurant parking lot. I was sure that the dangers were minimal.

But the student wasn't. When he saw what looked to him like a thousand cars, he froze and failed to make the quick-changing light. I waved to him from the parking lot and radioed instructions, but somehow he misjudged the driveway and clamped the front brake as he should have been accelerating over a little patch of gravel. His circuits were loaded with extraneous data (cars which posed no immediate risk), leaving no open pathway to relay a warning of the gravel.

The difference between "quick" and "hasty" often comes down to good visual habits. I've never subscribed to the theory that one must choose between a brisk pace and a look at the scenery. Scanning a large area enables you to continually upgrade information. Constant eye movement also enhances depth perception; a rider who fixates on a turning point or apex is more apt to miscalculate it.

A simple head check is a deceptively complex exercise in visual quickness. Since peripheral vision lacks the sharpness needed to make sound traffic decisions, every degree of head rotation adds one more degree of useful central vision. However, further rotation takes one's eyes off the road ahead for a longer time. A decent mirror/head check takes more than one full second. Add to that a half-second reaction time and—even with a two-second following distance—you're in deep peril, should the driver ahead of you slam on his brakes.

A quicker head check might help but would your brain keep up? The MSF, along with most drivers education courses, advocates the "SIPDE" system (Search, Identify, Predict, Decide, Execute). It may sound a bit cumbersome, but it's actually an oversimplification of all the data processing a skilled rider does.

Take a routine passing maneuver on a two-lane road. You predict that a car may appear over the crest, but you also calculate sufficient distance to accelerate and safely overtake. It's almost automatic; but now you need a moment to consciously verify your calculations. How long is a "moment?"

"How long is a piece of string?" my father would say. We all process information at different rates, but clearly the rider who can digest quickly—and *accurately*—has the advantage. My personal rule for approach/avoidance conflicts: If I have to *re*verify, I don't go. I may not always make the best choice, but I always err on the side of caution.

A quick street rider is a student of math. The other day I took a student to an area I frequently use for passing practice. I instructed him to watch for the passing zone, then safely overtake my bike, but alas, a truck appeared in the oncoming lane. The student demurred.

"How much time did you have to pass?" I asked the student afterward.

"Well, I didn't count," he replied. I did. It was 11 seconds. We reversed directions, and this time he executed the pass—in five seconds. His earlier decision not to pass was a sound one, based on his limited experience . . . but this side of West Texas, a six-second space cushion is a pretty good opportunity.

The goal of motorcycling isn't to pounce on ever-smaller windows of opportunity. However, a motorcyclist making a quick, well-calculated pass has less risk exposure than someone who straps the wife and kids into a $50,000 Swedish Safetymobile, then drives the speed limit for 10 miles in another driver's blind spot.

A wise old saying goes: "It's okay to ride fast . . . but never in a hurry." Conversely, it's okay to ride slow . . . but never sluggishly. Lazy steering has become the curse of both winding two-lanes and urban surface streets. Stand on any street corner and watch how many drivers make diagonals instead of crisp left-hand turns. With coffee or car phone in hand, they start a half-block too soon and cut a 90-foot swath through the opposing lane before settling on a viable path of travel.

Weak turning is a major source of traffic congestion, but more to the point, it places everyone behind the groundhog at risk, particularly in an environment of inattentive, tailgating drivers.

My experience on twisty roads suggests that many riders go into corners with a lot of speed, but when it comes time to actually turn, their steering is too weak and time-consuming. The strong rider rides point to point—entrance to exit. The weaker rider plods along, point to point to point to point, forcing numerous steering corrections. Try this experiment:

On a sheet of letter- or legal-sized paper, use a ruler to draw two parallel lines, four inches apart. Use your coffee mug to draw a circle inside the lines. Now carefully retrace half of the circle without benefit of the mug. See all the tiny wiggles and deviations? Now try the same thing on the other half, but much faster. Your mistakes become larger, don't they?

Now, instead of tracing, draw a new arc in your remaining space between the lines. Holding the pencil lightly, start toward the circle, then quickly *swoop* back the opposite way, finishing with a long straight. The arc isn't circular, but it's surprisingly steady, took hardly any time to complete and—with any practice—you can easily stay within the lines.

The benefits of quick turning are even more pronounced in a narrow driveway, where boundaries soon catch up to riders who are unturned. And I'm forever emphasizing to students the value of *aggressively* dodging potential hazards, such as a parked car. Could there be a child pedaling a tricycle out from behind it? A snappy two- to three-second swerve guarantees plenty of space; a lazy, diagonal adjustment either crowds the child or prolongs your exposure to oncoming traffic.

So, ride slowly if you like. But if you can't be quick, go back into your hole!

Four on a Bubble

April 1997

Marching an assembly of motorcyclists lock-step down the highway in staggered formation didn't fit Larry's concept of desirable conduct. He had seen too many lapses of judgment attributable to group dynamics, or just plain testosterone poisoning. Understandably, he always found an excuse to pass up invitations to join the annual "Transalps in the Blue Ridge" rally, even if he had plans to be Transalp-mounted nearby in the Blue Ridge at the time.

However, he acknowledged that social dynamics inevitably result in riders' meeting up for a ride. Accordingly, this column suggests ways of injecting a modicum of safety into group rides, starting with putting a cap on the group size at four.

Pete Tamblyn

There are two kinds of people in this world: those who believe that there are two kinds of people in this world and those who don't. Personally, I think the rainbow of personalities is far too vast to pigeonhole individuals—or for that matter, to even organize more than four for a motorcycle ride.

I've divided the people who insist upon riding in large groups into two categories (I'm not prejudiced, though—some of my best friends are group riders): the "gang bangers" and the "paraders."

A former student of mine (we'll call him "Biff" to protect his identity)—a solid Midwestern, 40-something sort of weekend rider—recently wrote me, describing an event sanctioned by a prominent national organization that degenerated into a gang bang.

"(There were) a total of 39 bikes . . . several Honda VFRs, a couple of ST1100s, lots of Wings, a couple of Ducatis, one lonely BMW, a couple of bright, shiny, huge Honda Valkyries," wrote Biff. "The coordinator divides us into three groups (by speed). I put myself into the fast group and we leave first—about 11 of us with (let's call him Alphonse) on a Honda CBR90ORR in the lead.

"... off the slab and onto some country roads and on the very first curve (15-mph, 90-degree left) a guy on a 900RR goes down. He broke his collarbone, and we wasted a half hour resolving that situation.

"Back on the road. Alphonse is setting a very fast pace. He passes anywhere, anytime, and he is frequently out of sight of the rest of us. After lunch the fast group re-forms (we are now down to six) and we head off in search of (famous racer road). About five miles later another bike goes down on a hard uphill right-hander—he just lost it. Bike was pretty banged up but still rideable. He had a nice scar on the side of his helmet but seemed unhurt (he was wearing one of those under-jacket armor vests). He decided to turn around and limp back home and another guy (the slowest of the group) went with him. Alphonse was so far ahead of us that it was about 20 minutes before he came back and discovered what had happened behind him."

Ever the deep thinker, Biff posed the question: whose fault is it that this guy went down?" His conclusion: "I put part of the blame on Alphonse for setting a pace that no one else was capable of."

However, according to Biff, "The consensus view completely exonerates Alphonse. 'He should be able to ride as fast as he wants . . . no one is forced to try to keep up with him . . . we're all adults here . . . ride your own ride,' etc."

I confess I'd rather listen to Salvadori talk about opera than participate in any event that necessitates a "road captain." Of the possible half-dozen highly-organized rides I've gone on, three probably were actual parades. According to my friend, Dr. Joseph Bark, who has authored several pop health books as well as a piece or two in this magazine, we receive "secondary gain" from participating in these see-and-be-seen events.

Although I'm more the primary gain type, I'll be the first to admit that the accident rate for "paraders" has to be much lower than that for "gang bangers." However, I do hear of accidents taking place on large, highly organized group rides. Usually it's a collision of some sort, though not necessarily with a car—sometimes with a fellow group member.

Simple arithmetic dictates that for 20 or more riders to remain a cohesive unit, the pace must never exceed the limits of the slowest rider. That alone practically guarantees that some motorist will lose patience and attempt an ill-advised pass or pull-out. You think it's tough to get around a doddering Lincoln Continental driver on a road with limited visibility? Try passing 20 touring bikes in an underpowered 4,000-pound sedan!

Staggering (forming two parallel columns in the car wheel tracks of a single lane with riders positioned catercorner rather than side-by-side) shrinks the "mass to pass" by nearly half, yet still enables riders to maintain the "safe" two-second following distance, universally espoused in highway safety liturgy. It can be a useful tool for keeping the group together on urban boulevards and freeways, but may be just as detrimental on the open road.

In a staggered formation, a rider may follow two seconds behind the rider directly in front, but he's still only one second behind the preceding bike. Even if all participants were exactly equal in skill and reflexes, a rider making an unexpected swerve could take out the unfortunate soul on his rear flank. On those occasions where I've been forced to ride long distances in staggered formation, I've often felt as if I had to ride *three* motorcycles.

My other serious gripe against staggering is that it forces individuals to ride where the group dictates rather than in the most secure and advantageous position. All riders on the right, for example, are dangerously exposed to driveways; riders on the left to oncoming traffic; everyone is forced to ride over surface hazards they would otherwise avoid. Make no mistake, staggering can be a useful tool, but in my opinion its use as a default mode is like carrying only one wrench in your toolkit.

Consider your response capabilities: you can slow down or accelerate, but you can't suddenly throw your motorcycle into reverse, nor can you move laterally without covering an even greater piece of ground in front. What you have is a sort of "response bubble" . . . i.e. an elliptical zone in front and to both sides where you can put your bike at a given moment. If you're traveling at low speeds, it's rather round and fattish; the higher the speed, the more elongated it becomes.

From the standpoint of accident likelihood, there's no question—riding solo is your safest bet. All you have to do is keep your bike's handlebars off the ground and maintain a bubble that's small and flexible enough to stay on the road without bumping into other bubbles. The psychology of "gang banging" stretches the bubble to the point where little or no response is possible. "Parading," on the other hand, squishes those bubbles like a hot tub full of delegates to a Weight Watchers convention. The group's conspicuity becomes the members' only defense.

My own experiences, training riders on the road, have convinced me that with more than four riders, the quality of the group ride erodes exponentially. When you're leading three riders you can see the others in your mirrors (on straight sections, signaling for a momentary stagger will give an unimpeded view and verify everyone's still there). Should something go wrong, you can send a rider in each direction and still have a friend at the side of the rider with the problem. Four forces us to discuss and resolve since neither side can rely upon a one vote majority. And there's really no reason why any size group ride can't break down into mobile little four-bike squadrons.

Make no mistake—even four can degenerate into a "gang bang," but a little common sense and ego management can be a powerful deterrent. Was speedy Alphonse really to blame? Let's just say he could have exercised a bit more judgment. When the same guys and gals ride together regularly, they generally know and respect one another's abilities. Some groups like to hang together curve for curve; others could care less if they become separated. In the latter case, the "last man waits" rule usually keeps the successive riders from missing a turnoff.

In the end, it's a question of personalities, but when you take a new gal to a party only to abandon her for the remainder of the evening, you probably don't get another date. Alphonse may be in luck, however. Counting Biff's negative vote, there remained three of the original 11 who hadn't crashed or spooked themselves out of the ride at the time the "consensus" was tabulated. So next time out, he's down to four—the perfect size for a group ride!

For the Love of Riding

October 1999

Re-reading this column, it struck me that we still have the same issue today that we had back then. Riders still fall down. We still get up. Sometimes group dynamics are suspect. We may, in fact, love motorcycling too much!

I did not take advantage of Larry's unique Talk/Ride/Talk/ Ride class during his visit to our rally in 1999. I wish I had, but as the out-going President, I was covered up with other rally-associated duties. Since then, the HSTA has continued to flourish; the STAR rally is still the focal point of our riding year. During our 25 years, we've had the National rally in 20-plus locations, with the mixed blessing of the many, challenging "new" roads that are available to us, and only a short week to explore them all.

Larry's words still ring true after all these years: "Safety on a motorcycle is a continuing educational process." Larry urged us to continue to strive for improvement, to ride smart, and to constantly look for those situations that may be hazardous.

I wonder if the road to Grandpa Zwick's Park is still in good shape? I think I'll find out the next time I'm in southeast Ohio.

Moose Parrish, past-president
Honda Sport Touring Association

They pass out business cards with models of motorcycles where their job titles should be; three's the average number. They profess to dislike rallies, yet they schedule vacations a year in advance so as not to miss their annual rendezvous. They're known as the "Honda Sport Touring Association," and although you'd best leave a few extra minutes to locate your VFR, VTR or ST1100 in the parking lot, a third of them don't even ride Hondas.

Is it possible to love motorcycling too much? The 466 men and women who've converged upon Marietta, Ohio, for HSTAs STAR '99, test the hypothesis. By 8 a.m. their red sea of machinery departs, leaving only trailers in dry dock. When faced with the preservation of Z-rated gumball tires and the impossible task of choosing a single mount for an entire week, "Touring" often takes a backseat, prompting some members to quip that HSTA stands for "Honda Sport *Trailering* Association."

Ohio is a non-helmet-law state, but voluntary usage (beyond the adjacent Wal-Mart) is 100 percent at this event, and a majority ride in fully armored suits. If gear and training are your measures of safety, this club is as safe as acidophilus milk. We shall see. The organization invited me to conduct three days of bite-sized training sessions in the surrounding hills of the Wayne National Forest.

The first evening, in the parking lot, I field the following question:

"I don't want to mooch off you or anything," begins the voice, a gentle mixture of temerity and beer, "but what is it exactly that you do in your course?" It's odd how apologetic the speaker is, as if safety trainers were apostles granting wisdom and eternal life in exchange for absolute contrition.

What we do exactly is talk, then ride, then talk, then ride for a little over two hours. Actually, all I do is talk, talk, talk, talk, since I communicate with the students via a *one*-way radio. Our scheduled sessions book up following the opening ceremonies, and most of the riders prove to be quite skilled. Like Tim Shook, whose BMW K1200RS comes equipped with a 70-pound smoothing device—10-year-old son John.

Grandpa Zwick's Park sits atop a breezy ridgetop on a remote road not shown on any of the rally maps. Our six-mile approach was repaved last August and the six miles after it were done literally days before the event. Both wriggle along exquisitely, and there have been times when we've taken 40-minute lunch breaks here and not seen another vehicle pass by. By the end of the first day, however, word of this treasure has filtered through the ranks, and on the second morning we pass the aftermath of an unscheduled off-road ride. The ST1100, according to eyewitness accounts, performed a quadruple axel, spitting off its rider, who has sustained a broken kneecap plus miscellaneous sprains, strains, and contusions.

Two years ago, at the STAR '97 in Oklahoma, the organization suffered a rash of accidents, prompting the formation of a "Risk Assessment Team" and an edict that any member involved in a mishap at a sanctioned event submit to an in-house investigation. That had some interesting findings according to the organization's outgoing president, Don

"Moose" Parrish: ". . . white males, 40s and 50s, hot weather, late in the day when they're tired." An inordinate percentage of ST1100 mishaps has become a pox on the house of those who ride the silky smooth 700-pound locomotives in the company of lightweight sport-bikes.

"You just don't realize . . ." begin so many doleful tales. The task force appears to have succeeded. The number of crashes at the '98 STAR in Taos, New Mexico: *zero*. But that was Taos, and by the second evening, the eerily pretzeled roads of southeast Ohio have already claimed four members by unofficial count.

"Moose," I say, as we watch the barges float lugubriously down the Ohio River on the first evening of summer, "This isn't Taos. You can't run 400 motorcycles up and down these roads for three days and not have mishaps."

Everywhere riders cluster, the conversations turn to State Route 555—one of the top 10 roads in the United States according to prominent lists, but a route which resembles a swoopy western mountain pass less than it does your small intestine. Scores of blind summits, any of which can go left or right. Virtually every turn entrance obscured by trees. Throw in decreasing radii, loose gravel, and a little horse dookey (it passes through a small Amish community), and you get the picture. No—you *don't* get it. Three days later, while off-road riding in Canada, I will finally figure it out: Southeast Ohio is an enduro course with paved trails!

"Maybe you're right," Moose sighs, "but I just wish . . ." Aptly nick-named, Moose has the mien of a big ol' country preacher, and the HSTA members are his flock, his friends, his family. When they go down you get the feeling that it hurts him worse than it hurts them.

The jungle telegraph here runs at 56K, and by the third morning Grandpa Zwick's has become *the* place from which to view all the knee-dragging action.

A six-pack of red bikes dives into a left-hander, the alpha dog slicing a neat incision through the freshly blackened asphalt. Rider four takes his tires right up against the yellow paint; rider five grazes it. Rider six, possessing the will but not the skill to keep pace with his buddies, runs right across the paint. Steering rates, traction values of painted lines, group riding mentalities . . . Zwick's proves a veritable laboratory of sport-riding instruction.

The psychology of group riding would surely fill a chapter in my doctoral thesis on cool roads. Seven times I follow riders toward the same fall-away right-hander. Seven times I caution them, "Easy, easy," as they near the vanishing point, and seven times I watch the brake lights flash in a panic at the turn entry. Each time the formation is the same: student A, then myself, then students B and C. How, I wonder, would the result differ if student A were merely tooling along by himself with no one to impress? We must install a hidden camera with a monitor back at the Zwick laboratory.

There are no fatalities. The aerobatic ST pilot hobbles into the closing ceremonies on crutches, having endured two nights of broken-bone camping to remain with his friends and to hear the keynote speaker, race commentator and AMA Hall of Fame inductee Dave Despain. Carefully, casually, Despain wraps tales of Freddie Spencer with stories of his own club racing heroics (battling wheel to wheel for 13th place in a 15-bike field) into a message no one expected—safety.

"Get your kids started on dirt bikes," he implores the audience. "The lessons they learn about bike control they'll later apply to street riding, should they decide to take it up. Sure, they'll fall down, they'll get hurt. They'll break bones. They may get *killed*."

A chortle starts to rise from the floor below. Professional after-dinner speakers have the ability to trigger that instinct—not the finest in man— to reject free will and laugh on cue. Despain's eyebrows arch almost cartoonishly into his high forehead; his hands stretch out beseechingly.

"No—I'm serious. They can get killed. They probably won't, but they can. You need to tell them that.

"When someone lives out their days rocking in a nursing home, we say that they've died of 'natural causes,' but when a young man dies in a racing accident, doing what he loves, I think that's natural, too. They've both died of natural causes; it's just that one's chosen to live his life a little faster."

Despain's eloquence subdues the lusty audience. We all want to believe him, but how many would trade their golden years for a trophy or a fast trip down a mountain road . . . even for a world championship? We're not champions. We're hobbyists.

And I still wonder—is it possible to love motorcycling too much?

Across an Ocean . . . in Seconds

June 2006

I remember clearly sitting at breakfast early one morning with Larry and our six students for the weekend training tour in the Blue Ridge Mountains. When asked about their expectations, several students identified challenges with slow-speed maneuvers. Larry replied that we would work on that, but the course is all about getting our eyes up, hazard perception, and various techniques for riding the "twisties" with control and smoothness.

The following article illustrates the benefits of Larry's teachings about situational awareness generally and getting our eyes up specifically. Larry posed an interesting question at the end of the article.

Mike Wisniewski, U.S. Gov't., retired,
MSF RiderCoach Trainer

Twelve hundredths of a second. In track and field it can mean the difference between "World's Fastest Human" and a chest with no medal. In World Cup skiing it's millions of dollars in endorsements, even though the opponents it separates never race head-to-head under equal conditions. In road racing it's about three bike lengths per lap, so GP and World Superbike teams take *very* seriously even smaller gains which might accrue over a 30-lap competition.

What about street riding? According to Dr. Horst Ecker of the Vienna University of Technology, .12 seconds is the mean difference in response times between motorcyclists who perform hard braking with the front brake *covered* vs. *uncovered*. Not surprisingly, Ecker's presentation at MSF's recent International Motorcycle Safety Conference evoked some lively dialogue, both during and after the official discussion period.

"We teach students *not* to cover the front brake," an animated Dutch trainer insisted in the post-session coffee-klatch. "What's the first thing people do in a stressful situation?" Before I had a chance to respond, he answered his own question.

"They *squeeze* whatever it is they're holding onto!" For dramatic effect, he clenched both fists and assumed his best zombie pose.

I've heard that argument before and, frankly, I've never bought it. You'd have to be Hakeem Olajuwon to be able to clamp a front brake lever while holding the throttle open even one-eighth of a turn. For those of us who cannot palm a medicine ball, forward rotation—a learned response—must precede any palpable braking force. My take is that a sudden lunge across the abyss between throttle and brake lever would more likely induce lockup than would a couple of fingers curved in delicate repose atop said lever. But that's just my opinion. The bounds of ethical research prevent either of us from launching live autos into the paths of approaching motorcyclists, thereby proving once and for all the superiority of one method over the other.

It was a good session—maybe the best, of the four-day conference— featuring papers by Joachim Funke of Germany's Darmstadt University of Technology *(Rider/Motorcycle Interaction: A Human Approach to Motorcycle Safety)* and Dr. Rudolf Mortimer, a retired University of Illinois professor *(A Survey of Motorcyclist Braking Techniques . . .* actually a survey of what motorcyclists *believe* their techniques to be). Following the presentations, the three speakers were joined in a panel discussion by Dr. Bert Bruer, also of Darmstadt, an engineering professor who has conducted extensive investigations in the area of integrated and antilock braking systems.

Having attended a few of these conferences, it strikes me as curious how differently academics on opposite sides of the Atlantic angle their approaches to safety research. Germanic investigators like to dissect the rider—to measure him as they would an assemblage of mechanical parts; their American colleagues would rather ask him how he "feels" about his riding. Surprisingly, their conclusions are often not so disparate. After submitting to the assembled his test group's mean braking performance of 5.6 meters per second squared—along with collateral data showing a modern Oldsmobile to produce nine m/sec^2 and a new BMW K1200LT with integrated and ABS brakes somewhere between 11 and 12 m/sec^2— Dr. Funke proceeded to the following conclusion:

"It would appear that they (his test group) were *lousy* motorbike riders."

All four researchers agreed that improvements in braking

performance are more easily attainable through technology than through rider training.

Now we at *Rider* have evidence that ABS on the wrong machine (i.e. one with a short wheelbase and sticky tires), or ABS designed only to engage on less-than-perfect surfaces, can promote nose wheelies and possibly front flips. Breur himself testified that "preventing the rider from leaving the machine" becomes one of the design challenges when riders take full measure of a superbike's speed and braking abilities. Notwithstanding these dots on the far periphery of the performance graph, arguments that a top rider can beat the "computer" in the real world simply don't wash. First of all, maybe one rider in a thousand can guarantee 100 percent efficiency in an emergency on a mysterious surface. Secondly, I haven't seen one of these confrontations published in close to a decade; microchips have evolved more in 10 years than humans have in the last million.

So, back to that .12 of a second. Concurrent to the conference, in a tent 200 yards away, various vendors had set up displays for a "rider fair." Three MSF instructors from Northern Virginia Community College sat by a VCR which played a tape of themselves coaching students on-street in suburban Washington. I'd seen the video many times (to be honest, it was a tape from my instructor course), and I was curious to see how all of the morning's theory squared with reality—or at least my perceptions of reality, based upon this seven-minute vignette of real-world riding. The footage I wanted to review was at the very end of the tape—a scene in which instructor Mike Wisniewski guides his novice student's eye toward a van attempting to cross a busy multi-lane boulevard.

"... *and a car that's partially hidden on our right ... slow down here ... and as I thought, it did pull out—and* another *one coming behind it ...*"

My hypothesis was that the tape would show Wisniewski's radio commentary arriving six seconds before the point of interception (the car which was obscured by the van *did,* in fact, turn right and into the instructor's path).

As I'd thought, the replay revealed a five- to six-second lapse between the verbal identification of the hazard and the moment in which an actual collision might have taken place (it's reasonable to posit that the car driver never saw the bikes). At the speed the bikes were traveling, a "dumb rider" (one who simply mashes the foot brake) might reduce his stop by 50 feet with a "smart bike," but the student on the video didn't even use his brakes; he simply rolled off the throttle when his teacher advised him to slow down.

A total of *10-and-a-half seconds* had elapsed when the student finally cleared the second car (which could have pulled out between the two bikes but did not). Time enough for a mirror and head check followed by a switch to a safer lane. Barring the availability of such a lane, time enough to roll off the throttle (or to roll *on* at the correct moment), to come to a full stop, or to toot the horn and hope for recognition—probably the *least* effective measure.

Aggressive skills training might improve emergency response times by .12 of a second and overall stopping performance by considerably more. If there are as many "lousy motorbike riders" as Dr. Ecker's research suggests, intelligent braking systems—ones that can prevent lockup *and* apportion the correct pressure to each wheel—would doubtless reap even greater performance gains.

We know lousy riders perform badly during emergencies—those split second intervals that separate a motorcyclist from a solid object on a collision course. In fact, the evidence is pretty strong that "good riders" choke as well. What the literature lacks is any record of what riders—skilled and unskilled—think about in the four to 10 seconds which determine whether or not a situation evolves into an emergency. Loyal readers, I ask you . . . .

How do you feel about *that?*

Responsibility

Drunken Research

January 1989

My memory of the night we performed our mildly inebriated vaudeville act for the rodeo crowd at the 1998 Rider Roamin' Wyoming Rally is sketchy, largely because when it was over there was still a bit left in that bourbon bottle, and Larry and I sat down in the grandstands with it and furthered his research late into the night. I do remember just how hard Larry must have worked on designing and laying out the cone course we would run on the rodeo dirt, as it was clear by the time I arrived—fresh from the feeding trough—that he was worn ragged and thirsty. I found out later that he hadn't eaten most of the day, either.

Two shots after the control run and Larry was giggling as he got on the bike for his first boozed run—with nothing but sour mash in his belly it's no wonder he took a tumble. That shook him up enough that I think the third shot before the next run merely served as a bracer. Larry describes the lap quite modestly in the 'Drunken Research' column that follows, but for being liquored-up on an empty stomach and just having crashed, he actually rode very well.

Since Larry wrote this column in late 1988, the data about drinking and riding has been updated, and it's still disappointing. According to NHTSA, in single-vehicle motorcycle crashes in 2001—the type of accident the rider is most capable of preventing—41 percent of the fatally injured were intoxicated with a blood alcohol content of .08 or greater, the legal limit in most states. Not only is that fatality rate much higher than it is for other vehicles, motorcycle riders in fatal crashes also had higher intoxication rates than any other type of driver.

It's really quite simple, as Larry says at the end of the column: Don't drink and ride. And don't let your friends drink and ride, either.

Mark Tuttle Jr, editor, Rider *magazine*

I swear it was all in the name of science. Or so it began, but somewhere things went awry. Maybe it was the cheers of the 3,000 people. Perhaps it was the TV cameraman, beckoning with his microphone to utter a few choice words of wisdom for the solid, sober citizens of Cody at the *Rider Roamin' Wyoming Rally II.* Or maybe it was when Mark Tuttle Jr. goosed me.

Tell you something about Tuttle: not since the word "party" became a verb has there been a more boring person to get drunk with. But get drunk I did—in the name of science.

The plan was simple: set up a few cones, weave around them, clock the time and count any cones that get knocked down. Then do a shooter and try again. And again. It's been done before, by magazines even squids can read. But never before had such an experiment been attempted publicly.

The problem (from a scientific standpoint) was our failure to control all the variables—chiefly Tuttle's vaunted stomach. The tight schedules we kept at Cody saw me adjusting the last of the cones and honing my baseline to a razor-sharp edge, just as Tuttle was returning from the Beartooth Pass photo tour and swallowing a side of Wyoming beef. There I sat at the west end of the rodeo—the crowd clamoring for action—vainly trying to explain the course's complexities as Tuttle made stab after futile stab at the mighty XR200's kickstarter. It was what scientists call a formula for disaster.

The course looked like this: As the clock starts, the bikes accelerate up to perhaps 20 mph. A weave consisting of seven cones placed at diminishing intervals follows, leading directly into a left-handed, decreasing-radius turn, or "corkscrew." Coming out of the corkscrew, a sharp right-hand turn leads into another weave, this time with cones staggered left and right. Next, we have to accelerate toward a barrier, whereupon a signal is given to swerve left, swerve right, or stop short of the cones. Lastly, we dismount, run around bike and barrier, remount and ride across the finish line. A fairly challenging course.

With Tuttle scrupulously watching my first run, I whistle through the grid in 35 seconds, keeping both feet on the pegs (as per our rules) and toppling nary a cone. Tuttle fires up his XR, then proceeds nicely through the tricky diminishing weave, but gets lost coming out of the corkscrew and misses two cones. Time: 50 seconds. Officer Chan Richards, of the Cody Police Department, helps us celebrate the first circuit by cracking the cap off a bottle of Jim Beam and pouring us each two shots.

I raise some dust sliding around the last two cones, but knock over none. I bank it into the corkscrew, leaning over and staying on the gas—smooth—but flopping right into the staggered weave, I see the ground inexplicably smack up against my foot. Never mind, I'm cooking. When I get the signal to stop, I'm traveling way too fast and suddenly the bike is swapping ends! I tuck and roll, leap to my feet, circle the barrier and push my bike across the finish. Time: 55 seconds.

Tuttle, a self-described "experienced drinker," rolls up to the line, two hundred pounds of solid liver. He rides smoothly, without charging. No cones this time; no feet down. Time: 45 seconds. He's obviously learning the course . . . and sabotaging the demonstration in the process!

Tuttle's third run is predictably boring. Minute and three seconds; well, at least he's finally showing some signs of decline. Under the dim lighting of the rodeo's west end, I observe with some satisfaction, a string of toppled cones.

Following rounds six and seven, I begin my third timed assault on the obstacle course. It's a trickier venue, now that the cones jockey back and forth, but generous helpings of throttle compensate for my total loss of stationary balance. Remarkably, I negotiate the first two phases without a mishap (I think), but slowing down, I just can't make the staggered weave without dabbing twice—maybe three times. Not bad for a guy who's at or near the legal limit.

A trip into town to blow into the Intoxicator 3000 will yield some amazing insights. En route to the station we make a bust. It's Tuttle who first notices the perpetrator weaving to and fro. Though he exhibits all the classic symptoms of DUI, it turns out the driver is merely scanning his radio dial in search of the Bronco's exhibition game. Twenty-five thousand people are killed each year by drunk driving; it's not known how many die searching for exhibition football games. I stand before the monitor, feeling lucid and alive. "I am not drunk!" I swear the computer will uphold my honor.

"You reek!" says the waggish Officer Richards and flatly predicts I will top .10 percent, the legal limit.

Vindication comes in the form of a .056 reading—enough to lose my driving privileges in Sweden, enough to be executed in Yemen, but perfectly legal in Wyoming and every other state. Chan is amazed and slightly disappointed; it's been nearly two hours since we started, so probably I've oxidized one or two.

Tuttle's turn. He breathes deeply, then blows into the tube. The computer whirs and clicks then spits out its result—.011—less than the charts predict for one drink! Chan's never seen anything like it in 12 years of law enforcement.

So what, if anything, did we learn from our mismanaged experiment? Before I answer, let me quote from a 1980 NHTSA study on alcohol absorption. Their conclusion: "It is recommended that further research be directed to the development of BAC estimate tables which will be more accurate than those currently available." Considering that the NHTSA study cost taxpayers $109,000, while ours cost *Rider* eight dollars worth of booze, we didn't do so badly.

What we showed was that an average-sized, relatively inexperienced drinker, imbibing on an empty stomach, will get drunker and show it more than a hefty, experienced one who's just eaten. NHTSA identified age, weight, body composition, and alcohol-use history as factors. In the NHTSA study, subjects given a 1,000-calorie meal a half-hour prior to drinking cut their peak BAC by about half. Tuttle's stomach proved to be an incredibly efficient mechanism for delaying the issue of alcohol into the bloodstream. It must be noted that food does not lessen the effects of alcohol; it merely serves as a sump, preventing the full dosage from circulating through the blood at one time.

It is widely assumed that alcohol absorption is almost instantaneous, but clearly, this isn't always the case. In a second NHTSA-funded study, drinkers were given an alcohol dosage of .68 grams per kilogram of bodyweight—an amount which would, theoretically, place each at .10 percent. All of the drinkers had been dosed on an empty stomach, but some didn't peak until an hour-and-a-half after they finished drinking. The women, who peaked higher, took 15 percent longer on average to sober up, but one 239-pound man needed four-and-a-half hours before his BAC fell to .03, the level at which subjects were released. If any one generalization can be made about today's BAC tables, it's that they underestimate the time it takes to get drunk and to get sober.

Drinking motorcyclists show a strong proclivity for killing themselves. Exactly 42.8 percent of the fatally injured riders in the Hurt Report tested positive for alcohol. In a 1977 study by Baker and Fisher, it was 66.7 percent. Average BAC for the deceased was .14 percent. That's nearly three times the level I had when I crashed on a closed course!

A couple of drunks wobbling dirt bikes around some cones is a lot of laughs. Running off the road at high speed isn't. Drunks don't get hit by left-turning autos; they simply lose control. You can look it up.

The NHTSA is presently taking bids on a study to identify drunk riders. I think the taxpayers' money would be better spent identifying the effects of lower, so-called "legal" BAC levels on rider performance and judgment. Three shots of hooch were enough to demonstrate my impairment in the least ambiguous way. If you insist on drinking before you ride, please never do it on an empty stomach, and allow at least an hour for each drink to be metabolized. You can control alcohol's entry rate, but you can't control its exit. Alcohol leaves the body at a fixed rate and nothing—exercise, cold showers, nor black coffee—can hasten its retreat. But the best advice is the simplest: Don't drink and ride.

Secrets of Smoothness

May 1995

I first met Larry Grodsky in the early 1990s as a novice rider on an FLHS Harley Davidson motorcycle. Reflecting Larry's generosity and patience, I received a three day private lesson riding the blue highways of southeast Ohio following cancellations by others in the group. It had to be Larry's slowest ride on a motorcycle.

I subsequently rode with Larry on IMT tours in Spain and group tours with Stayin' Safe in the Smokies. Even during his riding vacations in Spain, Larry offered his instruction free to everyone. He taught an excellent perspective on safe riding habits and I always learned important new street strategies from Larry's instructions.

Larry had a nice knack for turning the conversation to areas of my medical interests. As a practicing cardiologist among the seniors of Sarasota, Florida, I advocate regular exercise and cardiac fitness as a standard prescription for my patients. Larry and I chatted about the health and riding benefits of fitness. For myself, my patients, family, and friends over the age of 55, I have a conviction that cardiac fitness through regular aerobic exercise can produce a safer and happier ride. Physical fitness will increase our desire to ride, provide us with stamina, flexibility, and balance, preventing premature fatigue on long day rides. Physical fitness leads to mental alertness as well.

Larry left legacies of durable and safe riding strategies to me, offering his counsels with modesty, a sharp wit, and a willingness to listen to others. Larry was a professional with a generous heart; I and the motorcycle community will miss him.

> *Sam Kalush, M.D., cardiologist who had*
> *the privilege of riding with and learning*
> *from Larry Grodsky on several occasions*

In 1818, only two years after Baron Karl von Drais invented the first steerable two-wheeler, the draisine, rumors were already fanning across Europe of a steam-powered version! It would be another 35 years before the French would perfect the first reliable source of locomotion—the pedal crank—but one could argue that the motorcycle appeared before the first bicycle!

One thing's for certain: Even before there were pedals, pedalers were searching for a better way. Mechanically, motorcycles have it all over bicycles, yet pedal bikes haven't gone away. Top road racers and motocrossers have proven that they're a great way to hone physical skills—body steering in particular—and to develop the stamina needed to win big races.

How well-conditioned must a touring rider be? I wish I had an easy answer. Once, while researching an article on endurance riding, I visited a checkpoint on the Iron Butt Rally. The first rider in (and eventual winner) forever shattered my illusions of "ironmen."

Atop his fuel tank he'd perched 10 gallons of blubber, a load much less suited to his spindly bowlegs. Sway-back, he hobbled and creaked his way to the refreshment table—where he quickly downed a ham and cheese sandwich and a cup of coffee. Go figure.

Athletes have very definable fitness requirements; I suppose a touring rider's probably comes down to his personal expectations. Can fitness make you less likely to have an accident? Sure, one could make a case along those lines, but I'd rather work under the assumption that riding is just more fun when you're fit.

So I think what I'll do with my remaining space is a sort of general fitness overview . . . then see if there are any special implications for motorcyclists. My qualifications, by the way, are legit. I was once the girls' physical education teacher at Pleasant City Junior High School.

Cardiovascular Fitness

Overall Fitness Quotient (OFQ) 5; Motorcycling Fitness Quotient (MCFQ) 0

Would you believe the Gold Wing Road Riders Association has a video which instructs Mrs. Gold Wing on how to take over the controls should Mr. Gold Wing suddenly slump over the bars? I suppose it can't hurt to have a look, but really, isn't this a bit like purchasing asteroid insurance?

According to Dr. Sam Kalush, a Michigan Harley rider and cardiovascular surgeon, "Heart attacks are almost completely preventable." A low-fat diet and 20 minutes of vigorous exercise per day will give you a lot better odds against a heart attack than will any video.

Motorcyclists, especially when they're on the road, typically face two obstacles to such activity. Either they just don't *feel* like exercising or they can't find facilities to participate in their normal fitness regimen. When I travel, I like to pack a jump rope, preferably a "professional" model with swivels. Make sure the handles reach to your arm pits exactly when you stand on the midpoint of the rope.

Strength

OFQ 2; MCFQ 2

Strength isn't very important to motorcycling . . . unless you don't have any. Or if you're short-legged and have to support a big bike at rest. Often women riders lack the hand strength necessary for firm braking and good clutch control. Grip strength can be significantly improved by squeezing a tennis ball for several minutes per day.

If road trips mean leaving a gym or a basement full of weights behind, and you can't bear the thought of losing your "chiseled" appearance, there's always the old reliable—pushups. Any decent fitness book will have a variety of upper and lower body exercises. If you suffer from chronic back pain, chances are that your abdominals and lower back muscles have weakened over the years. Get a copy of *The Better Back Book*.

Muscular Endurance

OFQ 3; MCFQ 1

More than anything else, your muscular endurance needs are probably determined by your work. I've never been sorry that I laid down my brick hod in favor of a word processor, but a few times I've regretted neglecting to fill my gas tank.

Which reminds me: Do you know that you have $10,000 or more worth of exercise equipment in your garage? Pushing your bike is an unbeatable way to quickly get rid of a chill, and the workout potential is practically limitless. Whaddya say this July 4, we have the first annual "Pikes Peak Motorcycle Push?" If I'm not there by noon, start without me.

Flexibility

OFQ 4; MCFQ 4

Life just isn't much fun when you're stiff and sore all the time, but even lots of exercise junkies take no time to work on their flexibility. Too lazy to exercise? How about a hot, steamy bath? That's what ballerinas do to dilate their capillaries and deliver lots of good red blood to their muscle tissues.

Then they twist themselves up like pretzels (gawd, I love ballet). Serious stretching is intensely painful (and dangerous if you don't know what you're doing), but it can also be downright euphoric. Why not start by just touching your toes for 30 seconds, followed by a good calf massage. A "seated spine twist" is an exercise you can do on your bike (two to three 10-second repetitions per side). Stretch your shoulder muscles by extending an arm overhead against a wall or tree, lightly weighting it. Take a minute and bend your fingers back for five seconds each.

Habituation is the enemy of anyone engaged in repetitive activities—which in this age of specialization is just about everyone. That's why we now have doctors who treat nothing but music injuries (rub a viola against your neck for six hours a day, 365 days a year, and see if you don't experience any consequences).

As motorcyclists it's crucial to get off the bike and get blood flowing to all the traumatized parts: fingers, wrists, knees, butt, and the less obvious ones . . . stomach, liver, spleen. If you want to enjoy this pastime in your later decades, I'd strongly suggest buying a good book on yoga or t'ai chi.

Quickness

OFQ 2; MCFQ 2.5

If you can run a sub-10-second 100-meter dash, you're wasting your time reading motorcycle magazines. Amateur track stars make *millions* these days.

I was all set to dismiss quickness as a non-entity, but a couple of things made me reconsider. One is a newspaper article I recently read about Alzheimer's. The article discussed a nun who recently passed away. She was about 90 as I recall, but was still a vital cog in the charitable and logistical operations of her convent. So everyone who knew her was shocked to learn, following an autopsy, that her brain was riddled with Alzheimer's!

So what's that got to do with quickness? This: Both mental and physical skills work via nervous pathways. As the body ages, it becomes extremely difficult to establish new pathways, but repetition makes it surprisingly easy to maintain older, well-established ones.

Speaking from my own experience, I took up volleyball a couple of winters ago to get me through those months of cabin fever. It's becoming painfully obvious that I'll never be any good at it, but the diving and rolling—the things which I learned years ago in other sports—are still second nature. The next morning I'm reminded that a man my age shouldn't do those things, but I also realize, when I get in my car or on my bike, that I feel very alert and that my visual skills are extra sharp.

Declining visual skills (not acuity as measured by an eye chart) are probably the biggest cause of poor performance among elderly motorists. I'd bet that older drivers who play ball sports, like tennis and pingpong are significantly under-represented in traffic accidents.

Still, my highly arbitrary rating system dubs quickness a mere "2.5." You can ride motorcycles long after your winged feet have turned to lead, and you can probably maintain good visual quickness by sitting on a stool playing pinball or video games.

Let us not forget that the reason for building machines is to minimize our work. What makes us "fit" may be unclear, but this, I'm sure, is what makes us *civilized*.

A System Error Has Occurred

December 2000

It would have been easy for Larry to beat on Bridgestone here like a rented mule, but the easy way was rarely his way. He could routinely come up with four responses to a yes or no question.

As a recovering trial lawyer ten years ago, I didn't have that problem. I knew exactly what to do when I went down hard in a work zone in Washington, D.C. First I hired a lawyer with sharp teeth. Then I called Larry.

"A construction crew tried to kill me last night," I moaned. "You're going to be my expert witness at $250 an hour. Come to D.C. and I'll show you the scene of the crime. We'll both get rich."

The road had been milled except for a concrete bus platform that stretched for 60' with a two-inch lip. Traffic cones funneled unsuspecting riders into it at a lethal angle, a devastating, invisible edge trap on a dark night. They should have tapered the raised lip with asphalt, but that would have cost money and time.

A few days later Larry and I surveyed the scene. I leaned on my crutches while he walked around, silent and brooding.

"Stop thinking!" I finally yelled. "This place is obviously a minefield."

"I don't think I can stop thinking," he said.

And he really couldn't. He was a philosopher, and I needed a huckster. That wasn't Larry's style. When the case settled, I sent him a photocopy of the check. He just laughed.

Bob Higdon

As the rest of the world elbowed their way toward the cash-leaking hull of the Bridgestone/Firestone ship, I spent my weekend deliberately punching holes in my bike's Bridgestone radials, then plying them over some crumbly rain-sodden urban battlegrounds. I wasn't testing the tires per se, as they'd already comported themselves admirably over their intended life span, nor was I setting the hook for some lunker-sized product liability attorney. In actuality I was testing the puncture preventive "Ride On" for a future issue of this magazine.

Of the tragic Bridgestone/Firestone drama the less levity invoked the better. None of the jokes will seem the least bit funny to the families of the 134 fatal crash victims so far linked to tread separations on the company's tires in the United States and Venezuela. Nor will I, with 1 1/2 pages of editorial space and a few bits gleaned from other media, try to resolve what numerous government agencies and thousands of pages of legal briefs may never bring to closure. I do know, however, that this industrial giant's fight to remain viable will almost certainly fail, throwing many more thousands of lives into chaos.

In a world where a pot of gold—real or apocryphal—awaits at the end of every software rainbow, tire-making is one of the last reminders of our great, grimy industrial heritage. Among my memories of youth still lingers the noxious chemical dagger that was the original Firestone plant in Akron, Ohio—the "Rubber Capital of the World." The EPA, that much-maligned agency, has blunted the most poisonous of those fumes, but tire-making remains, at its core, a most odious process.

So it doesn't surprise me that journalists have had little trouble unearthing whistle blowers among the plant workers in Decatur, Illinois, and Valencia, Venezuela. How hard would it be to find a disgruntled line worker in a sardine cannery in New Brunswick, at a poultry plant in Delaware, or any place where workers perform noisy, smelly, monotonously essential tasks in grim anonymity?

I don't wish to add to or subtract from the mountain of responsibility that Bridgestone/Firestone must ultimately bear, but know this: These are tough guys who play in a very high stakes game. While software "engineers" brush aside their fallen bridges with pithy one-liners ("sorry, a system error has occurred") or obfuscate them in smoky jargon ("failed to parse?"), tire makers *welcome* the slings of zealous governments and the arrows of outrageous consumers. Who but tire makers would, in the jaws of a crushing blizzard, have the *cojones* to flaunt images of little cherubs wrapped sweetly and contentedly inside their steel and Kevlar belts?

When I was 19 years old I ran my first car out of oil and spent a sleepless night freezing my kazoonzies off on a deserted country road.

Although Fiats weren't exactly known for their hearty engines, I, as a consumer, bore the financial burden and learned a valuable lesson in maintenance. Two years later, having forsaken cars, I came within a few millimeters of a catastrophic tire failure on my Triumph motorcycle . . . even though the tire itself was probably defect free.

I'd fitted a new Dunlop K81 in anticipation of my longest ever motorcycle trip—Athens, Ohio, to Virginia Beach and back. I hadn't considered that the new tire had a greater rolling circumference than the K70 it replaced. For that matter, I can't say whether the offending fender bolt was the original or a longer one which I'd fitted during one of several tear-downs. I managed to discover the mounting crisis after I'd carved a 3/8-inch groove in the new tire, but before I'd worn through the carcass. Come to think of it, I *did* crash on the return trip—in a leafy, rain-slicked hairpin on Goshen Pass—but the thought of suing Dunlop never occurred to me at the time.

Considering our paltry numbers, two things amaze me about today's motorcycle market: 1) that giant tire makers still bother with us (peruse any bicycle magazine and see how East Asian "off brands" dominate that sector) and 2) that so many of the hard-earned (and hard-resisted) consumer protections have trickled down to us. Regarding the second point, we now enjoy solid warranties and service plans, websites and toll-free information lines—not to mention supremely accurate application charts to protect us from catastrophes like the one I nearly visited upon myself lo those many years ago. If you've bought a new bike and had it dealer-serviced, chances are technicians in every state know whether you've been naughty or nice with respect to basics like tire pressure and chain maintenance.

You can write your own position paper on the role of Big Brother in motorcycling. Same with the increasingly complex and "automotive" countenance of today's bikes. No matter the outside influences, the motorcyclist's need for self-expression will always triumph. Twenty years ago, the more visionary among us might have foreseen the coming of fuel injection, but who could have dreamed that we'd remap systems in our basements, using our own laptop computers? What makes motorcycles more responsive to tinkering also makes them more susceptible.

I don't have to tell you that small changes on motorcycles can have big consequences. We have, today, a renaissance of stylish aftermarket products; some excellent examples of low-volume, craftsmanlike manufacturing . . . and some equally pointed examples of products rushed to market without the sweat of research and development.

A front-running light kit I recently observed carried a particularly dire side effect. Both dual filament bulbs burned brightly until the rider activated the left or right turn signal. At that moment, the brighter filament on the signaling side cut out, while the dimmer one blinked on and off. Unfortunately, the low wattage blinker became virtually invisible, while the opposite side continued to burn brightly, so that oncoming traffic watched what ostensibly was a left signal for a right-hand turn and a right signal for a left-hander!

The National Highway and Traffic Safety Administration (NHTSA) has been criticized for not investigating Firestone in the '90s, a period in which they received 46 complaints about tread problems out of a pool of 47 million tires. In the world of motorcycles, there's only one watchdog who can successfully guard against low-volume accessory makers dumping uniformly shoddy pieces on the riding public . . . *you*.

To be honest, I don't think I've ever heard of a catastrophic tire failure on a motorcycle (*tubes*, yes—tires, no). The chances of you being injured by a flying truck recap are far greater than the likelihood that you'll experience tread separation on your bike's Metzeler, Dunlop, Pirelli, etc. I've little doubt, though, that riders have suffered injuries, some of them fatal, in low-traction situations where fresher, properly inflated rubber would have prevailed.

It's my hope that the Bridgestone/Firestone debacle will cause each of us motorcyclists to reflect upon the control we have over our own destinies. We know that hot weather was a factor in most of the tread separations, and some reports lead us to suspect that underinflation played a role. Most of today's street tires *like* running in good, hot conditions, but check those pressures. If the difference between cold and hot pressures is much more than four pounds you may be running underinflated or simply running too fast and long for conditions.

Think twice before you make modifications to your bike—what possible downsides might you experience? Little things matter; when you clean your bike, check for loose nuts and bolts. Instead of a new chrome gee-gaw this week, why not buy a torque wrench? Tonight, instead of watching a vapid sitcom, why not read (or reread) your owner's manual?

Jim Hansen, who is the publisher of the Rider Group, which of course includes this title, has a theory that the recent upsurge in motorcycle sales stems in part from the litany of sanctions which government and other societal monitors impose on daily life in the name of "safety." People, maintains Hansen, are saying, "To heck with all these restraints—I *want* to take some risks!"

The difference, I'd say, between motorcyclists and people who merely own motorcycles is that motorcyclists understand the risks. They might exhibit vastly different riding styles or attitudes toward things like helmets and protective gear, but if they're real motorcyclists they know what they've gotten themselves into. And they know that no one—not Congress, not NHTSA, not Johnny Cochran or F. Lee Bailey—can reboot for them after a serious system error has occurred.

Bearing Strait

August 1996

My take on LG with wrenches? This article on bearings is a perfect point of departure; I always told Larry he could "f—k up a steel ball with a banana." I enjoy a long-standing agreement with a shop that both employs me and allows me to work on my own jobs after hours. Discovering this, Larry showed up for occasional coaching that always led to hands-on help— mine! Once I suggested he get a full-time job so he could pay me for some work; he responded, "That is not what I want to do with my life." For reasons unknown, I have always let people I like take advantage of me; if somehow this "help" could be cashed in, the payoff would buy something nice.

In a way it did. I recently accompanied Larry on a training tour as a guest coach—an experience cash wouldn't have bought. We had no maintenance issues that trip but my trained eyes, ears, and riding feel detected that the tour master was the same guy that visited me late nights years before. Larry messed up some repairs (as he laments in this column) but at least he knew some repairs were needed; others ride on in total ignorance.

Travel was always his goal and he needed to learn the nature of his machines to deal with problems encountered en route. The guy went places on bikes and ultimately led others; if moving forward is the measure, he did well enough.

Neil Barker, mechanic, friend

It's a gray, contemplative morning as I sit at my desk, staring at number E32005JS/26, one of a pair for which the local dealer lightened my wallet by $60. Not surprisingly, the bearing warehouse down the road wants $24 less for American-made Timken replacements. Maybe I'll take these back . . . or maybe I won't. It's nice to know that 12 minutes from my home sits a half million dollars worth of parts—parts that no one will ask for today, but which tomorrow might mean the difference between walking and riding.

Incredible devices, bearings. I know not the words to describe their circular bridge between complex machinery and the elemental functions of component parts . . . but one effortless spin around the index finger makes it crystal clear. Even someone as mechanically challenged as I, can see why my bike, with 62,000 hard miles on its odometer, will continue to steer wretchedly until they're installed in its steering head.

This particular unit, a tapered roller bearing, consists of an inner and an outer race, a cage and 21 steel rollers. Who knows what other uses the E32005JS/26 is being put to at this moment? A tractor on a Siberian collective? A hospital generator in war-torn Liberia? Maybe there are even E32005JS/26s orbiting the Earth, helping to beam Australian rules football into our living rooms? But the question that *really* burns in my mind is: Who's going to put these bearings in my motorcycle?

When I was 10 or 11 years old, my classmates and I took the Cooter Preference Test. Besides spawning weeks of "cooties" jokes, it helped our teachers and counselors steer us toward courses and vocations which would make us productive citizens. According to the Cooter abacus, 94 out of 100 boys and girls my age liked fixing machinery more than I did. Today, not surprisingly, my list of equipment functioning below spec is considerable: typewriter, fax machine, stereo, TV . . . even the freezer needs defrosting. As long as they start and run, I'll ignore them, but the E32005JS/26s must go in at once, because sticky or loose steering head bearings make my skin crawl.

I just don't know who's going to install them. Last year I bought new head bearings for another bike, and it took me nearly a week of torching and banging to get the old ones off the steering stem. Any mechanic who knows a vacuum gauge from a torque wrench would have had me on the road in two hours.

"You've been working on bikes all these years," sighed a mechanic friend of mine not so long ago. "What'll it take for you to figure out that you're just not any *good* at it?" I dunno, the time I reversed the oil lines and blew up my Bonnie's newly rebuilt engine didn't stop me . . . nor the time I wrecked my GPZ's rear brake caliper by installing both pads on the same side of the disc.

But I've seen pros botch up routine tasks, too. On a recent tour, a wrench at a major dealership removed my bike's rear wheel, then forgot to reinsert a bushing. Just before the wheel bearings turned to metal shavings, I stopped at another authorized dealership for an oil change . . . and rode away with no filler cap!

Most mechanics are conscientious and vastly more qualified than you and I, but everyone makes mistakes, and either of those oversights could have caused a nasty accident. That's why, despite my limited mechanical acumen, I like tinkering with my bike. I like knowing the functions of individual parts—the difference between right and wrong and how to resolve it.

Where do you draw the line between maintenance and meddling? Last December, about 40 miles south of Austin, Texas, I felt that my bike wasn't handling solidly. Within another mile I *knew* it wasn't. I pulled over, and sure enough I had a flat rear tire, the first since I switched to heavy-duty enduro tubes several years ago. Because my bike has spoked wheels it can't run tubeless tires, and that means there are about 40 orifices for air to rush out of when there is a puncture. Armed with this routine mechanical knowledge, I made the decision to switch. Out in the sticks, I had the skill and the tools to get my bike back on the road in less than an hour. My hands and clothes were covered with grease . . . but not *blood,* which they may well have been had I experienced a sudden blowout at speed. At that moment I was very glad that I'd learned a thing or two about tire maintenance.

I always carry a spare tube, but not the two sizes (17 and 21 inch) which my bike uses, since I can cram the 21-inch tube into the 17-inch tire (but not vice versa). It's an acceptable temporary measure. I then rode another 800 miles and parked the bike, scarcely touching it over the next month. When the time rolled around to depart on another tour, I disregarded the oversized tube; the tire had 2,500 miles left, and I would replace it then.

Seventeen hundred miles later, running two-up with luggage at 75 mph in 95-degree heat, the tube burst. It took a quarter mile of bronc wrestling to bring the bike to a halt. By then the tire had twisted off the rim like a bow tie at 3 a.m. on prom night; inside, the tube was a mosaic of scuffs and creases.

So, what did I learn from the experience? Regarding motorcycles or tires, nothing . . . but I learned something about myself. From now on, when I decide whether or not to take my bike to a mechanic, I won't just ask if I'm able to do the job myself, but also what level of attention I'm willing to devote to it. My mechanic friend has an expression: "You can judge a mechanic by the way he mounts a license plate." A 10-minute job by a professional receives 10 minutes of his undivided attention, but few shade-tree mechanics share that clear-eyed, dispassionate focus. Without love we are nothing.

Back in the waning days of the Meriden cooperative, Triumph advertising lionized the owners of their maintenance-intensive Bonnevilles, labeling them "experts"; others (Honda owners) were merely "enthusiasts." Today, representatives of the reborn British marque openly confess to a "Japanese manufacturing philosophy." Simple math confirms that there aren't enough hours in a year to ride, pay off, and overhaul your new motorcycle.

I'm not sure what constitutes an "expert" rider, but I dare say some knowledge of what's going on between his legs is still a prerequisite. A musician who aborted a concert because he couldn't change a broken string or reed would likely find his career foreshortened. Motorcyclists who drop their bikes at the dealer with blanket instructions to "take care of everything" jeopardize the intimate man/machine relationship so important in smooth, safe riding.

Years of teaching Experienced RiderCourses (ERCs) and more recently taking to the road with my students have revealed some pretty consistent patterns of neglect. Number one would be tires—underinflated, dry-rotted, cupped, squared-off, or plain worn out. After that batteries (loose or corroded terminals, low water), cables (unlubed, improperly adjusted), worn, dry and maladjusted chains (too loose is better than too tight), mushy brakes, loose/missing bolts. Every spring I receive a rash of calls from students whose bikes won't start because they didn't store them with fuel stabilizer, and every summer I hit the road with riders who carry neither tools nor owners' manuals.

It doesn't require a trained mechanic to detect any of these maladies; they should be recognized by every motorcycle owner.

So who's gonna install my steering head bearings? Well, it happens I just got an offer on my bike from a guy who didn't even ride it. I may just take his offer and throw in a free pair of E32005JS/26s. Let someone else make the tough decisions.

Training

A Few Good Men

April 2004

Larry began his motorcycle safety teaching with the West PA Regional MSF program in the early 80s, and retained his certification with MSF until '97. While he eventually concentrated on his on-street program, he maintained his confidence in the good basic foundation the program provides. In this article, he encourages potential instructors to join up.

Pete Tamblyn

Even in the northernmost latitudes—where the crocuses require a jackhammer to pierce the permafrost—the days they are a lengthening. Machines pull men inexorably toward basements, to take up carb stix and timing light, and to simply dream. For of all the urges of two-wheeled man, the most primal is to spend warm days in the saddle.

And yet, there is a breed of motorcyclist—rarer than an albino buck, queerer than a duck-billed platypus—who chooses to spend his weekends, twisting neither throttle nor spanner, but rather pounding feet tortilla-flat, while those around him struggle to master the subtleties of piloting a motorcycle. People such as my friend, Chris Freed.

I'm proud to say that I recruited Freed into the ranks of safety instructors six years ago. Since that time he's trained many hundreds of fortunate motorcyclists. He rides about 8,000 miles a year, nearly every inch in city traffic, but the last time he took a recreational ride, Pete Rose was still signing autographs for free. From April through October, he averages 30 hours a week engaged in teaching and related activities; in a good week he might get paid for 10.

Perhaps even Freed lacks the patience of Ralph Duff, an instructor I trained alongside 10 years ago this month. This man once took 80 hours to finish teaching a 20-hour course. If Duff had a weakness, it was that he just couldn't bear to see another human fail. In fact it was rumored among his fellow instructors that Ralph had taught Helen Keller to ride a motorcycle!

One of the best women I know is Celine Nista—at least when she's dispatching opponents in men's racquetball tournaments. The rest of the time she's one of the best instructors and most unselfish people I know. A site coordinator and nine-year veteran instructor, Celine is a well-known figure to Pittsburgh area riders—especially women, for whom she's a symbol of poise, achievement, and self-assurance.

My favorite Nista anecdote involves a local sheriff who took umbrage at the ease with which she negotiated a series of esses on her Interceptor. Frustrated in his attempts to quantify her swiftness, said sheriff instead issued forth a citation for "reckless operation."

Not one to shrink from a fight, our heroine appeared in court armed with literature on safe riding practices—and bedecked in a form-fitting set of tri-color leathers! Not only did the judge dismiss the charges, upbraiding the sheriff for his shoddy police work, *Her* Honor demanded to know how she might register for one of "those riding courses!"

I wish that all my instructor tales were so cheery, but they're not. While unloading training bikes at Pittsburgh's Robert Morris College, instructor Bernie Zickefoose fell and broke his back. Six weeks later, he was teaching again.

Across town, Lynn Leskovic met with a similarly painful fate while directing a lane change drill. It was Leskovic's misfortune that after seven years of signaling students, he encountered one who couldn't tell left from right. Lynn hobbled through the remainder of the season strapped to a knee brace.

What makes these people carry on? I doubt that it's money. Average instructor salaries around the country are about $10–$15 per hour, which doesn't sound bad until you factor in the updates, the remedial lessons, and the hours spent setting up and tearing down. A realistic average might be half that amount, and in some programs, instructors work as volunteers—without pay.

One thing is certain: 3,431 MSF certified instructors to service an estimated 4 million street riders, nationwide, is no surplus. Presently, there are 34 state-funded programs, with legislation proposed in perhaps another 10. "But," says Bob Reichenberg, MSF education manager, "I doubt there's a state coordinator who would tell you he has an adequate number of qualified instructors."

Just what *is* a "qualified instructor?" MSF certification (not the only standard but the most widely recognized one) requires completion of a 40-hour instructor course that includes student teaching. Candidates gain admission to an instructor course by passing a basic riding skills test and, in some cases, completing an interview and a pre-course written assignment.

If you'd like to become an instructor, and you live in one of the fortunate 34, the road has already been paved for you. If not, you should know that every MSF instructor candidate in the other 16 states without legislated funding undergoes training in how to initiate, fund, and promote rider education courses.

A limited amount of highway safety (402) funds is still available to seed new programs in non-legislated states—states such as New York, which despite ranking third in new motorcycle sales, was only 29th in riders trained, with 617 in 1988. If there is no program available in your area, it could be because you and your club haven't started one.

As with anything worthwhile, there is a difference between doing it and doing it well. MSFs recertification policy requires instructors to teach a minimum of one 15-hour course every three years—a standard meant to keep people in the fold, not razor sharp.

"To stay sharp, one weekend every two months is necessary," says Reichenberg, who coordinates a Walnut, California, site. "In a seasonal program, probably one weekend each month."

I can appreciate that kind of dedication because, frankly, I don't have it. As a freelance writer, I *need* a part-time job, and one working with motorcyclists is a bonus. A sunny weekday and I'm on my bike—*gone*. Plus, I write for a magazine that (hopefully) sends me on several great trips per year.

But I share the same rewards as those other "average" instructors: the hope that my efforts might make someone a little sharper, a little safer; the taste of my own first rides each time I watch a new motorcyclist experience "rider's high;" and the energizing warmth in a grateful handshake, or a note of thanks.

Maybe you could, too. For information on instructor training programs contact the MSF at 2 Jenner Street, Suite 150, Irvine, California 92718 or on the web at www.msf-usa.org. In Canada, write to the Motorcycle Training Program, Canada Safety Council, 1765 Saint Laurent Boulevard, Ottawa, Ontario, Canada KIG 3T9.

Celine Nista recalls the following phone conversation with Larry immediately following her victory in traffic court:

CN: *"L.G.!"*

LG: *"That would be me!"*

CN: *"Guess what?"*

LG: *"What?"*

CN: *"I won!"*

LG: *"Get out!"*

CN: *"I dazzled the judge with my performance!"*

LG: *"I knew you could do it; after all, you ARE the Safety Princess!"*

CN: *"I think it was those leathers you bought me in England that got her attention, Larry! I looked so professional, it didn't matter what I said!"*

> *Celine Nista, Safety Princess and Pennsylvania Western Region Coordinator/MSF RiderCoach Trainer*

Rolling the Ball Out

February 2001

In 2000, the MSF (Motorcycle Safety Foundation) presented the BRC (Basic RiderCourse) curriculum to its instructors at a conference in Florida, and I attended. Larry then asked me to compare the BRC and the MSF's older course. He said he thought of getting re-certified to see for himself the current uproar within the rider education community.

At the time, concerns arose about the quality of the BRC. Instructors also questioned their title change to "rider coach." Coaching meant that just speaking from a lectern would no longer be acceptable. Thus, some fear and resentment set in.

Fast-forwarding to 2007 has not changed the level of commotion among rider educators nor has my own opinion of it changed. I remember telling Larry that students seemed to learn well and enjoy the content of a parking-lot course. I also said those with an instructor-centered approach would remain unhappy since education—as a field—underscores student-centered learning.

However, having taken Larry's own on-road course, among others, I also would highlight that the BRC has become part of motorcycle lexicon. It is a reference point for riders and rider educators, and it gives us a decent foundation—as well as insurance perks!

I also would tell Larry that learning how to ride in a parking lot in no way compares to learning how to really ride with him on roads offering random hazards as well as heart-pounding twisties, vistas, and charming pit stops. But then, he probably already knows.

Lee Uehara, New York City-based educator,
journalist, MSF RiderCoach

Many of you who read this column probably assume that I am a Motorcycle Safety Foundation instructor. Actually, it's been the position of the Foundation for some years that there are *no* MSF instructors, only MSF-*certified* instructors. But let's not split hairs. Although I taught MSF courses for more than 15 years, I'm not presently certified, and I do not intend to ever recertify as an instructor.

My credentials expired nearly two years ago, and because I teach a course of my own design these days, I just never bothered to retrain, although it has been on my "to do" list since my sheepskin first began to yellow. Now I'm told that none of the more than 5,000 dedicated men and women who pound their feet into pudding each weekend for the love of motorcycling will get the opportunity to renew their instructor credentials when their cards expire.

By 2003, the 15-year-old Motorcycle RiderCourse Riding and Street Skills (MRC-RSS) program which has spawned a whole generation of street riders, will be no more, to be replaced by the new Basic RiderCourse (BRC), a slightly shorter program, with a much more economical monogram. And while many of the same friendly faces will continue to bark signals at the local training sites, they'll no longer operate as "instructors" but rather as "coaches." It's a semantic change. Or is it?

Growing up in a sports-crazy environment, coaches provided my most steadfast role model. An "instructor," I always believed, was someone who presented a basic skill set or a standardized curriculum. "Teachers" or "educators" occupied a higher plateau—professionals who could write lesson plans and whose knowledge extended beyond a specific subject area to the subtleties of human learning. Back when I was in school, it seemed the best teachers were also coaches, and they were the motivators—the ones who took the success of their students as a moral obligation.

So why are MSF soon-to-be-coaches up in arms over the name change? Posts on the instructor email list currently run about five to one against the name change and the new curriculum in general . . . even though no one has yet seen a course syllabus, and few instructors have observed more than a handful of exercises. The rub appears to be the way in which the Foundation chose to break the news—in a video mailed to every certified instructor in the nation. Many unwrapped their packages expecting a breakdown of new teaching techniques, but what they found was a breezy 10-minute promo piece.

Wrote one list member: "Nothing gets my guard up quicker than being told, 'There's nothing to worry about—this is a good thing' without being told anything of substance about what they're talking about.

"... People handle change better when they're given the facts early," continued the instructor. "Start off with propaganda and you immediately put people on the defensive."

The word "change" is a highly suggestive one, and changes within the Motorcycle Safety Foundation can draw markedly different responses. Although millions operate under the misguided assumption that MSF "provides" training to riders across the country, their role is that of publisher, vendor, and standards enforcer. To their clients—budget-conscious administrators who purchase the books and films and who must coordinate statewide efforts to keep programs in compliance—the Foundation's six curriculum revisions in seven years made it a dervish of change, difficult if not impossible to keep pace with.

By contrast, many instructors see the Foundation as a woolly mammoth frozen in ice. To these men and women, mostly part-timers who bring a diversity of life and motorcycling experiences to rider training, MSF's strict standards often came across as the ministrations of a rigid and out-of-touch bureaucracy. Perhaps the most unpopular example is the soon-to-be-banished "armchairs" in which classroom instructors conduct the student body through an air-guitar suite written for clutch, throttle, shifter, and brakes. The omission of even one armchair movement would result in an unsatisfactory evaluation for an experienced instructor; for a student teacher ... the "death penalty."

Few enthusiasts have any idea how politicized rider education can be; those who do find it both amusing and embarrassing. Of the two Chief Instructors I solicited opinions from, one strongly favored the new curriculum, while the other felt only a "few good adjustments" were needed to the old RSS. Both agreed to speak only off the record. Later I phoned MSF's curriculum department, which referred me to their communications department, which declined to answer questions as innocuous as "Will the students cover more miles in the new course?" If the free world can tread water a little longer, we'll learn the answer to that question and others when the foundation presents the finalized curriculum at its International Safety Conference in Orlando during the first week of March 2001.

From the hints and snippets so far released, it appears the new course should squeeze in more saddle time, but include fewer exercises with less waiting in line. Classroom time has been reduced (a nearly 20-year trend). Opponents have used terms like "dumbing down;" however, the less-formal introduction of early skills mirrors a trend I've observed in beginner courses in three different countries. Call it a "roll the ball out" approach, but each of those other courses succeeded at getting novices to shift gears earlier and to execute tricky maneuvers like U-turns in a "more natural environment."

Ironically, what's bothering some instructors more than the "coach" designation is the implication that they'll actually have less coaching responsibility in the new course. We'll see. But surely no one will mourn the passing of exercise nine, "Sharp Turns." This 25-year monument to overcoaching has accounted for more training casualties than any other range exercise . . . including some instructors caught in the crossfire while flapping their arms in the mandatory "Braa-aake! LOOK!" pantomime.

Rolling the ball out doesn't have to be a bad thing. Were Little League dads not the death of pick-up baseball games? And soccer moms have merely turned the world's most popular game into a metaphor for suburban angst and inattentive driving. The balance of world power won't hinge upon the MSF's or anybody else's riding course. We should give it at least the same chance we'd give a Middle East peace plan.

Humble Pie

April 2003

In life it seems that all things eventually come full circle. Larry was once an MSF site administrator for Pennsylvania's MSF program, but had moved on to found his own on-road training curriculum by the time I met him. I learned to operate a motorcycle long ago in an MSF course, but I learned to ride a motorcycle from Larry. He was an exceptional teacher, with the ability to open the eyes of others to see the obvious in a different way. There was a Jewish proverb shared at Larry's funeral: "To save a life is to save the universe." Larry through his training efforts and writing has saved my life many times and I'm sure there are many others that feel the same way.

In this article, Larry kindly credits my small part as, with roles reversed, I counseled him (mostly in patience) while he re-certified as an MSF RiderCoach. Curious perhaps of the controversy stirred up by the new curriculum, Larry had opted to find out for himself. Once in the program, though, he questioned his motives and desire to continue; I'm flattered he credits my helping him hang in there.

Larry was a man of action and often took the road less traveled. This article details his returning full circle to his roots, and heading off once again to set his own path.

Leon Winfrey, instructor
Harley/Buell Rider Edge program

It was 4 a.m. in Colton, California, and the restaurant was as still as a Gays for Falwell rally. No surprise there.

"Would you like smoking or non-smoking?" asked the hostess, a fidgety bleach blonde.

"Well," I shrugged, "If you're offering a choice, I guess I'll take non-smoking." I ordered coffee and turned to my notebook. A minute later the hostess, bored with her graveyard shift, plopped herself in the chair next to mine. "You don't mind if I *smoke*, do you?" she asked.

That was the lightest moment in what proved to be two of the most stressful weeks of my life. It was 1989, and I'd held down this magazine page for half a year. It was time, I felt, to earn my field's highest credential: MSF's Chief Instructor certification. I knew it would be tough. Stories were legion of the severe tests to which prospective Chiefs were put.

My overseers, an elite gang of seven known in the fraternity as the Super Chiefs, were nice enough individuals. Collectively, they guarded the inner circle like a pack of wild dogs, ready to kill at the first sniff of weakness. Last man down was a father of two who would lose his job as a program administrator because he failed to flag *me* for speeding in a student teaching demonstration. How'd you like that one on your conscience?

My subsequent teaching partner was a black mark away from the funeral pyre—as was I—when he made a small but "fatal" riding error in the eyes of the Super Chiefs. Under the code of the day, I had to make a choice: step in and fry my partner . . . or spare him and kill myself.

I could have tried again a year later. They would've given me a second crack, but the wound to my pride was deep. By '93 I'd developed my own on-street course, and the chief status no longer seemed so important. By '97 I let my MSF certification lapse entirely, but Dave Surgenor, the Foundation's coordinator for my state of Pennsylvania, always kept the door open for me to come back.

This past November, my schedule cleared and I made the commitment to retrain, not as a Chief—that ship's sailed—but as a soldier in the army of RiderCoaches, as they're known in the parlance of the new Basic RiderCourse (BRC). A lot of controversy has greeted the introduction of MSF's new "learner-centered" curriculum—mostly from veteran instructors, inured to the 14-year-old course it replaces. I thought it best to learn the new course from the ground up, just like a rookie RiderCoach.

So I didn't tell my eight classmates about my day job, but most of my supervising instructors knew. And they were many.

For this was not merely a RiderCoach Prep session. We arrived on the second week of a RiderCoach Trainer (formerly "Chiefs") Prep session. A *double* one. By the weekend, the old Caterpillar plant in York, Pennsylvania, would rumble with 24 motorcyclists who didn't know how to ride but were being taught by 19 people who didn't know how to teach . . . who in turn would be taught by 22 people who didn't know how to teach people to be teachers! The survivors, I imagined, would be joined in holy matrimony by the Rev. Sun Myung Moon, who would burst out of the adjacent Harley factory on a 100th anniversary Heritage Softail in 24k gold.

To say that I was skeptical is to put it mildly, but I placed high expectations on myself. I would keep my mouth shut. And I would LEARN. The administrative nightmare was beyond my control, but the learning was mine for the taking.

Ray Ochs would love that last phrase. An old friend of the *Rider* staff (he was Program Coordinator of the Traffic Safety Institute at Eastern Kentucky University, scene of multiple *Rider* Rallies), Dr. Ochs is the architect of today's kinder, gentler MSF, the one that dictates that "Riders should attribute success to their own effort and ability, rather than the instruction/coaching of a RiderCoach" (page 28, RiderCoach Guide).

In this new curriculum, instructors are considered "facilitators" and not experts in their field. My teachers—the Coach Trainer candidates— were a surprisingly relaxed bunch, a far cry from the death-row inmates with whom I pounded rocks in '89.

The course we taught was as new back then as the BRC is today, but I have to admit these "non-expert" trainers were better prepared than we were. Many, like Leon Winfrey, a trainer with Harley/Buell's Rider's Edge program, were professional teachers. I met Leon five years ago when he enrolled in one of my training rides. Two years and another training ride passed before Winfrey, a junior high gym teacher at the time, told me that he was an MSF-certified instructor. I don't know why, but he chose me as a mentor, often traveling at his own expense to shadow me and to pick my brain. These days, when Milwaukee gives him time off, he often assists me on my rides.

But in York, Leon was doing the mentoring, patiently walking me through my lesson plans each evening, answering questions, reassuring whenever the new system frustrated me. I'm not a good student, and frankly there were times in the first half of the week when I thought I should just walk.

Leon was one of the best, but he wasn't atypical of the group. On Friday night, Bobbie Carlson, MSF's Senior Manager of Program Services, threw a dinner party for the new Chiefs and invited me along. All 99 candidates had successfully passed their training. Many, I realized, weren't yet riding motorcycles in '89 when I bombed out of the program. Their confidence wasn't that of grizzled survivors but of an elite corps, groomed for success in the Ivy League tradition: start with the best; finish with the best. If *they* fail, the *system's* failed.

Unfortunately, that approach doesn't work on novices performing risky activities in a public course. A goal of the new curriculum is a safer training environment, and it's known that accidents in the old course often befell older, less fit and—dare I say it—female riders. One of the first things I noticed when the actual novices arrived was the new waiver form—orally delivered. Listening to the graphic catalog of potential disasters for which they had to waive indemnity, I half-expected to see students walk.

They all stayed, however, and nine of 12 passed. Among my student teaching assignments was the last range exercise, the "skill loop," preparatory to the final exam. My partner, Scott Hertzog, and I kept right on schedule, but our students couldn't. Several still didn't have the hang of the figure 8s. We could wrap up the lesson or try some remedial, exceeding our time allotment and risking an "unsat."

"It's your lesson," said our supervising instructor, (6-foot, 4-inch Air Force Master Sergeant) Tim Becker, somewhat icily. Shades of '89.

"Let's roll," said partner Hertzog, or words to that effect. We ran 20 minutes over. Two of the struggling students nailed the 8s on their test. Master Sgt. Becker gave us both passing grades. I am now a certified RiderCoach (for two years).

What most impressed me was that not one handlebar touched the ground in 10 hours of training, even though our novices were trained by nine rookie instructors, shadowed by 11 neophyte chiefs. Although it'll be three years before all states have fully switched to the BRC curriculum, early reports indicate that the accident rate is lower by perhaps two-thirds in the new course. Less teaching pressure and more emphasis on low-speed control are the explanations most widely given.

The Foundation and state programs face some big hurdles. One reason, in my opinion, for the new "guide on the side" style of teaching is that it's so difficult to find enough talented, dedicated riders who like and are good at teaching (www.msf-usa.org if you wanna give it a try). The learner-centered classroom is touchy-feely in the extreme, and that's because market researchers hired by the Foundation reported that students felt MSF was mean (or at least pushed people too hard). So the pendulum swung completely in the other direction, but it will likely settle in the middle over time.

"If the wheels aren't *turning,* they're not *learning!*" is a popular coach's slogan, so riding time is up . . . but not by that much. I've personally observed five novice programs in three countries, and frankly, MSF's is the only one that even has a classroom. If I were King, I'd scrap the five-hour session and mail each student the video. Then I'd put them in smaller groups and see that they double their miles.

MSF, you have 23 more columns to revoke my credentials.

The Next Big Thing

September 1992

Following a decade or so working with the Motorcycle Safety Foundation, Larry observes that critical skills taught in the classroom and on the training range aren't making the transition to the street. Regrettably, it seemed then unlikely that the MSF would add a meaningful on-street component to its curriculum, apparently having decertified one state program that dared to do so on its own.

This prescient column hints what the next big thing in rider education will be for Mr. Safety—the following year he launched his own on-street curriculum, Stayin' Safe Motorcycle Training. Unfortunately, every training tour wasn't silk smooth. To wit:

Pete Tamblyn

In the summer of 2005, I signed up for a 2-day Stayin' Safe course in Wisconsin. Larry and his assistant, Leon Winfrey, were to be the instructors. The first day began with an hour of discussions at a restaurant, and on to a large parking lot to do some low speed drills. Then we advanced to the beautiful Wisconsin country backroads for on-the-road coaching. We were in one-way radio communication with either Larry or Leon, depending on whose group we were in.

We spent a full, hot summer day unlearning bad habits and trying to internalize good habits. It was hard work. After lunch, we got turned around (read: lost). Larry was unfamiliar with the Wisconsin backroads and we got lost several times that day. To make matters worse, we rode through a downpour that lasted close to an hour. By about 5 p.m., we were exhausted, hungry, and still a good hour's ride from our evening destination when we made our last gas stop.

This combination of factors conspired to create a predicament when it was discovered that Larry's tank had accidentally been topped off with diesel. Without going into detail, in hindsight one might say the students were too creative in resolving the crisis. Suffice to say the gas station owner was highly displeased by their genius, and before it was all over the words "hazardous waste spill" (along with a surfeit of expletives) were spoken and a confrontation with several levels of law enforcement ensued.

Larry was very professional about it and took full responsibility for his students' totally unacceptable behavior. He gave his information to the authorities but, to my knowledge, was never contacted.

I think the cops felt we'd had enough punishment from the owner.

Mike Doran, builder, Stayin' Safe Motorcycle Training student

Funny how things go. In a flagging economy and a legal environment where swimming pool owners must remove springboards in fear of divers who don't know which end to bounce on, suddenly, inconceivably, we have factory demo teams with shiny new motorcycles of every description for us to try.

I think Yamaha's latest attempt to stir up interest is especially sharp. I'm talking about the four truckloads of 600cc Seca IIs that the company dispatched to select dealers around the country this spring. Now the Seca is a nifty roadster that can satisfy all kinds of riders, but none more than the all important 18 to 27-year-old male, i.e. the sport-bike crowd. Reality dipped in Ferrari red or basic black, it perfectly balances the spheres of comfort, performance, and skill . . . and at $3,799 (discounted by up to $600 in some markets) it has the power to convert wannabe racers into honest-to-gosh riders.

At the request of a local Yamaha dealer, I spent a weekend accompanying groups of demo riders on a swoopy, green, 15-mile loop. During that time I became pretty familiar with the Seca, but I learned even more about the habits of the typical rider. I'm pleased to report that I didn't see any truly stupid behavior—just some odd quirks, "it can't happen to me" wardrobes, and too many reminders of the need for more education.

I had to chuckle at the number of riders trying to "hang-off" like GP stars, but I wasn't laughing when I saw how few of them comprehended the importance of "late apexing," particularly in left turns, where an oncoming car can knock someone's kneecap off. And of the dozens I rode behind, only *one* made regular lane adjustments to accommodate changing traffic conditions.

I noticed that a fair number of testers were rider-education graduates, so I must ask the obvious question: Why aren't they employing the street strategies that are emphasized in every Motorcycle Safety Foundation novice and experienced RiderCourse? Well, would you speak French if you had studied it for only one hour in school?

Interestingly, after they'd followed behind me or another safety instructor for a few miles, some of the riders began to pick up on our lane adjustments . . . moving to the right to distance oneself from a left-turning vehicle . . . to the left to avoid a car poking out of a driveway . . . to the right to establish a line-of-sight with cars tailgating tall trucks. I suspect that most of these riders could sit through a classroom session and snap off the correct answers to lane positioning questions, but without practical application they lacked any sense of the degree and the frequency to which lane adjustments are necessary.

On-street training isn't a new idea; it was an optional three-hour module in MSF's original 23-hour course, but one which never quite caught on. In 1976, less than a year after the original curriculum was designed, a feasibility study performed by an independent consultant group on 300 Denver area students found no measurable difference between the half that were street-trained and those who spent three additional hours on the range. Their field test was the "street oriented" MOST (motorcycle operator skill test), a tool whose complexity and high accident rate kept it from ever achieving widespread application.

Now few scientists would stake their careers on a sampling of 300 unpredictable humans, but more importantly—who makes the determination of what skills are "street-oriented" and which are "range-oriented?" And isn't a student's ability to *avoid* panic maneuvers at least as important as his skill in executing them?

Trainers in 1976 lacked the tools to make such an assessment, but today there are devices, such as the Michigan Driver Performance Test (Michigan State University), which evaluates riders' abilities to scan and recognize hazards. In Japan, as reported in our coverage of the 1990 International Motorcycle Safety Conference (*The Humans are Heard From,*

February 1991), high-tech "eye cameras" are used to record students' scanning patterns in concert with chase vans that videotape their lane adjustments.

High tech doesn't come cheap, and neither does insurance when a program suddenly decides to take its students from the womblike confines of the parking lot to the urban combat zones. Add to this increased instructor costs (this instructor would never assume responsibility for more than three students in traffic) and you've come up with a plot much thicker than the typical MSF course. Of the 40 state-funded programs in the United States, only Kansas has a mandate extending beyond the parking lot.

Cynics might argue that Kansas is a parking lot, but Gerald Christensen, the Director of Driver and Traffic Safety Education for the state's board of education, insists that on-street is the only way to go.

"It's like learning to drive a bus or fly an airplane," argues Christensen. "To develop the necessary cognitive and psychomotor skills you've got to get out there with the vehicle, and as an educator I can't conceive of any other way."

In the Kansas system, which is administered through local school districts, the MSF core curriculum (15 hours) is employed, but courses span 24 hours, of which six to eight hours are spent in traffic. MSF, which stresses nationwide uniformity, is less than enthralled with the maverick system and has stripped Christensen of his chief instructor credentials, but the Kansan doesn't seem perplexed.

"State government doesn't ask nonprofit corporations for approval. In the main, theirs (MSF's) is an excellent, state-of-the-art curriculum," he acknowledges. "We just take things further."

Indeed, 70 percent of the state's current instructors are certified teachers, and all of them must complete 84 hours of instructor preparation compared to MSF's 52. Although the insurance costs of putting bikes on the road add an estimated 20 percent to the program costs, Kansas, according to Christensen, boasts the lowest claim rate in the nation—only two serious accidents in 20 years. Despite higher insurance premiums and instructor costs, tuition has remained affordable (average of $60–$70; free in some districts) thanks to a surcharge of $1 per year on motorcycle licenses.

So why can't MSF acquiesce to an obviously good plan? Because MSF is the motorcycle *industry,* and the industry has already poured way more promotional money into the American market than any other in the world. The perception in other countries is that we Americans want neat, quick-fix solutions—helmet laws, air bags . . . convenient one-weekend courses.

We are, of course, more complicated than that. We're a nation of many extremes and untold contradictions. Maybe we don't know what we want, but we usually know a good thing when we see it. Just over the border, in British Columbia, more than 8,000 students have voluntarily paid for a 15-hour traffic skills course after completing the Canada Safety Council's 24-hour basic skills training. As with the Kansas program, only top instructors with extensive in-traffic training may assume the responsibility of leading neophytes onto the street.

Americans are willing to pay for a good product that fulfills a clear need. At a time when new motorcycle sales are dominated by second-generation riders and mature re-entry enthusiasts, the need is clearer than ever. Let's hope some enterprising educators will take up the challenge. It's the American way. It's the next big thing.

Fakin' It

July 1989

Back in the mid sixties I had the privilege of serving under a WWII era colonel. He liked to talk about his initial checkout in the F-102 Delta Dagger Interceptor, one of the USAF's early supersonic jets. Being as there were no two seat F-102 models available, the colonel's training consisted of classroom instruction and a thorough review of the aircrafts manuals. His initial flight was to strap in, by himself, and hang on. The military lost not a few planes, as well as good men, back then. Over the years training techniques have improved dramatically.

The human being is a unique creature. Given a traumatic dose of the unexpected there is a tendency for our brains to go numb. Reactions can be unpredictable and inconsistent. The end results may be good but are more frequently bad. Modern technology has provided a better means to not only learn systems and procedures, but to learn to consistently make the correct response to a given situation, even when our brains take a break.

Instructor and author Lawrence Grodsky saw, and understood, the potential benefit of utilizing modern aircraft training technology and concepts with motorcycles. It would be a wonderful thing if Larry's ideas were to become an affordable reality. This would save a lot of bikes and not a little skin.

Chuck Tame, motorcycle enthusiast, and professional civilian pilot with more than 35 years and 16,000 hours in various jet aircraft

My mother insists that I've wasted half of my life fooling around, riding motorcycles. I love my mom, but the woman exaggerates. I sat down the other day with my pocket calculator, did some ciphering and, as near as I can figure, about 10 months is all that I've spent aboard the many motorcycles I've owned.

Ten months. Of that total, perhaps a month was spent tilted over in curves, two weeks or so on the brakes, and—oh—maybe a minute sliding down the pavement. Funny how the briefest events compete for your memories.

I *hate* crashing. I needn't devote any space here to the reasons why. As organisms go, the human body is among the most adaptive, but asphalt polishing is something it was never intended to do. And I hate *watching* crashes, too. After my first year as a motorcycle safety instructor—a year in which I trained three or four hundred new riders and watched more than a handful dribble themselves across the driving range—I vowed that if I couldn't put an end to those unsightly displays, then I would do everything within my power to at least minimize them.

If I might be allowed a moment of self-aggrandizement, I think I've done a fairly good job. During one stretch of a year and a half, not a single student came off of a moving bike while under my tutelage. Never, during my first eight years, was a class of mine visited by an ambulance and there were no broken bones. But alas, motorcycles still balance on two wheels, and last summer the law of averages reigned over my site. *Man* I hate crashes.

And I know how *you* hate them. Putting aside your fears of serious injury, think about the expense you'd incur from a simple low-side on your new RT or Cavalcade. You work hard for your money, and you'd probably swallow hard before springing for $1,500 worth of cosmetic repairs.

So how'd you like to replace an F16 fighter jet at $9 million? Or a C130 transport costing $17 million? Or a Boeing 737 jumbo jet at a cool $33 mil? Grapple with those numbers for a few moments and then see if you can't figure out why the U.S. Air Force and the major airlines won't let a potential pilot climb into one of their cockpits before he's logged many hours on a computerized flight simulator.

Simulated flight has been a mainstay of pilot training for at least a decade and a half. With an average of 10 to 15 flights on the simulator, an Air Force pilot-in-training takes to the sky fully competent at the controls and ready to devote his attention to radio transmissions and other in-flight responsibilities. Each Air Force plane has its own specific simulator, which even veteran pilots continually train on.

Nearly every advantage attributable to flight simulators should, theoretically, apply to motorcycle simulators, if such devices existed. Beginning students could master clutch and throttle operation at a desk-top unit, while the computer metes out uniformly accurate feedback. Advanced students could learn to manage traction on live working models that would simulate real crisis situations such as blowouts and wobbles. Maintenance costs would be negligible, and accident potential *nada*. I can think of only one conceivable hitch.

"A motorcycle simulator would be relatively easy to develop," opined Captain Darryl Hartman, a C130 training specialist at Greater Pittsburgh Air Force Base. "You could probably do something for less than a million." That's *dollars*, bro, which is chump change compared to a full-motion, wraparound visual cockpit, with total roll capability and 20 to 30 degrees of rotation in any axis. A rig like that, which Hartman describes as "like riding in a big cartoon," will dent your Gold Card to the tune of $10 million. That would be roughly equivalent to the profit on, say, every Kawasaki street bike sold in the United States last year.

So there are some unresolved obstacles to the simulator concept. And yet, Kawasaki purportedly *is* at work developing a simulator; Honda too. When these projects shall reach fruition and exactly what form they'll take is a secret buried deep within the Japanese CAD rooms; great weight is placed upon their attendant rumor within the industry.

The Honda folks already have a venue for their experiment in ersatz motorcycling, their recently opened Rider Education Center in Colton, California. Four more regional facilities are set to open across the country within several years.

Skill development is the logical goal of every mature rider and every safety program, but a leading safety expert recently left me to chew on his own unique slant to skills training. "Any time you require emergency braking and turning skills," he told me, "you're experiencing a breakdown of the SIPDE process (Scan/Identify/Predict/Decide/Execute)."

SIPDE—or Search/Predict/Act if you wish to truncate the process—is a technique that's been taught to student drivers for quite a few years . . . and practiced on simple driving simulators costing far less than a million dollars. I'm willing to bet there's a teenager within shouting distance of my home who could write the software for a "street strategies loop" on his MacIntosh.

So in all, we need not one, but three simulator programs: one for basic controls; a "full combat" version that goes, stops, and leans; and a simple traffic replication. Once up and running, such a system could drastically reduce the costs of rider training, since it would lower the required number of instructor hours and the considerable wear and tear that training cycles (usually loaned by the manufacturers through local dealers) must endure.

I'm not advocating that new riders go from the video arcade to the streets without closed-course supervision, but people learn differently and at different rates. Simulators can help people reach their goals quickly and painlessly, so they can get on with *real* life. And if I had only 10 months left to live, I know how *I'd* want to waste them!

Stories from the Road

A Remarkable Individual

I looked forward to showcasing the quite fantastic roads of my own "backyard" when assisting Larry on the Stayin' Safe in the Smokies tour. His incredible memory for the labyrinth of roads matched my home-grown familiarity, and we could synchronize route changes on the fly with little more than a nod of the head. Our personalities and talents merged seamlessly in that aspect, but in others we weren't as similar. I'm the sort who needs his ducks in a row a day in advance; Larry wasn't nearly that uptight.

Out of convenience and friendship he would bunk at my rural outpost, arriving a scant afternoon before the training tour was to begin. In his inimitable style, he would still have "a few things I need to do." Sometimes that would include mounting fresh rubber. Once, the trip from Pittsburgh had fragged his drive chain; we managed to pirate one from my Transalp. Frequently there were electrical items to cobble together for the radios. A high-stress issue for me always was getting the rat's nest of radio gear he brought untangled and installed in my helmet and tank bag . . . and then trying to recall all the nuances of how it worked. It was rare to finish before midnight. The critical "Testing 1, 2, 3 . . . " usually happened the next morning as we made our pre-dawn dash-in-the-dark down my Driveway from Hell (a three-quarter mile gravel roller coaster), generally a smidge behind schedule to meet our new charges at breakfast. I would be frazzled.

For Larry, it was merely the start of another day. Yesterday's minutiae were just that; his antennae were tuned productively to the upcoming. Will that student, riding a bike with linked brakes, require separate coaching? What minor correction will improve this person's corner line? Which rider conceals an inability to forcefully steer his bike if caught by a tightening curve? Larry's calm demeanor reflected not indifference but self-confidence earned over years of honing his techniques. He knew that if the road got bumpy, his suspension could handle it.

These concluding eight columns—including his first and last—paint the self-portrait of a remarkable individual in a way no others' words can. A peek through this window reveals a well-rounded person who loved to travel by motorcycle, to sample other cultures, to experience new places and the people who lived there, to try daring things, but most of all—to have fun.

Safely? I'm afraid that depends on your level of risk acceptance. Lean back and enjoy.

Pete Tamblyn

Demonology

October 1988

*The Demonology column was first published almost a year be-
fore my son Parker was born and I was a mere demon-filled
young man of 27. Today, my now 18-year-old son, in addition
to taking after me, takes to the streets on two wheels. I know
how long it took to rid myself of my own demons (longer than
most) and I fear Parker will naturally follow suit. Larry knew
the cure; it was "middle age." But he left us without showing
how to effectively apply that cure to anyone under the age of
40. Or did he? I've been working closely with Parker. Sharing
Larry's philosophies, providing radio commentary in all types
of traffic scenarios and requiring his participation in a
Grodsky Stayin' Safe tour I conducted this spring are clearly
having an effect. He's reading the landscape and clearly recognizing where to place the motorcycle. He's selecting appropriate corner entry speeds. He's showing good—dare I say
mature—judgment. I even caught him listening to Aerosmith
in the car last week. Could it be that, while man has spent generations seeking the Fountain of Youth, Larry has successfully
led a young motorcyclist to someplace more relevant: the
Fountain of Middle Age?*

Eric Trow, senior instructor
Stayin' Safe Motorcycle Training

*Larry Grodsky was taken from us in a motorcycle accident in April, 2006,
but we're just not ready to let him go yet. Following is the first column he
wrote for this magazine in the October 1988 issue. We think you'll agree
that—like most of Larry's work—it is just as meaningful now as it was
then. Mark Tuttle Jr, editor,* Rider *magazine (August 2006)*

Safety Editor. Lofty-sounding title *that* is, one I hope I can live up to.
But I have to tell you up front, it looks like a setup to me. Safety Editor: A role model, a paragon of virtuous riding practices, fluorescent

orange vest, 99 yards of reflective tape, foot down for every stop sign and, of course, above all else, never a single, solitary tenth of a mile per hour over the speed limit. Hallelujah brothers and sisters.

OK, speaking candidly, this is my position on safety: I'm for it. I'm also for the people and against higher taxes, but I didn't get this job by kissing babies. How did I get it? The answer is, by default; it's a real loser of a job. Everybody's for safety; for rider education, for safer roads, for better licensing, but there's no quicker way to lose the room than to start preaching the gospel of safety.

Unless your name is Stuart Munro. That's the real reason I know I've been set up to take a fall. See, I never rode a Rudge Ulster or fired a rifle from behind the bars of a BSA M42 as it sped across the Sahara. I don't have 40 years of riding experience, and I can't quote Wordsworth. I don't have his curmudgeonly wit or grandfatherly wisdom.

And I've been a bad boy. "How bad?" you ask. I can't say. To admit publicly would be to kiss off this job before my first column sees the light of print, but this much I'll say: I like to fly. No, not 100 or 120. I'm talking about "flying"—like Icarus, like Lindbergh, like Eddie the Eagle. But only on a motorcycle.

Normally my flying is confined to the slag dump about two miles from my home. I'm not talking Snake River Canyon here, or even the double jumps that adolescents across the nation routinely perform, wrapped in the loving gazes of Mom and Dad, who have just shelled out three grand for a machine that will be scrap metal in another three months. My leaps are about the equal of a good high-school long jump, but they make me feel like a condor.

It was Super Sunday, and I was visiting my friend Mik at his farm in the Laurel Highlands. A freakish sort of a January day—sunny and 65 degrees, yet patches of clean snow laced the hillsides, and the lake was still dotted with orange-clad ice fishermen. We needed a quart of milk— a perfect excuse for a ride—so I jumped on my thumper and headed down to the store. About 200 yards from the house there was this little bitty bridge, shaped like the top of an octagon—the perfect jumping ramp. I've crossed that bridge a thousand times on all kinds of street bikes, and I always get a little rush when the thing starts to get light. Still I know the place to jump is the slag dump. But this was Super Sunday.

My best guess is that the average car hits that ramp at about 20 mph, the average bike maybe 30. My speedo said 45 just before I goosed the throttle, then I gave the bars a little tug and—whoosh—I was airborne. It was sinful. It was delicious. When at last my rear wheel kissed the pavement and I'd gently set down the front I knew I'd set new records for distance and style. A Super Bowl performance.

You be my judge. Is that the kind of behavior a motorcycle safety instructor should engage in? A Safety Editor? In my defense I'll stress that I never exceeded the speed limit. A case might be made for reckless operation, but I was wearing all of the proper protective gear, not a drop of liquor had touched my lips in days, and the road was absolutely free of traffic. I could see for miles ahead. It was a safe jump, a responsible jump, a thinking man's jump.

Still, I'm duty-bound to confess the truth, which is that I have a demon inside of me. Just how many motorcyclists suffer from this affliction? Meredith "Hoot" Gibson, Motorcycle Safety Foundation training specialist, asked me to assist him with his doctoral research a few years back. Gibson's hypothesis was that motorcyclists exhibit no more risk-taking tendencies than the population at large. My job was to administer a questionnaire surveying attitudes toward a variety of stimuli ranging from water skiing to body odors. We separated the respondees into riders and non-riders using an ingenious device concocted by Gibson with the aid of the Department of Motor Vehicles. It was a class act. That Hoot really is a learned man, but his premise stunk: Motorcyclists proved to be far and away the greater risk-takers. Demons.

Gibson's was hardly the first survey to backfire. Various studies have linked drug abuse to drug education, promiscuity to sex education, and traffic accidents to driver education. Alas, after 13 years of organized rider education in this country, safety pundits are fearful of uncovering just such a snake pit. In fact, a National Highway Traffic Safety Administration study (hotly contested by the motorcycle safety community as unscientific) showed trained riders in New York to be no safer than untrained ones. Nationwide, less than 10 percent of all riders have received professional safety training, but their numbers are statistically significant. And their statistics aren't good. Several states with well-funded programs are having a hard time showing that rider education works.

As one who's logged thousands of miles running up and down blisteringly hot ranges, coaching new riders on the finer points of motorcycle operation, I find that this is a bitter pill to swallow. See, I believe in rider education, and I know that studies, notably the Hurt Report, show typical riders to be painfully deficient in the fundamentals of safe riding, especially braking and countersteering. But if we're to believe that motorcycling is a "sport," as we're constantly told, then we must accept that a fundamental precept of sports participation is the challenge to better one's performance: "If I can take that turn at 50, then I ought to be able to take it at 55. If I can stop from 30 mph in 35 feet, then next time I'm gonna do it in 30," and "If that's the absolutely shortest distance this thing will stop in, then watch me stand it up on its front wheel!" Demons.

So knowledge is a two-edged sword, one that must be tempered daily with the white light of wisdom. As it happens, I know the cure for demons. Unfortunately it can't be bottled, and even if it could, I'd never sell the first case. It's "middle age." Middle age is less a numerical milestone than it is the realization of one's mortality, the ability to see a future in which the world exists independently of the self. This realization meshes perfectly with a concept safety professionals call "risk acceptance."

Motorcycle-accident figures, when served in the most academically digestible form—i.e. accidents per miles traveled, youth, and alcohol—bring motorcycles much more in line with other modes of transportation. Interestingly, the age differential can't be explained away as a mere by-product of experience. Even middle-aged novices enjoy better-than-average safety records. Safe riding isn't superior skills or encyclopedic knowledge of motorcycles, and it isn't the total elimination of risk. It's the personal acceptance of a level of risk commensurate with our skills, our expectations for life, and the needs of others whose lives are interconnected with our own.

If this column is to succeed, I'll need your help. I'll need your input and your understanding. I'm a mere mortal. Judge me not by one flight of fancy. A demon made me do it, but still I knew the risks. If I'd had a couple of kids at home, waiting for me to take them to Chuck E. Cheese's that night, I wouldn't have played Evel Knievel. But I didn't, so I did. When the time comes for me to have a family, my level of risk acceptance will simply have to change.

And if my kids one day approach me asking for motorcycles, I'll give them the best that money can buy and personally teach them how to ride . . . as soon as they turn 40.

One Hundred Months of Demons

January 1997

The title of Larry's centennial Stayin' Safe column refers back, of course, to his first—"Demonology"—and the 98 in between, all of which teach us the value of riding well and safely while acknowledging that ours is a fun sport with (a little) room for some demonic behavior. "One Hundred Months" is a brief ride down memory road, a few reminiscences that include how Larry got the job in the summer of 1988. You might imagine how the rest of the staff and I felt when my predecessor announced that he was making some guy who had just crashed because he forgot to raise his sidestand Rider's *new Safety Editor. Editor Tash Matsuoka gave Larry's talent a place to blossom, and after Tash left later that year it wasn't long before I realized what a gift he had given the magazine.*

Mark Tuttle Jr, editor, Rider *magazine*

The Volvo swung 'round the blind turn, then veered hard to the right, screeching to a halt, several yards short of the downed bike. Its door swung open and the burly driver strode purposefully toward me.

"Allo," he said. "I ahm a dok-tor. I haf a car phone. Vood you like some morphine?"

Although I was awake and alert, I had no sense of the scope of my injuries. Seconds earlier I'd stared into the steep, rocky chasm of Norway's fabled Gubrandsdalen, flying like Peer Gynt and the reindeer buck above my motorcycle and the guard rail; I was ecstatic just to have my life back.

No way could I have known how that life was about to change.

I'd blown the left-hander big time: a total failure of what the MSF's *Motorcycle Task Analysis* refers to as skill item 12-486. To you laymen, that's raising the sidestand.

Highway signs, you may have noticed, now call those steel barriers "guide" rails—in deference to litigious types who might not feel suitably "guarded" by the department which erected them. Guarded, guided—

whatever—I was grateful that it trapped my right foot against the bike and boomeranged me back onto the highway.

Of course my joy at receiving a second chance in life receded as reality set in. A struggling freelance writer on my first overseas assignment, I now had to deal with a crashed loaner bike and a foot that was fractured in 10 places. It was only the second day of the trip; things would get a lot worse.

On my last scheduled morning in Norway, some trolls frollicking in a coin-operated clothes dryer decided to hold my laundry (and thus me) hostage. The next ferry wasn't for four days, so I filled the time sightseeing in the historic port of Bergen and eventually hobbled into the local hospital for a checkup. There the attending physician coldly informed me that continued motorcycling had displaced all the fractures and infected the open wounds. He spoke perfect English, but just to be sure he'd made his point the doctor grasped my right hand.

"I was like you once," he said . . . and rapped my knuckles hard against his ceramic foot.

Was I shook up? Only long enough to miss one more ferry, forcing me to abandon the motorcycle and fly (at my own expense) to England, where I was to cover the International Motorcycle Show. I'd already missed the press day and, on arrival, I discovered that all my exposed film from the Norway tour article had vanished. On top of that, the "scoop" I'd promised the editor—a Soviet-made "sidecar boat"—turned out to be the creation of a discombobulated government translator; "boat" coming from the German *boot*—which happens to be what the English call an ordinary sidecar!

Crashed bike, broken foot, lost photos, no story. Add to that a 36-hour airline odyssey triggered by the worst storm in British history, plus a visit on my return home from two FBI agents—demanding an explanation for my recent commiseration with certain Soviets.

The phone rang. It was Tash Matsuoka, the enigmatic former editor of this magazine. He was calling about my "assignment," which had been dubbed "Falling Through Birmingham."

"This is great stuff!" gushed Matsuoka, whose editorship generated, among other such ephemera, a touring comparison of a Bimota vs. a Yamaha Venture, and a photo essay on body-builders and motorcycles. *"Exactly* what I wanted. We've got to get you on our masthead. What do you do when you're not writing for us?"

I had to think quickly. Hmmm . . . *hod carrier . . . temporary secretary . . . folder of underwear in discount clothing store?*

"I, uh—teach some motorcycle safety classes," I replied weakly "That's it!" Matsuoka exclaimed. "You're gonna be our new *Safety Editor!*"

So it was that in October of 1988 *Rider* reprised the legendary Stuart Munro's *Safety Forum.* Titled "Demonology," my inaugural column weighed the merits and demerits of a capricious little jumping event on one of my local back roads. I felt the jump was a perfect metaphor for the fun vs. safety conflict motorcyclists face on every outing.

I didn't know how long a safety column could run, but with such a narrow subject area, it was only a matter of time before I'd have to recycle ideas. Well, here I am, confronting my demons again . . . for the 100th month.

Is it really so? It must be because Editor Tuttle Jr. called the other day and told me it was time to supply the illustrator with yet another mug shot: number three in the continuing series, "Hair loss in America."

Tuttle Jr., of course, took over the reins from Matsuoka in 1989, and the two men's editorial styles were as different as their epicurian tastes. Matsuoka's avante garde vs. Tuttle Jr.'s friendly and informative; sushi vs. . . . the rest of the food chain. On this page he could have installed anything or anyone (well, he couldn't afford *anyone*), but Tuttle Jr. stuck with Matsuoka's impulse purchase, changing only the name to its present Stayin' Safe.

Before the switch, it was MTJ who helped me research column number four. The little treatise studying the effects of Jack Daniels on one's control of a Honda XR200 ended with me flat on my back in front of a crowd of 3,000 spectators and a local TV camera in Cody, Wyoming. Who'd have thought that being a safety editor necessitated so much crashing?

Fortunately, I found other ways to gather material, including two trips to Bochum, Germany: first to attend an international safety conference and later to collect data using the motorcycle simulator at the Institut für Zweiradsicherheit.

"Keep it simple," Tuttle Jr. continues to remind me. "People need the basics." Though we've had long and heated editorial discussions, let it be known that anything you've seen on this page has appeared almost exactly as I submitted the piece . . . except for the addition of those excruciating phrases "he or she" and "his or her."

Actually, finding subjects to write about hasn't been that terribly difficult. You, the readers, have proved an invaluable source of material as I learned when suffering through my worst case of writer's block in the bikeless winter of '92. It turned out my most attention-getting column was in my hip pocket, just waiting for us to put our heads together.

Finally, with several deadlines approaching, I turned to the scribbled questionnaire I'd carried for over a year. The "Rider Risk Survey," as it became known, prompted some 1,500 responses and resulted in a paper, co-authored by Professor Fred Mannering of the University of Washington (who did all the real work), which we presented before the Transportation Research Board in Washington, D.C.

The survey and accompanying comments produced some great variances—from riders who'd never exceeded the speed limit to several wheelie-mongering Gold Wingers. Most were guys (and gals) with life, not death, wishes, riders who confronted the occasional demon in uniform—and the one in their own clothes. Over three-quarters, for example, indicated that they'd ridden more than 100 mph and were willing to pass on a double yellow line, conditions permitting.

Of course, not everyone's real world approach is entirely realistic. When asked to estimate the likelihood of going down or having any kind of an accident in the next 10 years, the greatest number responded "10 percent." However, informal follow-ups at rallies and clubs unveiled precious few who'd ridden a whole decade without a tumble.

I'd have accomplished that feat if it weren't for demon No. 12-486, but then I might still be folding underwear in Marshall's and would've never ridden in the Alps and Africa and Central America—just a few of my perks from scribbling for this magazine.

So Matsuoka, if this happens to find you on whatever planet you're visiting these days, *kansha suru* for 100 really cool months. See ya' in hell.

Jean-Claude Grodsky

June 2000

Though Larry excelled as a writer and storyteller, he was first and foremost a teacher—an exceptional one; and this is where I saw his joy. As I watched Larry the ski student progress from tripping down the slopes to racing past me, I understood the immense satisfaction he derived from teaching, and how being a student inspired his approach to it.

Determined to teach motorcycling where it needed to be taught, Larry became a pioneer and made the street his classroom. It was fascinating watching him, like a mad scientist playing in the lab, test new and better ways to improve the student's experience.

During the off-season, whether at his desk, on the ski slopes or in Spanish lessons, he'd go into his laboratory mode, investigating his teaching technique and new technology. As a student and teacher, he examined how one learns and best absorbs skills and information.

Over the years I watched his technology and skills progress from the use of clipboard diagrams, hand-signals, and chalk talks, to radios for "real-time" coaching, video camera, laptop, projector, and speakers. Always, Larry fervently conducted research to find the best equipment for the job, then constantly tweaked it.

During and after training tours I'd get to experience his joy as he shared his success stories. He strove to give the best to his clients. And he achieved it because he worked so hard at being the teacher and the student, and because he symbiotically lived these two roles.

> *MaryAnn Puglisi, partner, Stayin' Safe Motorcycle Training, and director, EduVacations*

We lined up in two rows, facing each other. I wasn't the biggest in my class—a few of the two dozen sixth-graders were taller or heavier—but I was the only one who shaved.

"We can do this one of two ways," began our teacher, Cody. (Cody?) "You can pay attention, and we can be out on the slopes in an hour . . . or you can waste my time and we'll spend the whole lesson right here."

I would've cast my vote for option "B" but realized, before my hand was half raised, that it was a rhetorical question. Anyway, better to reach the bottom of the hill unconscious, a crumpled mass of broken bones, than to unmask the truth of my cowardice before all those giggly 11-year-olds. "You'll love skiing," my friends and students had insisted for years. "It's just like motorcycling." But I never bought the argument.

"Why pay to wait in a line," I'd reply with stubborn indifference, "when I can just jump on my motorcycle and ride?" But there was no backing out of this ski package, a Valentine gift from my skiing (and motorcycling) sweetheart, MaryAnn.

After the lesson and lunch, my classmates and I dispersed over the mountain. A succession of smaller and smaller children flew past me on the green (beginner) run. When a cherubic little girl in a pink snow suit—no more than 6—passed me for the fourth time, I seriously considered tripping her.

"It's easy for little kids," friends would later comment. "They're so close to the ground."

Despite my shame and degradation, the instructor in me took mental notes and experimented with various theories and calculations of this strange wheelless, engineless locomotion. I watched parents clasp their children—barely old enough to walk—under the arms and go shushing down the slopes with the babes tucked between their legs, almost like a mother kangaroo carries her baby in her pouch.

It's said that the children of sub-Saharan Africa learn their ancient tribal rhythms before they even learn to walk. Strapped to their mothers' backs, awake and asleep, they internalize the beat and the motion of daily life. I'm absolutely convinced of the soundness of such nonverbal instruction. One of my finest successes as a motorcycle instructor has been the discovery that I can teach countersteering in a similar way. Seated on the pillion with their palms resting lightly on the backs of my hands, it's usually no more than a minute before most students begin to apply their own pressure, initiating a forceful, yet graceful weave.

Conversely, I've known riders to take BRCs and ERCs, to read every available article on countersteering and still, after years of street riding, scarcely scratch the surface of bike control. Their knowledge was all cranial; they never felt the little bell go off inside signaling that the correct synaptic bridge had been made.

Have you ever laid your head to the pillow following a day of abundant twisties and felt all the day's curves return, dreamily washing over you like waves lapping against the shore? My first day of skiing revisited me that evening with all that intensity and more, for with each left/right combination I gathered speed and shed control until—as I would repeatedly that night—I awakened with another bone-shattering collision!

Day two began with a six-hour ice storm. We hitchhiked to the slope unable even to chip our way into the frozen car. The slopes were so foggy I couldn't tell if anyone was out there, but I suspect there were damn few souls.

"Man, it's nasty out there!" instructor Cody said to no one in particular as he returned from an early run. Very confidence-inspiring.

I allowed MaryAnn to persuade me onto the frozen mountain, this time in the company of a private instructor named Dave, a good-humored insurance salesman from Philly. The lesson was less an expression of my winter sports aspirations than an affirmation of belief in instruction. I actually got the idea for private motorcycle training after reading a magazine article years ago on top ski instructors.

Dave took me by the hand (literally). I knew at once he was a skilled instructor and trusted him—but not like a baby on the back of his Xosa mother. I was *scared*, and riding a bald-tired Tour Glide in the Swedish ice-racing championships could've been less frustrating. We made perhaps four runs down the icy beginner slope during the one-hour lesson and probably spent more time discussing motorcycles than skiing. The slowest lifts are on the beginner slopes, and Dave took advantage of this, knowing that unlike children, who absorb new ideas like sponges, we adults need them translated into concepts we already understand.

Dave gave me something tangible to take with me—a fundamental explanation of the principles of turning. I was glad I'd taken the private lesson, but the truth was I felt even less able than I had the previous day. Things didn't get much better the rest of the morning. The green slopes were horrible—an icy minefield of fallen beginners. I'd gather a little speed, try to dodge one of the casualties, and—*shoom*—my crisscrossed skis would pitch me off the high side.

"Come try the blue (intermediate) run," urged MaryAnn after lunch. "What are you *nuts* or something? I'll never make it down, and I'll take everyone else out with me!" "No you won't. It's like motorcycle racing—the faster skiers have to safely go around the slower ones." Against my instincts, I yielded and discovered, with some surprise, that I finished the blue run less bruised and battered than the green ones. But it looked to me like Mount Everest with other skiers hurtling at me as if launched from a catapult. Applying the principles of the morning lesson, I slowly zigzagged to the bottom in nearly horizontal lines, falling only once. And, yes, the other skiers did miraculously avoid me.

I tried another, less-crowded blue run. I discovered that, like a cone weave or a set of tight switchbacks, a good, quick cut gave the most control. And *head turns*—no one had to remind me of those! The lines were short. A third and fourth run quickly followed. I *passed* people! I passed a *lot* of people! It really *is* like motorcycling, I thought . . . and then in a blinding flash of sky/snow/sky I whammed myself silly. As I sorted my head from my feet, enough real skiers sluiced by to shatter my brief illusions of speed, but I'd done it—I'd really skied.

Ski instruction has been a mainstay so much longer than formal motorcycle training. The best schools and instructors become famous, like hospitals and surgeons, for their pioneering techniques. Perhaps we'll catch up before long. Already we can book time on Keith Code's "slide machine" or on one of Fast Freddie Spencer's telemetry-equipped Honda CBR600F4s. Popular as they are, those celebrity-taught schools don't serve anything like the numbers trained each year by MSF Certified programs. How many people ever ski under Jean-Claude Killy's tutelage?

Just hours ago, I returned from another ski slope, but this time on my own terms. Just up and back one time; a perfect motorcycle road, were it not for the end-of-season ski traffic on the ride back down.

So I've been thinking. Skiing is seasonal. To offset their warm-weather losses, resorts pump millions into marketing new activities such as mountain biking. Why not a fleet of Buell Blasts? What MSF instructor wouldn't trade one weekend a month of blistered feet for a few days of strafing apexes in the cool mountain air? Imagine the possibilities.

I see it quite clearly. It's February, and the bike's in the barn, but I'm relaxing in the sun, sipping cappuccino between runs at the Chamonix School of Skiing and Motorcycling. *Formidable!*

Mikey Likes It

March 1998

Mike Tyson started riding motorcycles in the fall of 1997. The first time he showed up at the shop, he was in a stretch limousine with 4 to 5 staff and bodyguards. Being a new motorcyclist, he was very excited and set out purchasing a BMW K1200RS and a few Ducatis (a perfect addition to the two Ferraris in his garage).

We helped him ride the bikes to his home in nearby Bethesda (adjacent to the, ahem, Congressional Country Club). On the ride I realized that he needed some training. The following day, at my suggestion, we met in the parking lot of the nearby Great Falls Tavern Visitor Center to work on some rider training exercises. I hoped to keep Mike disguised in full face helmet and riding gear, but a few park services employees in a refuse truck stopped and asked if it were Mike riding. To avoid a crowd, I denied it.

Realizing the need for professional training, I forwarded Mike's business manager's information to Larry. And now he can tell you the rest.

Tom Buzas, sales manager, Battley Cycles

It's 2 a.m. somewhere in the Mojave Desert, one of the Earth's most forlorn landscapes, and the one to which Mike Tyson's bodyguard has kidnapped me.

Scratch that—the word "kidnapped," my lawyer warns me, is potentially libelous. I could have climbed out of the vehicle at 10 p.m. back in Compton and hailed a cab to Beverly Hills, where a hotel had a pair of satin sheets with my name on them. How had I, a humble shuffler of six-inch traffic cones, become a pawn on the chessboard of the rich and famous?

Unbeknownst to me, my fate began taking shape one day in mid-October when the former heavyweight champ walked into Battley Cycle in Gaithersburg, Maryland, and spotted a gleaming new Ducati

916 . . . then an ST2 . . . and a Monster . . . and a BMW K1200RS. Sensing that Tyson's countersteering might not be on a par with his counterpunching, Battley's manager, Tom Buzas, summoned him to an empty parking lot for a quick tutorial.

"Mike," Buzas told the pugilist after an hour of coaching, "I don't do this for a living. I think you need to get some professional training."

Now I'm not saying that I could have sprinkled holy water on him and prevented an accident. That's what I told the *Washington Post* gossip columnist who phoned me two weeks later, following the tumble which cost Tyson a broken rib, a punctured lung (according to wire service reports), and a $77 ticket for riding without a motorcycle endorsement. "But we would have at least prepared him for the basics." The ex-champ had scheduled—then postponed—a training appointment four days before the spill. Gossip spreads, and soon my quote was on *Newsweek's* "Perspectives" page, alongside those of Chinese President Jiang Zemin and Michael Jordan.

My fame was short-lived, but not Tyson's interest in riding. He checked out of Hartford Hospital, purchased a new Bimota Tesi, and scheduled lessons once again.

"Yeah, I'm glad you called," said his minister without portfolio, Abdullah Muhamed, when I called to confirm a *third* attempt. "I forgot—we're out of town."

I was sure I'd heard the last of this flaky crew, but two days later Muhamed phoned to see if I could deliver the training in California. Within an hour, I'd booked the Honda Rider Education Center in Colton and a testing appointment with an MSF official.

"Stay the whole weekend," Tyson's secretary told me as she booked the Beverly Hills room in a conference call. "You might as well enjoy yourself."

Twenty minutes after the driver met me at LAX baggage claim, I learned of the new itinerary . . . Las Vegas!

"We've got some business we have to take care of," said Muhamed when I reached him on the cell phone. "Isn't there a track we can use in Vegas?"

"Listen," he continued after covering the receiver for a minute, "we've got to at least get you two gentlemen together face to face." Fine, I thought, the guy's on a two-bout losing streak; I'll take my shot.

The moonlit crossing of the Mojave is the second in a row for Tyson's bodyguard/driver, an amiable fellow named Marvin Kinsey (". . . like the sex survey"). To keep awake, we prattle on senselessly, concluding a comparative analysis of Dolly Parton vs. gangsta rapper Tupac Shakur about the time we descend into the great neon oasis. It's 7 a.m. back home when I finally hit the sack. At four in the afternoon, Muhamed picks me up and drives me to the champ's mansion. I have no training bikes—not even a traffic cone. Perhaps I'm to parachute into Caesar's Palace while Siegfried and Roy produce a safety course from a cloud of purple smoke!

In the driveway, upon a yellow Triumph Daytona T595, sits a helmeted figure in a Levi's jacket, jeans, and Timberlands, nearly as broad across as he is tall.

"Hello Lawwy . . . are we gonna go for a wide?" I recognize the voice from an old Simpsons episode.

"No, Mike," I reply. "We're gonna hit the books." He assumes a hangdog expression but obligingly wheels the yellow superbike inside the gate beside his Porsche Boxster and Yamaha YZF1000.

Smiling shyly, he gestures toward the Triumph like a tot showing you his toys. "I like the British bikes. I like British people. They're real mellow." The most savage puncher since the dawn of *Homo sapiens* is too cute to stay mad at.

"Larry," he says, munching a cookie during a break from the cram session, "I think I'm crazy."

"Why's that?"

"I've been riding motorcycles for one month and in that time I haven't driven a car. I own 30 cars, and I haven't driven in a month!" He flashes a gold tooth and rolls his eyes back in their sockets. "I just *love* motorcycles!"

Fade to the MSF film and a dog chasing down a motorcycle in the classic 45-degree pursuit.

"My tigers like to do that."

"You have *tigers?* Are they *tame?*"

He twists his face and shrugs. "As tame as they can be, but they're still wild animals. One minute they can be playing with me, licking my face, and the next minute they're sinking their teeth into my arms."

After class, in the driveway, Kinsey has Muhamed on the cell phone, discussing how we're to get to Colton in time for the morning training. Kinsey and I agree we should hit the road this evening. Muhamed says he'll speak to me at the hotel, but once outside the gate, Kinsey kills the engine.

"If we leave Mike alone, he'll get on the bike and we won't see him until 3 a.m.," he says. So it's come down to playing nursemaid to the man who, according to *Forbes* magazine, was the world's highest paid athlete in 1996. Yet, according to Marvin, Tyson suffers not from immaturity but from—believe it or not—innocence.

"The man lived in the street—literally—until he was 11 years old. And then to have all this and to have gone through what he has—going to jail and all. You'd think he wouldn't trust anyone, but he doesn't retain any bitterness.

"He sees a guy beggin' in the street and he gives him a hundred dollars. I'll say, 'Man, y'know the guy's just gonna spend it on crack!' But he says, 'I leave it to Allah to judge him.'"

Tyson's secretary phones my room at 4:45 the next morning. By 6 a.m. our chartered jet is in the air, and 20 minutes later we land at Ontario airport.

"I need to get one of these," I sigh.

"Don't waste yer money," says Tyson, the first time I've heard him use the "M" word. "Thirty million dollars—it's not worth it. Think of all the people you could help and feed for that much money."

His private stretch limo is waiting on the ground. It has three telephones and a GPS receiver, but the driver can't locate the Honda Center, so I boot up my laptop to find a phone number. Tyson practically doubles over with laughter.

"You should have wrote it on a piece of paper, man! That's too complicated!"

Incredibly, we make it to the Center as the doors open, albeit one day late. It's Friday, and I just pray that my MSF connection, Greg Hedgecock, is willing to hang around long enough for us to get through the basic exercises needed to satisfy the Foundation and earn Tyson his Nevada motorcycle license. In the lobby, Tyson picks up a copy of *Rider* and flips through it. "You gotta write about this, man. It'll be *wild!*"

Perhaps some other adjective would better describe the sight of Iron Mike Tyson aboard a Honda 250 Nighthawk.

And Mick Doohan he's not. Despite owning all the high-performance motorcycles, Tyson's a true novice. After about an hour of basic drills, Hedgecock shows up and together we drill him for the remainder of the day. Tyson, who looks to be about 20 pounds over his fighting weight, takes his lunch from a candy machine.

By three in the afternoon, he's looking pretty whupped, but fatigue has perhaps softened his touch. On the final exercise, a turning-speed-selection drill, he's looking almost smooth.

Hedgecock administers the test and though it's not pretty—Tyson's really tired now—he squeaks through and earns his completion card. I'm relieved, but also disappointed, knowing how much more we would have accomplished with a full two days.

A Latin friend of mine who's just learning English says, "Every man has animal inside. Some man have domestic animal . . . another wild animal."

I know there's a very wild beast inside Mike Tyson; we've paid billions to feed it. But the Tyson I've met is the one who's struggled to learn a new skill, who's scheduled himself to be in too many places at one time, who engages strangers with a gentle touch on the shoulder and the politeness of a young boy taking his first communion.

Back in Vegas we stop at a light behind a pickup with a bumper sticker, "Tyson Bites." I'm sure the driver, who sits behind locked doors and tinted one-way windows, is just having some fun.

Have fun with the new toys, Mike.

This Safe Land

April 1996

I never knew Larry Grodsky and, truth to tell, this may be the first column of his that I've read, but he sounds like a nice bloke, with impeccable literary taste. I wish I could have been the guy on the Guzzi. We would have talked, and not just about bikes.

I like to think that in this column he was subtly hinting at something I can afford to say out loud: which is that I'd prefer to be riding almost anywhere in the world rather than the USA, this land of gas stations, franchises, lunch counters, Wal-Marts, and old men whose worlds end at Memphis. The idea of America is magnificent and unrivalled, but the man-made physical reality is mostly dull and tasteless. Sure there's great natural beauty, but then there's plenty of that elsewhere, in the Andes, the Himalayas, Europe, and the whole sweep of Africa, where it's combined with fascinating cultures and interesting architecture.

I've lived here now for 25 years, and I love the place I live in. I'm American too, as well as British, and I'm not knocking America, but for a rider in search of adventure it's not that great.

I hope Larry made it to Guatemala. Every American should ride to Guatemala, and then keep going. As for feeling safe in America, all I meant by those words was that I didn't have to keep looking out for potholes. Otherwise, safety is something you create for yourself, and I'm sure Larry knew that as well as anyone. It's a real shame that fate tripped him.

Ted Simon, *world traveler, journalist
and author of* Jupiter's Travels

It was actually the giant turkey hay-bale sculpture and not the historical marker that made me stop. The passing rider on the Moto Guzzi Lario gave me a glance over his right shoulder, braked, did two 180s and

docked at my side. Call me a bigot, but I still find something incongru-
ous about a red Italian flashbike in the heart of rural Alabama.

"Y'all right?" he asked with a faint drawl. "I just thought I'd check," he
nodded when I assured him I was. Then he tipped his visor and rumbled
off. I thought he would stay and talk bikes for a few minutes, but that's all
right; it was nice that he stopped. Anyway, I was ready to roll, so I
punched the button on my TransAlp . . . and then tried again.

The problem—some slipshod maintenance come back to haunt me—
was quickly bandaged with a roll of duct tape. Earlier in the morning, I'd
stopped for gas along the interstate when a man—wearied from car sleep
by the looks of him—emerged from a rusted Chevy that wouldn't crank
over.

"Damn," he groused. "I need a new battery. Where *you* goin'?" he
asked, turning to the overloaded motorcycle. Mexico, I guessed, was
more than he'd expected to hear, and if that be so, Guatemala would
sound like some kind of taunt.

"Texas," I replied.

"I gotta git t'Memphis," he grumbled.

I didn't offer to help. I had no jumper cables, wanted to make time,
and something told me he was used to being in such jams. I imagine the
pioneers always aided their fellow travelers. Or killed them.

I decided not to get back on the federal conveyor belt. It would cost 15
minutes per hour, but I figured it was worth the price. Talladega Scenic
Highway wasn't the most thrilling road, but it hugged the rolling hills
with a tranquil wrap of pine scent and blowing leaves. They haven't yet
"double yellowed" every inch of two-lane in Alabama, and I was surprised, that some of the "legal" passing zones actually lacked the visibility to gain my trust. *Personal responsibility.* What a concept.

Every so often, I'd crest a hill and there'd be a car, fixing to turn left
across my path onto some red clay lane. Or—even though traffic was
fairly light—a gang of cars would stack up and I'd have to move to the
right to make myself visible. Even riding a relatively unchallenging two-
lane, it was clear how much safer the interstates were; why our highway
fatalities continue to drop, even as speeds (and speed limits) rise.

The last Appalachian foothills melted into cypress swamp; creosol, a
sure sign of the Deep South, filled my nostrils. Suddenly, winking headlights warn of an impending speed trap. I think of all the lower-than-B
movies in which a redneck Southern sheriff turned a routine traffic stop

into someone's personal Gallipoli. There—on the right. Even at 50 mph, the dynamic of authority is easily decoded. The car is new and German, but its driver is pale and deferential. The trim, neatly uniformed officer has made his decision.

Approaching the town, there are scattered brick houses where tarpaper shacks probably stood a generation ago. On the bypass I note signs of economic vitality: a 24-hour Wal-Mart superstore, some national motel chains, and all the major fast-food outlets. After three miles, I reach the end of the strip and turn around. I ride slowly, looking for a sign, but there's none.

Any other town as pretty as this one would be pounding a drum to attract tourists, but not Selma. Victorian and Antebellum mansions along the main street are curtained by ginkgo trees full of bright yellow fans. A Gothic church with handsome wrought iron work. Fountains. New stone benches and brick sidewalks, but no one on them; they're all in cars.

Downtown, between the Selma Times Journal and the 21st Century Youth Leadership Movement, a few doors from the bridge where National Guardsmen ushered marchers past Governor Wallace's troopers—safely—there's now a civil rights museum. It's Sunday and I can't go in, but through the window I can see the signs and photos: pictorial reminders of America's apartheid.

I'm hungry—hungry to eat among the locals and feel the undercurrent of town life, here where America fought its most important battle of my lifetime. But there's no lunch counter like the ones Martin Luther King gave his life to sit at. Selma's been peacefully integrated into the culture of the bypass. Watching the ingress and egress of McDonald's patrons, I note nothing extraordinary in their bearing. After 20 minutes it dawns upon me: none are old enough to remember 1965.

A billboard in Mississippi asks, "Why Raise Emus?" but I quickly forget the 800 number. In Monroe, Louisiana, I save some bucks by sleeping in a very bad motel on the poor side of town. I'd rather camp under the stars, but where would I go at 11 p.m.?

These days, I read about car jackings and sometimes, at night, I've heard the drive-bys. I know that several hikers have been murdered in recent years along the Appalachian Trail. But only once, in all the years I've been around bikes, have I heard of a violent assault on a motorcyclist.

He didn't deserve to be gunned down by the police, but it was well known in his Miami neighborhood that he wasn't on a tour.

On the other hand, there's hardly a week goes by in summer that I don't hear on the news that some motorcyclist ran head-on into a tree; usually about the time the bars close. We must write our congressmen and the AMA. Trees kill.

My parents, when I began traipsing around the country on motorcycles, assumed that it was a youthful phase and that I'd outgrow it. Curious, how differently motorcycle touring is viewed nowadays.

"That's one of those bikes old guys use to go riding cross-country," I overheard a college boy tell his companion when they passed a Gold Wing in the Honda dealership. It troubles me deeply that America's young people no longer seem to view motorcycles, or even the open road, as a gateway to the mysteries of a vast and complex land. Do they view it as too risky an activity . . . or has the speed of communications demystified the country itself?

As of this writing, I'm still unsure about Guatemala. The uprising in southern Mexico has subsided, and veteran travelers have assured me that I'll be fine . . . *so long as you don't take photos, talk to children, or go off the main road.* A pretty short list of everything I enjoy about motorcycle touring.

At Brownsville, where Texas knifes 300 miles into the gut of Mexico, the daily paper reports three cases of dengue fever. A few years ago killer bees were advancing on us, but we seem to have staved that one off, as we did communism and the other menaces. Another article tells of thousands dying in the rain forests to the south of diseases that haven't yet been named.

Our poets use the word "sanguine," to describe someone hopeful or radiant. But across the border, *sanguineo* is just the common word for blood. English author Ted Simon, whose *Jupiter's Travels* must be the finest work of motorcycle travel writing penned, described his feelings upon crossing that border from the south, after two years in the Third World on his 500 Triumph.

"Suddenly I feel safe. Why? I didn't feel unsafe before. It's just that now I don't have to think about it. Here I don't have to think at all."

No Bluff

November 1994

Larry wasn't the kind of guy who demanded perfection from his friends. "So you're blind?" No problem; "Jump on behind; we'll grab a sandwich and then take in a jazz concert." He focused on abilities rather than handicaps.

Larry's friend Dick hadn't ridden since losing his eyesight to diabetes years earlier. I tracked him down by phone, and gathered that this incident happened much as Larry describes it with Dick, relying entirely on radio guidance, relearning to ride a trainer bike on a grassy soccer field.

The whole experiment wouldn't have been nearly so outrageous if they hadn't been caught red-handed by Larry's MSF supervisor-friend, Dave Surgenor. Dick recalls that part of the venture in vivid detail, and obviously delighted in tap-tapping with his cane to reveal his lack of vision to Dave.

If you have to ask "Why?" then it probably can't be explained; the satisfaction derived by these two simply made the challenge worth the risk. It seemed perfectly normal to Dick, who's even flown experimental aircraft since losing his vision! (with a sighted co-pilot, of course).

Pete Tamblyn

Testing—one, two, three—testing . . . The *radio*—if there's one thing I can't afford, it's for the radio to screw-up!

This is something that Dick and I have talked about for some time, but just never got around to until today. Dick Simko is in his 50s and hasn't ridden in a while, making him one of the growing legion of "re-entry" riders. But he suffers from diabetes and hasn't much feeling left in his feet; plus, the degenerative disease has left him fairly brittle in recent years. He knows all the risks—he's a big boy but *I'm* nervous as heck. After all, he's my friend, and I don't want him to fall down, even if it's only on soft grass.

That's another thing. We shouldn't be here. It's July—too hot for the kids, or maybe they're all watching the World Cup on television, but it's clear from the ankle-high grass that the soccer field hasn't been used in weeks. It's soft, gigantic, and billiard-table flat. *Perfect.* I just hope we don't get busted.

Well, he's pretty wobbly. Oh, man, was this such a good idea? I mean, what are the chances he'll seriously get back into riding? He starts to smooth out slightly, but I'm still afraid to give him the reins. I decide to ride pillion the first time he attempts to make turns.

BAD idea! In a panic (half his/half mine) I grab the bars, and it takes all the strength I can muster to wrestle the 185 to a stop without capsizing. For better or for worse, I decide I must give Dick his freedom.

Gradually, the old skills return. Even with the diabetes, he's retained good clutch and throttle control, and unlike my novice students, he never needs to be reminded to get his eyes up. On the 60-foot circle he really comes around. Then we begin some ovals, and before I can give the command, he's cleanly upshifting and downshifting. This is going surprisingly well.

It's been 45 minutes, and I haven't seen a sign of life anywhere near the field, but in the distance I hear the throaty bark of a four-stroke trail bike. Uh oh! It's not the police. That wouldn't be so bad; the local motor cop looks the other way when I sneak the occasional student up here. No, I can't believe it. It's Dave Surgenor, our state's chief instructor—official *snitch*—the guy whose job it is to ensure that every instructor and every range is 100-percent regulation. Forty-five thousand square miles in this state and where does he pick to go trail riding?

So Surgenor closes in for the kill, pausing on the sidelines. He stares, then nods his head. A faint smile creases his face. He doesn't *know* . . . in fact he *likes* what he sees! Well, why shouldn't he? It's just a remedial session on some soft grass—no big deal. He splits for the woods, but before he hits the trail he just has to show us a big 'ol roost. Surgenor was a pretty fair off-road rider in his youth, or so he tells us.

Whooomph—down he goes.

Well, Surgenor's pretty embarrassed, and I'm not going to let him slink silently away. I radio Dick to ride to the far end of the field, which he does, coming to a Motorcycle Safety Foundation video-perfect stop, 15 feet from the soccer goal.

"See that, Dave—*that's* smooth riding," I gloat. "Maybe you should watch my student here, until you get the hang of it." He blushes but takes his ribbing good-naturedly.

Dick's off the bike now and craning his head toward us. "Be there in a second," I holler. Surgenor already looks bewildered.

Then Dick unfolds his articulated cane and, with a halting yet cocky gait, pecks his way toward the voices. "Dave, would you look at my helmet?" he asks, extending the undistinguished lid for inspection.

"Yes, what about it?" replies Dave, reasserting his chiefly mien.

"Well—you see this helmet coming down the road," warns Dick, " . . . you better get the *hell* out of the way!"

Blind man's bluff.

Dick Simko is the kind of guy you'd want by your side in a bad bar. Affable, even tempered, and ever ready with a sardonic quip, he'd grab a beer bottle and fell that 280-pound lughead before your friend the karate black belt had spotted the closest exit. He has the mark of any good species; he adapts.

A Brit bike enthusiast in the '60s, Simko drifted into stock-car racing, then back to bikes when the eyes began to weaken. An early retirement followed by a divorce left him with time on his hands—time he invested heavily in motorcycling. Then, in the spring of '93, his Yamaha Virago went inside the garage with 80,000 miles on its clock, to await the results of his operation. The news came as little surprise.

The garage is still home to the Virago, which is rewarded with occasional workouts whenever Dick's Retreads pals pay a visit. Still an avid race fan, Simko stays current through a longtime friendship with Indy car owner Chip Ganassi. Another of his passions is aviation, and he recently snuck a few minutes at the stick of a friend's "Very Easy," a home-built two-seater about the size of a Honda ST1100.

"But of all the things I've done," he says, nodding with satisfaction, "I'd have to say I like motorcycling the best."

Early this spring, with the weather still in flux, my friend joined me for an afternoon ride. Nothing special—I had some errands to run and we hit some rain—but I tried to make the route somewhat interesting (Simko can pinpoint his coordinates more accurately than Doppler radar). Along the way, a secretary, well meaning, but with a face and desk sculpted from solid monotony, eyed our helmets and attempted small talk.

"My husband rode a motorcycle once," she began. "Then one day, he nyahh nyahh nyahh and it grawwk grawwk, grawwk, and he broke his blah, blah blah blah blah . . ."

"Yeah. Well, I burned my lip once on a cup of coffee," Dick Simko replied.

He still talks the talk. Some motorcyclists (e.g. my Ducati friends) can't do U-turns to save their lives. Another friend—a safety instructor admits that he's totally handcuffed by sharp, downhill right-handed turns. So Dick Simko can't see where he's going. He can still unfold that cane and walk the walk.

Medical experts warn us that *everybody's* eyesight fades inexorably, almost from the time we get our first driver's licenses. People like Dick Simko remind us that, while the lights may dim, the vision is inextinguishable.

Safety Third

July 2005

When L.G. first approached me with the proposition to join his Stayin' Safe program as an instructor, I began looking for my escape route. I didn't know him well and surely, I thought, he mustn't know me. Although I was an MSF instructor (sorry, "RiderCoach™"), I enjoyed the thrill of motorcycling and often pursued activities that pushed my personal limits. I was clearly the wrong choice. Besides, his "safety" thing was going to suck the fun right out of everything for me. Then I discovered Larry embraced the thrill as much as I. He did track days, got kicks sliding a supermotard around a parking lot, never missed a chance to do hot laps aboard a friend's BSA ice racer, and loved exploring the limits of braking. He did these things in a controlled environment where he was willing to accept a greater level of risk and then applied what he learned to his road riding in careful measure. He proved that safety wasn't always slow and it didn't have to be boring. Years ago, MG sports cars of England had a simple slogan that I loved—especially when spoken with a British accent. "Safety Fast." I think that fits Larry beautifully.

Eric Trow, senior instructor
Stayin' Safe Motorcycle Training

Everyone wants to be a good rider . . . but for some, that means being a bad boy.

I know of this parking lot, and it's huge. It's also in very good condition and is usually closed off to automobile traffic. Those are all the details I'm going to reveal, because I've been practicing my riding skills there for several years under the premise that it's easier to beg forgiveness than to ask permission. And so far, I've not had to get down on my knees. Except by choice, that is.

See, I haven't been going there to practice figure-eights in a box, I've been motarding. Or at least practicing my own humble interpretation of the tire-smoking spectacle that stars like Jeff Ward, Ben Bostrom, and Kevin Schwantz have made into America's fastest-growing motorsport. Seventeen months ago I bought this aggressive-looking but actually quite docile Suzuki DR-Z400S from Louisville BMW dealer Jeff Cooke. A dry wit, Cooke removed all references to the Japanese marque and affixed a pair of BMW roundels to the royal-blue gas tank. The bike is a real conversation starter—many of those conversations beginning with the words, "Wow—cool Beemer!"

My supermoto is a work in progress. I spent last season making it more civilized—quieting the bark of its open Yoshimura can, affixing turn signals, getting the clocks to communicate with the 17-inch front hoop. This year I'm spending my money to make it less civilized, having already completed a winter engine hop-up. Mostly, I want to learn to ride it in that uncivilized way; you know—wheelies, stoppies, and big, long asphalt-streaking slides.

It's not gonna be an overnight process. People pay me to ride with them and to critique them, yet my bike handling skills are not exactly world class. Sometimes, when I'm coaching riders whose skills are more developed than mine, I begin to fear that I'm a fraud . . . but ironically those people are usually among my most enthusiastic students. I suppose people who truly ride well and know it would rather open their minds to another rider's ideas than demonstrate their technical superiority over him.

Throughout my riding career I've had friends who were stronger riders than me, many of them street riders who chose racing to test their personal limits. In every case they grew to become much more skilled riders. The most recent example is my friend and co-instructor Leon Winfrey, who for want of a better word I'd have to call my protégé. Leon started taking classes from me about seven years ago, and—to be blunt—he needed them. But he didn't just take classes from me. He did all four levels of Keith Code's California Superbike School, devoured everything written on the subject of riding skills, and became an MSF RiderCoach Trainer—what we used to call a chief instructor.

Watching Leon surpass me as a rider was a gratifying experience, but as he grew more serious about his track time and racing, I noticed an unanticipated change in his street riding. There'd be times when I'd up the pace over a favorite section of road only to look in my bike's mirror and see him casually clipping the apexes, indifferent to my change of tempo.

I'd nearly forgotten how utterly unimportant it is to most riders with genuine go-fast skills to impress others with their speed on public roads.

Leon has been steadily bugging me to do track days with him, and I have the ideal tool for the job—not my motard, but a Suzuki SV650, which entered my life as a twisted ball of metal and has since emerged fully road- and trackworthy. Combined with my Dainese race leathers, snagged off a bargain rack last summer, I have maybe three grand invested, so I can now go to the track secure in the knowledge that my financial and physical risks have been minimized. But in spite of the fact that I live only 50 minutes from the excellent BeaveRun Motorsports Complex, I only did two track days in 2004—not exactly the fast track to an AMA pro license.

So what I've done is to schedule regular track hours—but at the aforementioned parking lot, not BeaveRun. I started with the SV, but its 65 horsepower and tall gearing—so modest among the supersports on the 1.6-mile race course—brought the lot's poles and curbs closer to the field of play than I cared for, and those painted parking lines claimed too much of my concentration to explore the limits of traction. I don't have such reservation aboard my DR-Z. In my flaming red leathers, I'm confident that I can survive a simple lowside without serious injury. (I try not to think about highsiding, though I know it's a possibility.) Of course, the essence of supermotard is sliding, and though I've hung it out there on dirt bikes in deep snow and on dry lakes, (little) dirt ovals, and frozen ponds, I remain far from conquering my fears of riding sideways on asphalt.

Some might think it heresy for a safety expert to deliberately look for such trouble, but I never claimed to be the world's safest rider. Many of you reading this have better safety records than I. My good friend in Austin, Texas, Richard Black, frequently tries to push my buttons with barbs like "safetycrat," but it doesn't work. One of his favorite sayings is "Safety Third," an intended gibe, but in reality an accurate reflection of my personal philosophy. Safety isn't the reason I ride; it's a goal. I ride number one for pleasure and number two for transportation. Safety fascinates me professionally and intellectually because it is a kind of chess game—the challenge of attaining a sensory high, reaching an interesting destination and deflecting all of the ambient risks along the way. When I don my helmet and Aerostich suit, I acknowledge that around the next bend I could strike a diesel spill and land in a ditch (I have). So, too, could a car turn left into my bike, but with all of my training and experience, it would take a serious mental lapse on my part to permit such an occurrence.

So please don't judge me harshly if one day you see me with my arm in a sling, the result of an errant stoppie on my favorite playground. You may have all the necessary restraint to ride for the next 20 years without so much as a close call, but I need an occasional adrenaline rush. I need to know that I'm mastering new skills. I need to know that I'm a more complete motorcyclist than I could ever show you on a Sunday ride. And I damned sure need to stay off any track where the likes of Ward, Bostrom, and Schwantz are bumping elbows!

On my desk sits a well-thumbed edition of *Motorcycle Accident Cause Factors and Identification of Countermeasures* (a.k.a. The Hurt Report). Believe me when I say that I know something about how motorcycle accidents unfold. But it ain't all book larnin'. . . .

The American Idiot Tour

July 2006

Immediately prior to writing this column, Larry had attended a major 3-day international motorcycle safety conference during which the baffling rise in fatalities among motorcyclists received much attention. Here, Mr. Safety refuses to apologize for others' choices which seemed to him so patently unwise.

Rider *magazine editor Mark Tuttle Jr penned the following preface when the column originally was published: "Larry Grodsky wrote this excellent and final Stayin' Safe column the day before he died in April (2006) after colliding with a deer. Some may find the subject ironic, but in reality it has no relation to the way Grodsky died. The topic is indeed controversial, and if Grodsky were alive, I might debate him over one or two of the conclusions he draws and his choice of words. But he's not alive, so out of respect for the man and his body of work—which has run uninterrupted in Rider since October 1988—we present it unchanged."*

Those unfamiliar with George Wolfe's character may be curious to know the rest of the story. One version relates that during the Jack Pine enduro, a competitor crashed and was launched through the air in a lurid arc. The body landed in a limp pile directly in front of George who, rather than dodge, ran smack over it at full speed. His sidecar passenger shouted, "Why didn't you go around him?" It was then George offered his callous retort indicating since he was obviously dead, it didn't matter.

Pete Tamblyn

A fatal accident can claim any motorcyclist . . . but it's usually more selective.

In my hometown of Pittsburgh, nearly every motorcyclist of a certain age has a story about the late George Wolfe, peerless mechanic, multi-time Jack Pine Enduro champion (sidecar division), and leathery old curmudgeon. My favorite tale—which was passed down to me, but which Wolfe himself would not deny—captured George's legendary impatience and ended with the punch line, "Ah hell, we can't hurt him—he's already dead!"

Lord knows there are enough people on this side of the grass to pick on, but the dead aren't always as blameless as we tend to portray them. Many were idiots—uniquely "American Idiots," to borrow a title from the rock group Green Day and the 2005 tour promoting their hit album.

The two-wheeled American Idiot Tour begins and ends in Daytona Beach, Florida, with stops along the way at Sturgis, Laconia, Myrtle Beach, and thousands of little juke joints in thousands of towns and cities across this great land. In case you weren't paying attention, the final body count at this year's Daytona Bike Week was 18. That's the kind of number we expect to see posted from Bagdad or Falujah, not a social event noted for Jello wrestling and—once upon a time—world-class racing.

I confess the number of Bike Weeks I've attended can be counted upon the fingers of one hand. In 1973, I got to touch the cords of Johnny Cecotto's still-warm rear tire, minutes after he'd outdueled King Kenny Roberts in a blistering 200-miler. In '83, my girlfriend and I two-upped a thousand miles each way to watch Freddie Spencer triumph on a 750 Honda Interceptor that looked outwardly similar to ours. In 2001, the noise got to me so bad that I hopped an early flight home, skipping the 200 altogether. My singular memory of that Daytona is of the idiots cruising Main Street in their fake helmets. I call them idiots because that was the first Bike Week following the repeal of Florida's mandatory helmet law. Who, I wondered, were they faking out?

Themselves, I reckon. A not-so-scientific study of helmet opinions I conducted several years later shed a little light on the thinking of the American Idiot. Shown a custom-painted novelty helmet—i.e. one with *no* energy-absorbing liner whatsoever—numerous riders acknowledged their awareness of its legal status and intended use, then opined, " . . . but at least it gives you *some* protection." Didn't they make a similar reference to Saran Wrap in junior high? In my home state, three years after the helmet-law repeal, fake helmets remain as integral a part of every biker bash as the two products that made Milwaukee famous.

Normally I don't give much thought to the American Idiot, but I write this on the heels of a three-day MSF-sponsored safety conference, attended by more than 300 representatives from 20 countries. The National

Highway Traffic Safety Administration (NHTSA) posted a solid contingent of at least seven speakers and presenters, most of them visiting and revisiting what I will call the three pillars of American Idiocy:

1) Riding unlicensed
2) Riding under the influence of alcohol
3) Riding with no helmet

Understandably, fatalities are what most concern government safety officials, but we motorcycle instructors should know better than to regard our labors as life-or-death matters. Just as locks are for honest people, safety courses are for responsible riders—and responsible riders usually don't die on their motorcycles. Who needs a safety course to know that they should get a license? That they shouldn't drink and ride? That a helmet will reduce injury severity should one's head collide with a hard object?

Surely other countries have their idiots. A 2001 Thailand study, aided by the Hurt Report's Jim Ouellet, and the first to use the *Common International Methodology for In-Depth Motorcycle Crash Investigations,* reported alcohol impairment in well over 30 percent of the crash victims— more than double the rate found in California! But Dr. Nicholas Rogers, who delivered a summary of the European *Motorcycle Accidents In-Depth Study* (MAIDS) told the assembled that alcohol and helmet use "... were simply not issues." Not surprisingly, Euros crashed at higher speeds than Californians and Thais.

Demonstrating a cause-and-effect relationship between fatal accidents and alcohol or helmet use is an easy construct, but how about unlicensed riders? A little-known finding of the Hurt Report is that accident-involved riders were more likely than average to have tattoos—"a traditional symbol of the risk taker." So, is a simple U-turn test any more effective a countermeasure than laser tattoo removal?

I'm thinking that the level of compliance with licensing regulations is a fairly accurate measure of a society's respect for authority in general and government in particular. One of the conference presenters, Dr. Horst Ecker, of Austria's Vienna University of Technology, indicated that in his career as both a researcher, and an accident investigator, he had *never* come across even *one* unlicensed motorcyclist! I contrast that with my own recent experience, shopping for two-way radios. On at least three occasions I was advised by radio dealers not to apply for the required license.

"It's not like you're going to be interfering with air traffic controllers," said one dealer. "It's just an excuse for the FCC to take your money." I don't know enough about radio communications to comment on that view, but I suspect it mirrors the thinking of many motorcyclists—that two-wheelers don't really have an impact on the overall safety of the traffic grid and should just be left alone.

Perhaps the most interesting window to the psyche of the American Idiot was opened by Mr. Robert Rowe of Irwin Broh & Associates in his paper, *Contemporary Attitudes Toward Motorcycle Riding Safety and Riding Risk Factors.* If Rowe's data are valid—and that remains a large "if," as they're drawn from voluntary responses to a national survey—the American Idiot may not be at all who we think he or she is. Seeking an answer to the question, "Who is most likely to drink and ride?" Rowe found that the incidence of such behavior rises—repeat—*rises* with the following:

1) Age
2) Income
3) Education
4) Riding Experience

I was as shocked as you probably are.

"When you think of other social ills," says Rowe, "it skews younger, uneducated. You picture the guys you see on *Cops* with no shirts. My interpretation is that confidence is a risk factor. Riders are saying, 'I can handle this. I'm an experienced rider.'"

NHTSA's Michael Jordan (a "short, white guy" by his own characterization), reported that in an agency-sponsored focus group, sport-bike riders voiced the belief that cruiser riders are more likely to drink and ride, while cruiser types, maintained that it was the sport-bike crowd! Rowe, whose research is ongoing, sees a trend toward more accidents and fatalities among cruiser and touring riders. Something to think about the next time some idiot on a sport-bike passes you on the freeway doing a 90-mph stand-up wheelie.

Not everyone who rides without a helmet is an idiot. Few people are idiots after the first drink. Why people would risk getting caught without a license is anyone's guess. We all make mistakes, but idiocy—American Idiocy—is a way of life with deadly consequences. George Wolfe would've pointed out that death solves the problem with utter finality.

An Uncle's Eulogy

If memory serves, I once heard the television journalist Ted Koppel relate on his ABC Nightline show that his wife, knowing of his yearning to take up motorcycling, had given him a first-class motorcycle for his sixtieth birthday. A motorcycle dealer suggested to Koppel that he consult my nephew, Larry Grodsky, for road safety instruction.

Larry afterward strictly observed a required promise that he not utilize his experience with Koppel in any way to publicize himself or his Stayin' Safe instructional training program. But he passed along a story to me.

He and the TV star had taken a break for lunch. From their booth in a modest Washington restaurant, the two soon noticed a middle-aged man staring at them. Many of the famous pick up on such behavior from the corner of their eye but condition themselves to ignore the stare lest they encourage an interruption of their meal. In any case, the stranger soon walked to the Koppel-Grodsky booth and pointed an index finger.

"I know you," he said. "I've seen you on television."

He was pointing not at Koppel but at Larry.

It occurs to me as I recall the lunchtime incident that the last thing Larry himself ever sought was recognition. He combined his passion for riding the world's roads with a talent for writing; the magazine *Rider*, one might say, gave him a vehicle, featuring his writings and thus drawing to him a wide following whose members surely recognized the lives and injuries he spared by sharing his expertise. Only in that sense did Larry seek attention.

In his hometown of Pittsburgh, however, I was surprised to pick up my *Post-Gazette* and see Larry's obituary spread prominently across the top of the page and was startled to learn that the motorcycle community regarded him as one of Americas foremost experts on safety.

Why didn't you ever tell me? I asked his father, Hal Grodsky, at the funeral home. Larry's parents and I were from a generation that supposed motorcyclists to be daredevil fools, even thugs; otherwise, we took no interest in the growth of two-wheeled transportation and the pleasure it has given many.

"We never knew," Hal exclaimed. "He never told us."

At family gatherings I attended, Larry hung in the background, content to listen to others chatter rather than regale us with stories from his motorcycling travels abroad, where he made friends just being himself. Only occasionally at those family get-togethers did he pipe up to put in his good-humored two cents. I did not learn until after his death—an ironic death for an expert on safety—that in conversation with one or two friends he more or less had predicted his fate. If I'm ever killed on the road, he said, it'll be a deer.

Deer at night can leap from roadside brush so swiftly, how can even the best rider have time to react? So it was that Larry at age 55 met his end on a dark country road in Texas. He had departed a conference in California to bike to Pittsburgh for his mother's eighty-fifth birthday. His father, during World War II, fought in the historic Battle of the Bulge and upon returning home went straight to work to support his small family; in retirement he enrolled in college at age 77 for the pleasure of the education he had missed. He excelled and was even offered a scholarship to continue. But the loss of his only son robbed Hal of his interest in life. About six months later, he died in his sleep.

"Celebrate?" Larry's mother, Violet, said to me when another birthday came 'round. Her and Hal's only daughter, Marcia, had stayed strong to assist and comfort Violet, but knowing Larry's final biking destination, Violet said, I'll never celebrate another birthday again.

Yet she should know that many others have lived to celebrate birthdays because of lessons Larry gave them as a teacher and widely-followed writer. He taught techniques and uses of mechanisms many never had given a thought.

Earlier, back in his twenties, Larry had gotten the itch to write. In his thirties, he sent me a sample of his prose. I had been a professional writer and author and then a broadcaster, so he sought my opinion. I told him I thought I detected talent. As matters turned out, he wrote with humor and passion and insight. In fact, his portrayal of one of his more difficult pupils, the heavyweight boxing champion Mike Tyson, presented a view of Tyson I had never come across. I'm of the belief that readers have gained from this collection of Larry Grodsky's work. That comes from one who sat upon a motorcycle—a mini version—just once and squeezed the start-up gadget on the handlebar and found the bike roaring across the rental lot straight into a concrete wall. Where were ya, Larry?

Myron Cope

Index